JESUS—
WORD
AND
PRESENCE

JESUS— WORD AND PRESENCE

AN ESSAY IN CHRISTOLOGY

PETER C. HODGSON

FORTRESS PRESS PHILADELPHIA

The author gratefully acknowledges permission granted by The University of Chicago Press to make use of material contained in his article, "Heidegger, Revelation, and the Word of God," *The Journal of Religion*, Vol. 49 (July 1969), pp. 228-252, © 1969 by The University of Chicago; and by the American Academy of Religion for use of the material contained in his review article, "Pannenberg on Jesus," *Journal of the American Academy of Religion*, Vol. 36 (December 1968), pp. 373-384, © 1968 by American Academy of Religion.

Library of Congress Catalog Card Number 70-157538

ISBN 0-8006-0039-8

1875C71   Printed in the United States of America   *1-39*

To

MY MOTHER *and* FATHER

CONTENTS

vii

Contents

Contents

ABBREVIATIONS

of Frequently Cited Books and Journals

AJC — Gerhard Koch, *Die Auferstehung Jesu Christi,* 2nd ed., Tübingen, J.C.B. Mohr (Paul Siebeck), 1965.

AJN — Willi Marxsen, *Die Auferstehung Jesu von Nazareth.* Gütersloh, Gütersloher Verlagshaus Gerd Mohn, 1968. Translations from this book are the author's own. Page references are also given to the English edition, *The Resurrection of Jesus of Nazareth,* trans. by Margaret Kohl. Philadelphia, Fortress Press, 1970.

BT — Martin Heidegger, *Being and Time,* trans. by John Macquarrie and Edward Robinson. New York, Harper & Row, 1962.

CD — Karl Barth, *Church Dogmatics,* G. W. Bromiley and T. F. Torrance, eds., 12 vols. Edinburgh, T. & T. Clark, 1936—.

ChrG — Friedrich Schleiermacher, *Der christliche Glaube nach den Grundsätzen der Evangelischen Kirche im Zusammenhange dargestellt,* 7th ed., Martin Redeker, ed., 2 vols., Berlin, Walter de Gruyter & Co., 1960. English translation: *The Christian Faith.* H. R. Mackintosh and J. S. Stewart, eds. Edinburgh, T. & T. Clark, 1928.

ENTT — Ernst Käsemann, *Essays on New Testament Themes,* translation of selected essays from *Exegetische Versuche und Besinnungen,* Vol. I, by W. J. Montague. London, SCM Press Ltd., 1964.

GuV — Rudolf Bultmann, *Glauben und Verstehen: Gesammelte Aufsätze,* 4 vols., Tübingen, J.C.B. Mohr (Paul Siebeck), 1933—.

JGaM — Wolfhart Pannenberg, *Jesus—God and Man,* trans. by Lewis L. Wilkins and Duane A. Priebe. Philadelphia, The Westminster Press, 1968.

JRel — *The Journal of Religion.* Chicago, The University of Chicago Press.

JThC — *Journal for Theology and the Church.* New York, Harper & Row; Herder and Herder.

RRF — Jürgen Moltmann, *Religion, Revolution, and the Future,* trans. by M. Douglas Meeks. New York, Charles Scribner's Sons, 1969.

STh — Karl Rahner, *Schriften zur Theologie,* 8 vols. Einsiedeln, Benziger Verlag, 1954—.

SynT — Rudolf Bultmann, *History of the Synoptic Tradition,* revised ed., trans. by John Marsh. New York, Harper & Row, 1968.

TDNT — Gerhard Kittel, ed., *Theological Dictionary of the New Testament,* ed. and trans. by Geoffrey W. Bromiley, 6 vols. Grand Rapids, Wm. B. Eerdmans Publishing Co., 1964—.

ThI — Karl Rahner, *Theological Investigations,* 6 vols. Baltimore, Helicon Press, 1961—.

ThNT — Rudolf Bultmann, *Theology of the New Testament,* trans. by Kendrick Grobel, 2 vols. New York, Charles Scribner's Sons, 1951, 1955.

ThP — Gerhard Ebeling, *Theology and Proclamation: Dialogue with Bultmann,* trans. by John Riches. Philadelphia, Fortress Press, 1966.

US   — Martin Heidegger, *Unterwegs zur Sprache.* Pfullingen, Verlag Günther Neske, 1959.

WF   — Gerhard Ebeling, *Word and Faith,* trans. by James W. Leitch. Philadelphia, Fortress Press, 1963.

WM   — Hans-Georg Gadamer, *Wahrheit und Methode: Grundzüge einer philosophischen Hermeneutik,* 2nd ed. Tübingen, J.C.B. Mohr (Paul Siebeck), 1965.

ZThK — *Zeitschrift für Theologie und Kirche.* Tübingen, J.C.B. Mohr (Paul Siebeck).

PREFACE

This essay in christology is not intended as a dogmatic treatise, inclusive of all the traditional themes, but as an exploration in a christological framework of certain fundamental questions emerging from the contemporary cultural experience of the absence of God. An attempt is made to move through and beyond interpretations of God's *absence*, of which the death of God theology and the theologies of the future are important recent expressions, to a fresh understanding of his *presence*, definitively so in the words and deeds, death and resurrection, of Jesus of Nazareth. In the course of the argument, a number of methodological, historical, and systematic issues with which christology must concern itself are examined, but only as they relate to the central theme, "Jesus—Word and Presence."

Work on this project began during a leave of absence at the University of Tübingen in 1968-69, supported by a Faculty Fellowship of the American Association of Theological Schools. I am especially grateful to Professor Gerhard Ebeling, now of the University of Zürich, who made available his study at the Institute for Hermeneutic, whose studies in christology, hermeneutic, and related subjects have been an important guide for my own work, and who allowed me to read a manuscript of his lectures on christology from the summer semester of 1967. I have also benefited from my contacts with Professor Jürgen Moltmann, whose recent essays and whose lectures on christology during the winter semester of 1968-69 helped to crystallize the problems with which I find myself engaged in this book.

During the course of the year I had conversations with Professors Wolfhart Pannenberg and Karl Rahner, whose writings have been of basic importance for my work. I am indebted to these men for the courtesy they showed me. The possibility of developing a christology oriented to the concept of "presence" was first suggested by Professor Hans W. Frei, whose continuing influence I am happy to acknowledge. Professors Edward Farley and Paul Meyer read the manuscript and suggested many improvements. I also appreciate the contributions of other colleagues and students, especially Sister M. Aquin O'Neill, who helped in correcting proofs.

Financial support in various forms has been provided by Vanderbilt University. I am indebted to the University Research Council and especially to Dean Walter Harrelson of the Divinity School for his support and encouragement.

PETER C. HODGSON

Vanderbilt University
May 1971

PART ONE
INTRODUCTION

1

CONTEXT: THE ABSENCE OF GOD

1. INTERPRETATIONS OF GOD'S ABSENCE IN RECENT THEOLOGY

At the center of the Christian faith stands the confession that God's presence in history was definitively revealed in the person, ministry, and death of Jesus of Nazareth, and that this presence continues to be efficacious because Jesus has been raised from the dead and is now present in the world as the agent of reconciliation and mission. Yet precisely this confession has become the most problematic aspect of Christian faith today, for it is not God's presence but his *absence* that is the hallmark of our time. Contemporary literature, philosophy, and social science, and a good deal of contemporary theology, are agreed that the characteristic religious experience of twentieth-century man is that of the absence of God. Perhaps two basic reasons for this experience can be isolated.

(1) The challenge of modern secularism. Secularism has rendered the so-called "God-hypothesis" implausible. God cannot be an absolute and transcendent cause that "explains" relative and empirical effects. Modern science insists upon the empirical verification of causal hypotheses, and the existence of God cannot be empirically verified. Nor, according to secularism, is God the real object of subjective religious experience, the feeling of dependence on and presence to the divine, for such religious feelings are merely the expression of man's striving for self-transcendence: "God" is the hypostatized ideal of the hidden human essence. In both objective and subjective forms, the God-hypothesis has

been challenged, and with it not only traditional supernatu-
ralistic theism but also postcritical attempts to identify God
with subjective religious experience. The modern secular
man perceives that he does not need God as a fulfiller of
human longings and a solver of human problems, for man
himself has become a master at practical and theoretical
problem solving—or at least so he thinks.

(2) The experience of radical evil. Evil has always been
a factor in questioning the efficacious presence of God in
history. Witness the ancient formulation: either God cannot
abolish evil or he will not; if he cannot then he is not all-
powerful; if he will not then he is not all-good. Responses
to this dilemma have usually included the argument that evil
is a by-product of God's gift of freedom to man, which necessarily includes the freedom to sin, or that God uses evil as
an instrument for his own purposes, e.g., as a punishment
for sin or as a necessary precondition of a greater good. But
these arguments lose their force in face of the radical experiences of evil in our time: the murder of six million Jews, the
use of atomic weapons, the meaningless war in Southeast
Asia, the systematic oppression of black people in America.
Moral catastrophes the magnitude of Auschwitz, Hiroshima,
and Vietnam represent a manifestation of evil in history that
transcends individual freedom and guilt. Moreover, it is
absurd to argue that the death camps were a punishment for
Jewish sins, or that God has used the slavery and oppression
of black people to some higher end. After Auschwitz, it is
not unreasonable to conclude, with Rabbi Rubenstein, that
the God of history is dead.[1]

It is not my purpose in this chapter to evaluate these and
other reasons for the experience of the absence of God.
Rather I want to examine several theological alternatives,

1. Richard L. Rubenstein, *After Auschwitz: Radical Theology and Contemporary Judaism* (Indianapolis, Bobbs-Merrill Co., 1966), esp. Chapters 2, 3,
14. Emil L. Fackenheim's excellent response to Rubenstein, *God's Presence
in History: Jewish Affirmations and Philosophical Reflections* (New York, New
York University Press, 1970), was published too late to be used in this book.
Its appearance, however, is indicative of a new theological mood to which
the present work also hopes to contribute, namely, an effort to rediscover the
presence of God through and beyond the experiences of his absence.

based on different ways of interpreting this root religious experience of our time, which have been set forth in recent discussion. God might be experienced as absent: (1) because of his hiddenness, eclipse, or abandonment; (2) because he has "died," in which case God-substitutes will be fashioned; or (3) because his essential being is his futurity or "not-yetness," a condition that demands a "representative" of the absent God in the present. A quest for the presence of God is a hidden theme in each of these interpretations of his absence.

(1) God is experienced as absent because of his hiddenness, eclipse, or abandonment. Here three variations are encountered on the same basic theme that God in some sense still "exists," yet for one reason or another is or has become inaccessible.

(a) The experience of God's absence may result from his *hiddenness* or *withdrawal*. Of course there is a proper sense in which God is "hidden," for he is not an object of worldly perception, a thing at hand, whether conceptual, visual, or oral. His hiddenness is the meaning of his transcendence vis-à-vis the world. Although we may hold to the objective reality of God, and even though in some instances objectifying language about him may be appropriate (as Schubert Ogden contends[2]), nevertheless he is not an "object" of man's empirical observation. The question is whether God's hiddenness is taken to mean not merely his transcendence (as the fundamental condition of his presence[3]) but also his withdrawal or even his antagonism toward men, so that God in one of his modes becomes the "enemy" of man, the "godless God," "the dead and absolutely absent God." Such, apparently, was Luther's understanding, as expressed by the formula, *Deus absconditus et*

2. Schubert Ogden, "Theology and Objectivity," *The Reality of God and Other Essays* (New York, Harper & Row, 1966), pp. 71-98.
3. Carl Michalson, "The Real Presence of the Hidden God," *Faith and Ethics: The Theology of H. Richard Niebuhr,* Paul Ramsey, ed. (New York, Harper & Brothers, 1957), pp. 245-267.

revelatus.[4] It became a basic principle of dialectical theology (especially Barth, Brunner, Gogarten), and is ably summarized by John Dillenberger's early book, *God Hidden and Revealed*.[5] The attempt to convert God's hiddenness into a positive principle of inaccessibility (the *Deus absconditus*), paradoxically contrasted with his mysterious approach in Jesus Christ (the *Deus revelatus*), has not proved religiously satisfying for the generation following that of the dialectical theologians. "Existence between God and God" may characterize the *Anfechtungen* of Luther or the sense of divine judgment and otherness experienced by the early Barth, but it does not really speak to the religious experience of contemporary secularized man.

(b) According to Martin Buber, God is experienced as absent not because he "hides" himself or is unapproachable in his glory, but because something comes between God and man, *eclipsing* the vision of the beholder. For Buber, it is the displacement of the I-Thou relationship by I-It relations in the modern scientific and philosophical consciousness. However, Buber does not contend that the eclipse is total, and he continues to hope that it may come to an end; for if *all present* access to God were severed, the God of Judaism would be dead.[6]

(c) In view of the unsatisfactory character of both these theological interpretations of God's inaccessibility, it is not surprising that this position has been radicalized by recent novelists and poets who contend that God has *abandoned* the world while continuing to control it from inaccessible distance in malevolent or inscrutable fashion, permitting the proliferation of human suffering and evil. God in some

4. Gerhard Ebeling, "Existence between God and God: A Contribution to the Question of the Existence of God," *JThC*, Vol. 5 (1968), pp. 150-154.
5. Philadelphia, Muhlenberg Press, 1953.
6. Martin Buber, *Eclipse of God: Studies in the Relation between Religion and Philosophy* (New York, Harper & Row, 1952), esp. Chapters 2, 8; and P. A. Schilpp and Maurice Friedman, ed., *The Philosophy of Martin Buber* (La Salle, Open Court, 1967), p. 716. The latter text is quoted in Fackenheim, *God's Presence in History*, p. 61; cf. p. 79.

sense continues to "exist," but man cannot believe in such
a God, or at least cannot venerate him. We find here a
curious retention of the two-world mentality of popular
theism and of the reality of the divine combined with a loss
of confidence in the beneficence of the "other" world. An
absent God *eo ipso* cannot be good; the divine becomes
purely demonic. Pursued consistently, this view could lead
to a thorough-going Manicheanism and, consequently, has
not been seriously entertained as a theological option in our
time. Perhaps only a tortured soul like Simone Weil, in her
book *Waiting for God*,[7] could attempt to articulate it theologically. The Manicheanism is especially evident in the
novels of Franz Kafka, especially *The Trial* and *The Castle,*
where it is part of an essentially tragic vision of man's situation.[8] On the other hand, in the philosophical and literary
writings of Albert Camus, the inaccessibility of God becomes
the basis for a new humanism, a cautiously optimistic hope
that man can live meaningfully in a God-abandoned world.[9]
Nevertheless, even this radicalized interpretation of God's
inaccessibility is essentially transitional, and it is only a short
step to the more consistent conclusion that God is dead.

(2) For William Hamilton at least, the death of God theology emerged from the failure of the *Deus absconditus* to
work any longer. In some of his earlier essays, Hamilton
spoke of waiting for the return of God after a period of
withdrawal, a hopeful waiting in the world with the neighbor. It was just this respect in which he intended to distinguish his position from an atheistic one.[10] But in later

7. New York, Putnam, 1951. On Simone Weil, see Susan A. Taubes, "The
Absent God., *The Journal of Religion* (January 1955), reprinted in *Toward
a New Christianity: Readings in the Death of God Theology*, Thomas J. J.
Altizer, ed. (New York, Harcourt, Brace & World, Inc., 1967), pp. 107-119.
8. See Erich Heller's chapter on Kafka in *The Disinherited Mind* (New York,
Meridian Books, 1959).
9. See especially *The Rebel: An Essay on Man in Revolt* (New York, Vintage
Books, 1956), Chapters 1-2, and his novel, *The Plague* (New York, The Modern Library, 1948).
10. William Hamilton, "The Death of God Theologies Today," in Thomas
J. J. Altizer and William Hamilton, *Radical Theology and the Death of God*
(Indianapolis, Bobbs-Merrill, 1966), pp. 41-42, 46. This essay was written
in late 1963 and first published in 1965.

essays, this theme disappeared in proportion to Hamilton's growing clarity respecting the irretrievability and finality of the absence of God. What Hamilton means by the phrase "death of God" is no longer merely the disappearance, withdrawal, eclipse, or hiddenness of a God who someday will reveal himself or return. Hamilton believes that the time has come to move beyond the neo-orthodox dialectic of the presence and absence of God, i.e., to the undialectical absence of God.

> The theological reasons for the deterioration of neo-orthodoxy are beginning to become clear. Neo-orthodoxy was a striking protest against the liberal confidence that God could be possessed, and its return to the dialectic of the presence and the absence of God testified to the way believers felt during the years before and after World War II. The reason neo-orthodoxy is not working today surely has something to do with the collapse of this dialectic, a collapse which is the overcoming of the presence of God by the absence that men are calling the death of God. . . .
> . . . Absence has won a decisive victory over the presence.[11]

The death of God, then, does not mean just the hiddenness or withdrawal of God. Nor does it refer to the failure of conventional modes of religious piety and language or of traditional concepts about God. Nor does it accept the classical atheist position that God does not, and never has, existed. Rather, in Hamilton's words, it means "that there once was a God to whom adoration, praise and trust were appropriate, possible, and even necessary, but that now there is no such God."[12] The God who once existed is now undialectically absent; irretrievably lost. Why? Hamilton is not very clear about the reasons, at least in a systematic way. Two factors seem important for him, both of which involve a shift in cultural mood rather than a change or process within God himself. The first has to do with the apparent inability to move beyond purely human experience in any sort of empirically verifiable way to a reality called "God," and

11. William Hamilton, "The New Optimism—from Prufrock to Ringo," *op. cit.*, pp. 157, 168. See also "The Shape of a Radical Theology," *Christian Century*, Vol. 82 (Oct. 6, 1965), pp. 1220-1221.
12. *Radical Theology and the Death of God*, pp. x-xi.

the second with the discovery by man "come of age" that
he no longer needs a God to solve his problems or to satisfy
his deepest longings.[13] The second factor in particular opens
up the possibility of a new "worldly optimism," a post-tragic
mode of existence of which Jesus is the model in which man
no longer finds himself beholden to a transcendent deity but
rather discovers latent capacities to solve his own problems,
to become his own master. In his essay, "The New Optimism," Hamilton isolates three areas where he believes this
worldly optimism to be discernible today: literature and the
arts (Saul Bellow, Lionel Trilling, John Gage, the Beatles),
the social sciences (technological optimism), and politics
(the pragmatic optimism of the Johnsonian Great Society
and the civil rights movement). The essay concludes:

> This is not an optimism of grace, but a worldly optimism I am
> defending. It faces despair not with the conviction that out of it
> God can bring hope, but with the conviction that the human con-
> ditions that created it can be overcome, whether those conditions
> be poverty, discrimination, or mental illness. It faces death not
> with the hope for immortality, but with the human confidence that
> man may befriend death and live with it as a possibility always
> alongside.[14]

In short, for Hamilton man's worldly optimism and his problem solving capabilities become an effective substitute for
the dead God.

In his own way, Thomas Altizer agrees. For Altizer, the
absent God—the primordial, transcendent Beyond of Christian tradition—is a terrifying being who represses men,
causing acute feelings of guilt and resentment. Such a God
cannot be tolerated; he must be put to death. Or better yet,
according to the "good news" of Christian atheism, the primordial God has put himself to death, has annihilated himself and enters into an absolutely immanent identity with
the world. Thus, unlike Hamilton, for Altizer the death of

13. See my article, "The Death of God and the Crisis in Christology," *JRel*,
Vol. 46 (October 1966), pp. 451-52.
14. Hamilton, "The New Optimism," *op. cit.*, p. 169; see pp. 165-69. See
also "The Shape of a Radical Theology," *loc. cit.*, p. 1219; and "The Death
of God Theologies Today," *op. cit.*, p. 40.

God is not so much a shift in cultural mood as it is a process within the divine life itself, by which God empties himself of divinity and radical transcendence is converted into radical immanence. Altizer oscillates between absence and immediacy, and his book, *The Gospel of Christian Atheism,* is a striking instance of the pathos for immediacy that arises out of the experience of the absence of God. Altizer's Jesus is a radically immanent, actual, immediate Jesus, so much so that in the final analysis he is simply identical with a "new and transfigured humanity," whose principle is love. The incarnate word is not to be confined to a particular man of the past, Jesus of Nazareth. "No, the totally incarnate Word can only be the Jesus who is present in what [William] Blake called 'Experience,' the Jesus who is actually and fully incarnate in every human hand and face." The God who died *is* this Jesus; as he "becomes ever more deeply incarnate in the body of humanity, he loses every semblance of his former visage, until he appears wherever there is energy and life." The love of God is "a love that eternally dies for man." The God who *is* Jesus is "the expanding or forward-moving process who is becoming 'One Man.' "[15] Thus the transcendent, alien, absent God must die because he is the enemy of man. Altizer's God-substitute is the "new and transfigured humanity" that arises through the "love that eternally dies for man."

(3) However, it is just the ephemeral character of the God-substitutes offered by Hamilton and Altizer—"worldly optimism," man as "problem solver," "new and transfigured humanity," "totally incarnate love"[16]—that has led to the third of the ways the absence of God has been interpreted in recent theology: the experience of God's absence does not mean his death but his futurity or "not-yetness," a con-

15. Thomas J. J. Altizer, *The Gospel of Christian Atheism* (Philadelphia, The Westminster Press, 1966), pp. 25-26, 71-75, 133-157; quotations from pp. 71, 74-75, 145-146.

16. After the emergence of racial polarization, further urban decay, environmental pollution, the political assassinations, the escalation of Vietnam, Czechoslovakia, and other events of the late sixties, it sounds rather premature to speak of a "new optimism" in literature, the social sciences, and politics.

dition that demands a "representative" of the absent God prior to his final coming. This is an intriguing "post-death of God" attempt to develop the experience of God's absence into a constructive theological principle. In this respect, it parallels the earlier efforts of dialectical theology to interpret God's absence constructively as his hiddenness or withdrawal.[17] Yet it parallels the death of God theologies in its conviction (at least in its more radical forms) that, strictly speaking, God does not now "exist." Now is a time of "waiting" for God—not because he is hidden or withdrawn, but because he has not yet come. A whole new theological genre has sprung up around this conception, radicalizing the eschatology of the New Testament: Dorothee Soelle's christology of "representation," Jürgen Moltmann's theology of hope and his categories of *novum* and revolution, Wolfhart Pannenberg's definition of God as "the power of the future," and the synthesis of many of these themes in the work of Carl Braaten, Robert Jenson, Harvey Cox, Rubem Alves, and other American theologians.[18]

17. It is not without significance that the major exponents of this position were students of the dialectical theologians—Moltmann and Pannenberg of Barth, Soelle of Gogarten, Braaten of Tillich.

18. Dorothee Soelle, *Christ the Representative: An Essay in Theology after the "Death of God,"* trans. by David Lewis (Philadelphia, Fortress Press, 1967); *Atheistisch an Gott glauben: Beiträge zur Theologie* (Olten, Walter-Verlag, 1968). Jürgen Moltmann, *Theology of Hope,* trans. by James W. Leitch (New York, Harper & Row, 1967); "What Is 'New' in Christianity: The Category *Novum* in Christian Theology," "Religion, Revolution, and the Future," "The Future as New Paradigm of Transcendence," "Hope and History," and other essays in *Religion, Revolution, and the Future,* trans. by M. Douglas Meeks (New York, Charles Scribner's Sons, 1969). Wolfhart Pannenberg, *Theology and the Kingdom of God* (Philadelphia, Westminster Press, 1969); "Der Gott der Hoffnung," *Grundfragen systematischer Theologie* (Göttingen, Vandenhoeck & Ruprecht, 1967). Moltmann and Pannenberg are discussed at greater length below, pp. 233-239. Carl Braaten, *The Future of God* (New York, Harper & Row, 1969). Robert W. Jenson, *The Knowledge of Things Hoped For* (New York, Oxford University Press, 1969). Harvey Cox, *The Secular City* (New York, Macmillan, 1965); *God's Revolution and Man's Responsibility* (Valley Forge, Judson Press, 1965). Rubem A. Alves, *A Theology of Human Hope* (Washington, Corpus Books, 1969). See also the works of Continental Catholic theologians, especially Karl Rahner, Eduard Schillebeeckx, and J. B. Metz. The theology of the future has been developed in part through conversation with recent Marxist philosophers who have sought an authentic vision of transcendence—a transcendence of the future that overcomes the alienation of present society, that does not require the sacrifice of means to ends, that offers points of contact with the Christian concept of

The most radical and consistent of these efforts is found
in Dorothee Soelle's excellent book, *Christ the Representative: An Essay in Theology after the "Death of God."* Soelle
shares with the death of God theologians the conviction that
God does not now "exist," but she views much more soberly
than they the possibility that man and his products can
function effectively as a God-substitute. Just for this reason,
God's absence must be interpreted not as his death but as
his futurity: in the absence of a *future* God we are not to
seek *substitutes* but means of his *representation* in the present. Soelle is at pains to argue that the German word
Stellvertretung means representation *(Vertreten)* without
substitution *(Ersatz, Ersetzen).*[19] She believes that neither
society nor any other human product can offer a satisfactory
God-substitute. Society, she says, "is unable to satisfy a
religious longing which always reaches beyond it, the
longing for meaning and purpose in life, the longing for
personal identity and for the kingdom of identity. The unre-
solved problematic character of an absurd situation midway
between meaninglessness and the longing for meaning forces
us to the non-logical conclusion that God must be represented."[20] Indeed, society has replaced nature as the enslaving power over man: in it the individual has become a
utilized, manipulated, exchangeable, nameless object; his

God, and whose basic principles are freedom and love. Among the most
important writers are Ernst Bloch, *Das Prinzip Hoffnung* (Frankfurt, Suhrkamp Verlag, 1959); Roger Garaudy, *From Anathema to Dialogue*, trans. by
Luke O'Neill (New York, Herder and Herder, 1966); and Vítězslav Gardavský, *Gott ist nicht ganz tot*, trans. by E. Dederra (München, Chr. Kaiser
Verlag, 1968). See Moltmann's discussion and criticism of Bloch in "Hope and
Confidence: A Conversation with Ernst Bloch," *RRF*, pp. 148-176; and his
introduction to the German edition of Gardavský's book.

19. Soelle, *Christ the Representative*, pp. 19-23; cf. the German edition,
Stellvertretung: Ein Kapitel Theologie nach dem "Todes Gottes" (Stuttgart,
Kreuz Verlag, 1965), pp. 21-26, 52-64.

20. *Ibid.*, p. 132. For this reason Helmut Gollwitzer is wrong in arguing that
for Soelle, "God" is merely the religious title for "the attained identity of
society with itself and the attained identity of man with society," and that
therefore her position is implicitly one of atheism. Gollwitzer, *Von der Stellvertretung Gottes: Christlicher Glaube in der Erfahrung der Verborgenheit
Gottes. Zum Gespräch mit Dorothee Sölle* (München, Chr. Kaiser Verlag,
1967), p. 74.

work is reduced to meaninglessness and endlessness by the circle of production and consumption and the dominant category of material goods.[21] In short, the individual is merely alienated by society, not brought to identity with himself.

An even more forceful critique of post-industrial, automated, cybernetic society is offered by Jürgen Moltmann. He sees man becoming entrapped in an ever thicker network of social institutions, political bureaucracies, and industrial giants, whose control over the individual is enhanced by automation and the computer. Hence, the theme of philosophy and theology has become the quest for a new mode of transcendence which will liberate man from the estrangement produced by his own labor. The "boundary" of this transcendence no longer lies in the finitude of all things (as with Greek metaphysics), nor in the subjectivity of man (as with rationalism and existentialism) but in the rigid, dead forms of his own objectifications and in the dominance of man's work over himself. This is a transcendence vis-à-vis the present system, and hence it can be directed neither "above" nor "within" but "ahead," toward a qualitatively new future in which the present antagonistic condition of man will be fundamentally altered.[22]

Out of this situation the explanation of God's absence as his not-yetness or futurity has emerged. In such a world, God cannot be alive, effective, omnipotent, presently at work. If he were, he could justly be indicted for the suffering of the innocent. The only way to save the God-concept is to argue for his absence, his powerlessness, his present non-involvement. Soelle speaks more freely of the absence of God than Moltmann; indeed it is the central theme of her book. "So long as God 'lives'—so long as men can say, 'And a God exists! A holy will lives!'—there is no compelling theological need to reflect upon Christ's representation of God as the representation of one who is absent." For the first time in a post-theistic age "the truth that Christ repre-

21. Soelle, *Atheistisch an Gott glauben*, pp. 20-21.
22. "The Future as New Paradigm of Transcendence," *RRF*, pp. 180-187.

sents the absent God . . . takes on its full significance."[23]

Formerly, "representation" meant that in Jesus Christ *God* steps into our place, taking our guilt and alienation upon himself, mediating himself by his revelation. But in a post-theistic age, God can no longer be thought of as a presently acting subject and accordingly cannot be the agent of representation. Rather, *Christ* steps into the place of the absent God on our behalf.[24] *Stellvertretung,* we may recall, means representation without substitution. Hence Christ as the representative of God is not to be thought of as a God-substitute. Rather, "he holds the place of this now absent God open for him in our midst," granting him a future, allowing him the time to appear on his own, to become "the one he could be." This representation, however, is provisional (albeit with Christ an "ultimate and final provisionality"), so that God himself remains outstanding, and something more is to be expected of him. The provisionality of Christ permits a genuinely open future as well as responsibility on our part.[25] Soelle sums up her point most effectively in poetic language by speaking of Christ as "God's actor" (*der Schauspieler Gottes*). "In this changed world [where he is no longer immediately experienced], God needs actors to take his part. So long as the curtain has not rung down and the play still goes on, God's role cannot be left unfilled. The protagonist of God is named Christ. Christ takes the part of God in the world, plays this role which without him would remain unfilled." And because of the "provisional character of all theatrical performances," "we, too, can now play God for one another."[26] It follows that when God himself comes to the stage and takes over his own role, he will no longer need a protagonist. With God's final coming, Christ's role will be at an end.

23. Soelle, *Christ the Representative,* pp. 130-131, 137, 150-151.
24. *Ibid.,* p. 130. Cf. Gollwitzer, *Von der Stellvertretung Gottes,* pp. 105, 135.
25. Soelle, *op. cit.,* pp. 102, 107, 132, 134, 137, 138, 143, 148-149.
26. *Ibid.,* pp. 140, 142. Translation modified slightly; cf. *Stellvertretung,* pp. 189-190.

Moltmann does not speak of the absence of God as such.
Rather, he defines God as "the power of the future," the one
who is "before us," who is yet to come,[27] and he argues for
the qualitative newness of the future. The future can offer
a genuine transcendence vis-à-vis the "present system," not
when it involves merely the capacity for transcendence that
lies within history itself, but only when it brings the "qualitatively new," the "wholly other," only when it involves a
"fundamental alteration [*grundsätzliche Veränderung*]" of
the present order of things, only when it represents, in
eschatological-religious language, the "end of history." This
coming of the future is not a matter of "historical transcending" but of a "transcendence lying above history [*geschichtsüberlegene Transzendenz*]"; it is not merely "future history"
but the "future *of* history."[28] For such a future, the most
appropriate category is *novum;* it is a *novum ultimum,* a
nova creatio ex nihilo. Such a *novum* cannot be conceived
and interpreted by intrahistorical analogies, for it stands in
a contradiction to the old that shatters all continuities. For
Christian hope, this *novum* is the resurrection from the dead,
by which the true divinity and power of God are disclosed
(cf. Rom. 4:17).[29] What is the role of Christ in this context?

27. Moltmann, *RRF*, pp. 60-61; *Theology of Hope,* p. 16. Cf. Pannenberg,
Theology and the Kingdom of God, p. 56.
28. *RRF*, pp. 190, 196-198. Translation modified (see below, n. 36); cf. "Die
Zukunft als neues Paradigma der Transzendenz," *Internationale Dialog Zeitschrift,* Vol. 2 (1969), pp. 8-9, 12-13. This point is argued against the Marxist
concept of transcendence, which remains in the context of a dialectical historical process. "Christian eschatology . . . cannot be turned into a utopia,
nor yet into the 'principle of hope' of an immanent world consummation, by
dint of non-transcendent transcending; . . . rightly understood it also 'ex-
plodes' the 'principle of hope.'" "Hope and Confidence: A Conversation with
Ernst Bloch," *RRF*, pp. 152-160 (quotation from latter page).
29. Moltmann, "Die Kategorie *Novum* in der christlichen Theologie," *Perspektiven der Theologie* (München, Chr. Kaiser Verlag, 1968), pp. 176-179
(the essay by the same title in the English edition of Moltmann's essays is
quite different); *Theology of Hope,* pp. 179, 302. In a later essay, Moltmann
qualifies the non-analogous character of the future as *novum.* He acknowledges that analogies influence our "vision" of the "leap" to the qualitatively
new, but they do not bring about the leap itself. Furthermore, this "vision"
of the qualitatively new future can become the transcendental horizon that
opens up and stimulates intrahistorical transcending. He argues for a "link-
ing" of suprahistorical and intrahistorical transcendence, but is not very clear
about what this connection entails concretely or how it is accomplished.
(*RRF*, pp. 197-198.)

As with Soelle, he is the representative of the now absent, coming God. Moltmann speaks of the *Christus anticipator* and is seeking to develop a messianically oriented christology "from before."[30] Such a Christ can be defined only in terms of what he brings and, strictly speaking, is not an intra-worldly possibility. In strikingly Tillichian language, Moltmann describes Christ as the one "in whom [the] qualitatively new future is present under the conditions of history"; Christian faith "finds in him the end of history in the midst of history."[31]

Several questions may be raised concerning the effort to interpret God's absence as his futurity. First, it may be asked whether an *absent* God can still be conceived in any meaningful way to be *alive, active,* and *beneficent*. Have not the death-of-God theologians and the literature of abandonment drawn the more honest conclusion regarding the meaning of the absence of God, namely, that such a God is either dead, powerless, or malevolent? How can a powerless God or an evil God truly be God—at least a God in whom we can believe, trust, and hope? Helmut Gollwitzer has rightly noted that in the wake of Bonhoeffer, the accentuation of the powerlessness of God has taken on the character of a "romantic play with paradoxes."[32] If there is not some way of understanding God's power in the context of his objective powerlessness, and his fidelity in the context of his forsakenness—or, to put it most starkly, if there is not some way of understanding God's death on the cross as his most radical living presence among men—then it would be more honest to acknowledge that his absence implies not merely his futurity but his demise.

A second difficulty with this interpretation of God's absence is an ambiguity toward human activity and the possibilites of political and social change. On the one hand,

30. In his Lectures on Christology, University of Tübingen, Winter Semester 1968-69. See below, pp. 63-64.

31. *RRF*, p. 198.

32. Gollwitzer, *op. cit.*, pp. 123-124.

if God is absent and ineffective we cannot live from his
gift and are referred to our own action. We must represent
God to each other and do for each other and for God what
he, unfortunately, cannot do. Soelle's book ends with, "[God]
put himself into play, made himself dependent on us, and
identified himself with the non-identical. Now is the time
to do something for God."[33] Theology after the death of
God is based on a fatalism that becomes law, says Gollwitzer.
"The fatalism says, 'We can no longer . . ., we can no longer
. . . ,' and enumerates what earlier supposedly still could be
done but for us today is impossible. The law that follows
says, 'We must . . ., we must . . .,' and enumerates what we
must do because we can no longer believe that something is
done for us. The fatalism began with the manifestation of
our weakness, our impossibilities; the law ends with the
unheard of demand, . . . with the illusion that we ought and
are able to 'represent God.' "[34]

Yet, on the other hand, despite the call to activism, this
position has tended to take a pessimistic view of creation in
general, of present society in particular, and of purely
intrahistorical possibilities for change (political, social, economic, cultural). This pessimism is especially evident in
Moltmann because of his insistence upon the "qualitative
newness" of the future and the lack of any continuity between the old and the new. In *Theology of Hope* he has
spoken of the necessity of Christians taking up the role of
"Babylonian exiles" in modern society,[35] and throughout his
work he calls for "resistance," "solidarity with the oppressed,"
"alteration," but not "transformation" in H. Richard Niebuhr's sense of the term.[36] Just because the old order is not

33. Soelle, *op. cit.*, p. 152. My translation; cf. *Stellvertretung*, p. 205. See
also her essay on faith as a mode of practice, "Atheistisch an Gott glauben?",
in *Atheistisch an Gott glauben*, pp. 77-96.
34. Gollwitzer, *op. cit.*, pp. 144-145, 146-147, 130-131.
35. Moltmann, *Theology of Hope*, p. 324.
36. He uses the word *Veränderung* ("alteration"), rather than *Umbildung*,
Umgestaltung, *Umwandlung*, *Verwandlung*, or a similar term whose more
natural connotation is "transformation." The nuance of meaning is different
in both German and English, especially when *Veränderung* is combined with

"transformable," it must be "wholly altered" into the qualitatively new.

Finally, the interpretation of God's absence as his futurity
tends to issue in a horizontal dualism—a "supernaturalism
of the future"—because all continuities between past and
future, history and eschatology, have been exploded. This
supernaturalism is clear in Moltmann's distinction between
"transcendence lying above history" (*geschichtsüberlegene
Transzendenz*) and "historical transcending" (*geschichtlicher
Transzendieren*), or between suprahistorical and intrahistorical transcendence. To be sure, Moltmann calls for a "link-
ing" *(Verbindung)* of these two. But for him, the linkage
remains abstract and external. It does not belong to the
structure of history or of temporality as such. It occurs
essentially in miraculous, episodic fashion, so that one cannot
analyze it or lay out its horizontal structure. Thus, in the
final analysis, a new form of other-worldly religion emerges
here, although now the "other" world ("the kingdom of identity," the *nova creatio ex nihilo*) transcends "from before"
rather than "from above." God is not the "wholly other"
(*Ganz-Andere*) of traditional theism but the "wholly altering"
(*Ganz-Ändernde*).[37] In this context, it might be well to heed
Karl Barth's warning of the dangers inherent in making
eschatology the systematic focus of theology as a whole: creation withdraws into a dim dualistic distance; history loses

---

an intensifying adjective like *grundsätzlich, qualitativ*, or *ganz* ("fundamental"
or "qualitative" alteration, "wholly altering," etc.). Unfortunately the English
edition obscures matters by translating *Veränderung* as "transformation." For
H. Richard Niebuhr's transformation-theory, see "Christ the Transformer of
Culture," *Christ and Culture* (New York, Harper & Row, 1951). In terms of
Niebuhr's typology, Moltmann's position is closer to that of "Christ Against
Culture" or "Christ and Culture in Paradox." For Moltmann's position, see
"Die Kategorie *Novum* in der christlichen Theologie," *Perspektiven der
Theologie*, pp. 183-185; and "The Future as New Paradigm of Transcen-
dence," *RRF*, pp. 190, 195-199. In the latter essay he warns that an over-
emphasis of the "qualitative distinction" can result in an abstract negation of
the world and its history as a "vale of tears." But in his own work he has
not yet applied the needed corrective.

37. *RRF*, pp. 190, 198. Cf. "Die Zukunft als neues Paradigma der Transzendenz," *Internationale Dialog Zeitschrift*, Vol. 2 (1969), pp. 8-9, 13; and "Gott
und Auferstehung," *Perspektiven der Theologie*, p. 41.

its concrete, positive qualities; the doctrine of God acquires the character of a massive postulate; and present reconciliation evaporates into a longing for coming redemption.[38]

2. THE PRESENCE OF THE FUTURE GOD IN WORD

A quest for the presence of God is already a hidden theme of the theologies of absence and futurity we have just reviewed. The time has come to let this theme become an explicit one and to direct specific attention to the problem of God's presence in history. Several beginnings in this direction have already been hinted or ventured. The dialectical theologians proclaimed a *Deus revelatus* through and beyond the *Deus absconditus*. Martin Buber hoped that the eclipse of God, which is not total, will come to an end. A pathos for immediacy permeates Altizer's celebration of the death of God, and both he and Hamilton retain a worldly optimism. In response to Richard Rubenstein's contention that after Auschwitz the God of history is dead, Emil Fackenheim argues in his recent book, *God's Presence in History,* that Jews can and must reaffirm certain root experiences of "saving and commanding divine presence": Exodus, Sinai, and now Auschwitz. The "commanding voice of Auschwitz" requires that the tale of what happened there be told, that survival (of Jews and of humanity) is a supreme value, that pagan cynicism and pseudo-Christian otherworldliness be avoided, that protest against God not lead to his denial—for otherwise Hitler would be handed a posthumous victory, the total destruction of Judaism.[39]

Dorothee Soelle begins her book with the question, "How can a man become identical with himself?", and "identity" is what she believes can be accomplished by Christ's "representation." Although she equates "presence" with "immediacy," what she describes as "identity" is, in fact, what I mean by "presence." Life in identity is life "with God,"

38. *CD*, Vol. I/2, pp. 875-876.
39. Fackenheim, *God's Presence in History*, Chap. 3.

"in the presence of God" (*Bei-Gott-Sein*). The "kingdom of identity" is her translation of "kingdom of God," which is the "older terminology" for "God's identity." Christ who was "with God" left the kingdom of identity and entered into the kingdom of estrangement, promising identity as man's destiny by representing God to man and man to God. His task was "to represent the kingdom of identity which has not yet appeared. This kingdom has 'come near'—in this representative, who holds open God's place in the world and, by so doing, allows God a future."[40] But if the kingdom of identity has "come near" in Christ, then God is not, strictly speaking, absent but rather present *in the mode of representation.*

Of greater interest, however, is the emergence of "presence" as an important motif in the more recent writings of Moltmann and Pannenberg. Moltmann is no longer concerned to polemicize against the "eternal presence" of God, as was the case in *Theology of Hope*,[41] but rather to recognize God's presence as the "home of identity," the *nova creatio ex gloria Dei,* the *participatio in Deo,* to which we are called by resurrection from the dead and which even now we can anticipate.[42] God's being is now defined as his *coming,* and the coming God is *present* in Jesus the Crucified and Risen One.

> In the modern conflict between a theism that affirms "God is" and an atheism that negates God, saying, "God is not," eschatological theology can say, "God's being, the Kingdom of his identity, is coming." *God is* present in the way in which his future takes control over the present in real anticipations and prefigurations. *But God is not as yet* present in the form of his eternal presence. The dialectic between his being and his being-not-yet is the pain and the power of history. Caught between the experiences of his presence and of his absence, we are seeking his future, which will solve this ambiguity that the present cannot solve. By

40. Soelle, *Christ the Representative,* pp. 9, 130-131, 132, 145-159 (translations modified; cf. *Stellvertretung,* pp. 7, 176, 178, 196-201); and "Gottes Selbstentäusserung: Eine Meditation zu Philipper 2:5-11," *Atheistisch an Gott glauben,* pp. 18-19.
41. Moltmann, *Theology of Hope,* pp. 27-31.
42. *RRF,* pp. 33, 35-37, 61, 106.

future ("advent") we do not mean a far-away condition, but a power which already qualifies the present—through promise and hope, through liberation and the creation of new possibilities. As this power of the future, God reaches into the present.[43]

Similarly, Pannenberg, partially in response to his American critics,[44] has stressed in more recent essays the dialetic between present and future and the "coming," "arrival," or "presence" of the future God in definitive events of the past. "In the ministry of Jesus the futurity of the Reign of God became a power determining the present. . . . Wherever [obedience to God] occurs, there God already reigns unconditionally in the present, and such presence of the Reign of God does not conflict with its futurity but is derived from it and is itself only the anticipatory glimmer of its coming." The relation between present and future is construed on the analogy of the relation between appearance and essence (or being): being (as future) *must* appear (become present) in order to be, yet is never to be confused with its finite appearance.[45] Furthermore, writes Pannenberg, "the notion of the futurity of God and his Kingdom most emphatically does not 'remove' God to the future. It does not mean that God is only in the future and was not in the past or is not in the present. Quite to the contrary, as the power of the future he dominates the remotest past."[46]

In brief, for both Moltmann and Pannenberg *the futurity of God no longer signifies his absence but his presence, his mode of being present as the coming God, whose power already qualifies the present.*[47] With this understanding of the futurity of God, I have no quarrel. However, certain questions remain unanswered: What is the *means* or *mode*

43. *Ibid.*, pp. 208-209, 212-214 (italics his).
44. John B. Cobb, Jr., "Past, Present, and Future," *Theology as History*, J. M. Robinson and J. B. Cobb, Jr., ed. (New York, Harper & Row, 1967).
45. Wolfhart Pannenberg, "Appearance as the Arrival of the Future," *Theology and the Kingdom of God*, pp. 127-136, 141-143; quotation from p. 133.
46. Pannenberg, "Theology and the Kingdom of God," *ibid.*, p. 62; cf. pp. 53-64, 70, and "Der Gott der Hoffnung," *Grundfragen systematischer Theologie*, pp. 393-394.
47. Pannenberg, "In Jesus' message it is only *as future that God is present*," *Theology and the Kingdom of God*, p. 68 (italics his).

by which the future God is present? What *is* futurity in
essence and in what sense is God to be defined as "the power
of the future"? These questions are not satisfactorily
answered by either Moltmann or Pannenberg. To address
them, I shall propose another way of interpreting the
experience of God's absence and a corresponding way of
understanding the means of his presence.

God is experienced as absent because of the failure of
language. When language fails, God is still *experienced*
because men are unable to escape an awareness of the radical questionableness of their existence. When language fails,
they become most conscious of their insufficiency and powerlessness and are driven to speak of God but are unable to do
so. The God who is experienced only in the failure of language, who is implied by the questionableness of human
existence, and whose name we are unable to name, is the
absent God, the *Deus absconditus.*[48]

A twofold failure of language may be distinguished. First,
the language of traditional religious piety is no longer effective and meaningful for large numbers of contemporary men.
For a multitude of reasons—including the rationalization and
technification of life, empirically oriented modes of verification, the experience of radical evil, and the devaluation of
religious speech by irresponsible or traditionalist usage—
Christian language has largely become a ghetto language in
our time. This applies to the word "God," which is in
danger not so much of idolization as it is of anonymity,
pseudonymity, and decay,[49] as well as to other elements in
the language of Christian piety: prayer, sermon, sacraments,
sin, salvation, religious community, church vocation, and the
like. Second, and potentially more ominous, is the failure
of "secular" modes of language by which authentic human

48. Cf. Gerhard Ebeling, *God and Word*, trans. by James W. Leitch (Philadelphia, Fortress Press, 1967), Chapter 1; and "Existence between God and
God," *JThC*, Vol. 5 (1968), pp. 150-154; Robert W. Funk, *Language, Hermeneutic, and Word of God* (New York, Harper & Row, 1966), pp. 8-9, 55-56;
Wolfhart Pannenberg, "The Question of God," *Interpretation*, Vol. 31 (July
1967), pp. 294 ff.
49. Ebeling, *ibid.*, pp. 2-5, 34-37, 47.

existence is constituted. The language of non-oppressive authority, of truthfulness, of self-identity and community, of freedom and responsibility, is placed in jeopardy by the network of political ideologies, administrative bureaucracies, mass media, and military-scientific-industrial conglomerates that now dominate the Western societies and whose control over the individual is enhanced by technology, automation, and cybernetics. Under such conditions, language is more often used to oppress and conceal, to render powerless, to produce estrangement and hatred, than it is to liberate and unconceal, to upbuild and to gather. Thus, the temporal and spatial structures of man's very existence in the world are threatened. In some measure, the revolt of students, blacks, and the dispossessed of the Third World is an outcry against the abuse of language and the concomitant dehumanization of life by the present "system."[50]

If God is experienced as absent because of the failure of language, then by implication it is precisely language that can also become the medium of his presence. God is present, if at all, by means of word. Clearly God is not a thing at hand, an object of empirical, sensory, or even extrasensory perception. For this reason we may properly refer to his "hiddenness." As Ebeling points out, " . . . *it is the business of word to make present what is not at hand, what is absent, . . . what is even utterly hidden.* Everything that is expressed in language is dependent on language only to the extent that hiddenness is involved in one respect or another. However true it may be that our language cannot say everything, because many things are beyond its reach and call for silence, there is nevertheless all the more need to underline the experience, banal and trite as it has become, that language can say infinitely more than is perceived by the senses."[51] God is that reality which can be experienced and expressed, if at all, *only* by means of language, for he is that

50. On the failure of language, see further Sec. 5, Chapter 3.
51. Ebeling, *op. cit.*, pp. 24-25 (italics mine); cf. "Existence between God and God," *JThC*, Vol. 5 (1968), p. 151.

reality which is utterly hidden as far as empirical perception is concerned. In the face of such a reality, silence may indeed at times be the appropriate mood, especially when words fail. God is experienced as absent not because he conceals himself, withdraws, abandons the world, dies, or is not yet fully born, but because it is in the nature of God to be present only by means of words, which are finite, fragile, and susceptible of failure. Words fail not because God ceases to communicate himself but because men refuse to listen, because they abuse language and destroy it. If God's presence is to be experienced afresh, then what is required is a rebirth of language. The task of this book is to document this thesis and to explore the paths along which a rebirth of language might occur. These paths lead ultimately, for the Christian, to the one who was the definitive word of faith and who remains the agent and norm of authentic language today.

Before undertaking this exploration, several pointers charting the way are in order.

(1) A rebirth of language will involve not just "religious" discourse in the traditional sense, but also the secular modes of authentic speech that have been most acutely challenged in our time: the language of authority that liberates rather than enslaves, of truthfulness, of self-identity and community, of freedom and responsibility. By means of these secular language-structures, words that correspond to the word of God, participate in the power of God, and obey the will of God, may also be spoken. Accordingly, authentic and vital secular speech can be characterized as "faithful."

(2) Faithful language is not something at man's disposal, an innate human capacity, even though it is the fundamental definition of what it means to be human. True and faithful word always is a power that comes as an unexpected, unexacted gift, but which, of necessity, remains dependent upon human speech and action as the means of its expression. Man experiences the transcendence of the word precisely in his function as its essential instrument. The word does not

transcend "from above," as a supernatural word that invades
from another sphere of reality and is inserted into or between
human words, nor "from within," as the *finitum capax
infiniti*, the existential word of decision by which a man
determines his existence. Rather, we may define such a word
as the power of the future, which by its coming gathers man
into presence with himself and the world, constituting the
temporal and spatial horizons of existence. "Word" and
"presence" are fundamentally temporal, historical categories.
Presence signifies the "gathering" accomplished by the
"coming" of the future through the past into the present.
It is the antithesis of immediacy and absence, both of which
are atemporal, time*less* concepts in the strict sense. We must
not think of future, past, and present as mutually exclusive
modes of time but as dialectically related: the "coming" of
the future toward the present through the past, and the
"gathering" of the present in anticipation of the future on
the basis of past promises. "Presence" in the most fundamental sense means the dynamic, living unity of future-
past-present, accomplished by means of *word*. The power
of being and of time is the power of the future, whose
means is word.

(3) The word that is the power of the future and that
gathers into presence by its coming is, according to Christian
faith, the word of God. God is the one who "has word"
absolutely. We experience his transcendence as his futurity,
because he is the one who has the word that is the power
of the future absolutely. Nevertheless, it is misleading
simply to identify "God" and "future," as is implied by the
definition of God as the one "with future as his essential
nature,"[52] or as "the power of the future."[53] Such an identification encourages the hypostatizing of the future or its
apotheosis—the "God hope," *Deus spes*, as Ernst Bloch wants

52. Ernst Bloch, *Das Prinzip Hoffnung* (Frankfurt, Suhrkamp Verlag, 1959),
p. 1458; cf. *Man on His Own*, trans. by E. B. Ashton (New York, Herder and
Herder, 1970), p. 173.
53. Pannenberg, *Theology and the Kingdom of God*, p. 56; *RRF*, p. 61.

to say.[54] Rather, as the one who *has* the word that is the power of the future absolutely, God *is* presence. His being is the primordial unity of time, constituted as such by the power of the (future) word that gathers into presence. He is not simply our future but also our past and present. He is "behind us" and "with us" as well as "before us." He *transcends* us as the future, because he communicates himself to us or is present to us by his word, which is the power of the future. Thus futurity can serve as an appropriate model of God's transcendence, but it is not to be equated with his essential being, which is presence.[55] As Moltmann and Pannenberg have already recognized, the futurity of God is not to be taken to signify his absence but his presence, his mode of being present as the coming God, who gathers into presence by his word.

(4) According to Gerhard von Rad and others, the name of YHWH revealed in Ex. 3:14 is best translated, "I will be there" *(ich werde da sein)*.[56] Hence the word "God" means "the promise of presence." Israel found the focus of its existence in the hope for the redemption of that promise. According to Christian faith, God's promise of his presence has been definitively fulfilled in the person and work of Jesus Christ. He is the "there" of God's "being," the concrete "place" where God's presence is actualized and his promise fulfilled. The name of God has become the name of Jesus Christ, the name by which the word "God" is defined. There is no a priori philosophical or theological reason why this should be the case. The efforts by nine-

54. Moltmann, "Hope and Confidence: A Conversation with Ernst Bloch," *RRF*, pp. 153-159.
55. For my definition of God as the one who *has word* absolutely and *is* primordial presence, see below, Sec. 4b, Chapter 3.
56. Gerhard von Rad, *Theologie des Alten Testaments*, Vol. 1, 5th ed. (München, Chr. Kaiser Verlag, 1966), p. 194; see pp. 193-200. Helmut Gollwitzer, in *Von der Stellvertretung Gottes*, pp. 75 ff., 107-111, 121-122, discusses this name at length in his critique of Dorothee Soelle. In addition to von Rad, Gollwitzer refers to the work of T. Vriezen, M. Buber, F. Rosenzweig, H. Rosin, L. M. von Pakodzy. He points out that with this translation of the "name," many passages are given a meaning that otherwise would be lacking, e.g., Is. 42:8; 49:23; Jer. 16:21.

teenth-century speculative theology to "prove" the necessity of the incarnation failed. It is, rather, the fundamental
confession and experience of Christian faith that, in the
midst of a world where language constantly fails and God
is experienced as absent, Jesus of Nazareth is the definitive
and irrevocable, but by no means exclusive or final, place
of God's self-presentation in word. Thus, a christology oriented to Jesus, not only as the one who was the definitive
word of faith but also as the constant agent of faithful word
and *praxis*, may be able to provide a basis for rediscovering
and bringing to birth anew that vitality of language by which
the presence of God can be experienced. We must look for
the occurrence of such speech not just in the religious community or in the language of piety, but also in the parlance
of the world, whenever and wherever a free and truthful,
wholesome and salvific, responsible and obedient word is
spoken in the midst of bondage and deceit, estrangement
and destruction, indifference and pride. There the risen
Jesus is present and there also the future God.

The argument by which these themes are elaborated will
be developed under two systematic foci, comprising Parts
Two and Three of this book. Part Two will seek to understand the *person* of Jesus as the one who *was presence* in a
primordial and definitive sense, for he was the one in
whom faithful speech and free, responsible, and obedient
action came fully to expression in virtue of God's self-
presentation in word. In the word of faith, as it is fully
accomplished in Jesus of Nazareth, not only is man gathered
into presence temporally and spatially, but also God and
man are co-present, for God's word-presence is the transcendent horizon and power of man's faithful word and act.
The argument will entail a philosophical and theological
analysis of "word" as the medium of presence (Chapter 3),
and an exegetical study of materials from the Synoptic
Gospels under the theme of "Jesus as the word of faith"
(Chapter 4). Part Three will address the question of the
work of Jesus as the one who is *now present*, the one who

is risen from the dead and comes to stand in the world as the agent of a new humanity, engaged in the practice of presence (Chapter 5). The two focal themes—Jesus as presence and as present—will be developed in dialectical fashion, showing that the mode of Jesus' past presence (his definitively faithful word) determines the way he is now present to us, and conversely that his contemporary presence is the hermeneutical "forestructure" of our access to his presence as past historical figure. In Chapter 2, on the method of christology, the hermeneutical principles that support this dialectical movement between Jesus as presence and as present, and thus serve as the basis of the systematic structure of the argument, will be examined.

2

METHOD: THE HERMENEUTICAL STRUCTURE OF CHRISTOLOGY

1. CHRISTOLOGY, FAITH, AND HISTORY

The task of christology is to interpret faith's confession that Jesus is the Christ—the one in whom the co-presence of God and man was definitively accomplished and who is now present as the agent of reconciliation—by reference to the historical Jesus as the ground, criterion, and witness of faith, and vice versa. Christology stands at the juncture of faith and history. In it, historical research and present responsibility, exegesis and kerygma, historical theology and dogmatic theology are inseparably related themes and must really merge into a single hermeneutical endeavor. Awareness of this fact has fully dawned only during the past two centuries as christology was freed from an exclusively dogmatic approach and as its emphasis shifted from the divinity to the humanity of Jesus under the impact of modern historical consciousness. This awareness is expressed in recent definitions of the task of christology, of which two may be taken as representative: "Christology deals with Jesus as the basis of the confession and the faith that he is the Christ of God" (Wolfhart Pannenberg);[1] "the success of Christology depends on one thing: whether we can show convincingly that in Jesus God has 'come to expression,' in such a way that faith must constantly return to its roots in Jesus" (Gerhard Ebeling).[2] Both definitions indicate that the task of christology is to establish a basis for faith—the faith that

1. *JGaM*, p. 21.
2. *ThP*, p. 33.

28

Jesus is the Christ—by reference to the historical Jesus. If they are correct, they mean that the christological task becomes coterminous with the question of the identity of the historical Jesus—when this question is rightly pursued by a hermeneutically self-conscious historical method, one that recognizes the dialectical interplay between critical investigation and the forejudgments and responsibility of the interpreter.[3]

These definitions mean that ultimately Jesus himself is the content and criterion of christology—not the kerygma and the dogmatic traditions of the church, nor the present experience of redemption that derives from participation in the community of faith. The tendency to make contemporary Christian experience normative for christology had its roots in Schleiermacher[4] and the Erlangen school of neo-Lutheranism; it was perpetuated by Kähler and the Ritschlian theologians, and it has been given contemporary expression in existentialist theology (especially Bultmann). It represents a post-critical tendency (one that recognizes the necessity and validity of historical research) to soften the often damaging impact of historical criticism on the claims of faith. It has rightly been criticized by Pannenberg,[5] who insists that christology must move behind the confessions (both ancient and modern) to Jesus himself; in this respect he is at one

3. In "Jesus and Faith" (1958), Ebeling writes: ". . . the quest of the historical Jesus cannot somehow take the place of Christology. Rather, the quest of the historical Jesus and Christology are tasks that have to be distinguished," *WF*, pp. 204-205. But in "The Question of the Historical Jesus and the Problem of Christology" (1959), he says quite unequivocally: ". . . either the question of the historical Jesus destroys Christology, or else the question of the historical Jesus must show itself to be identical with the Christological problem—*tertium non datur*," *WF*, p. 290. The dialectical character of this identity—which perhaps caused Ebeling to draw back from asserting it so boldly in the earlier essay—is a theme that will have to be examined in greater detail below.

4. Schleiermacher's christology starts with the consciousness of grace in the corporate life of the redeemed and moves from this "effect" to its "cause," the historical Jesus. See *ChrG*, Secs. 86-89. Schleiermacher also clearly downgrades the importance of historical exegesis for dogmatic statements about Christ. See *ChrG*, Sec. 99, Postscript (Redeker ed., Vol. II, p. 86; Eng. tr., pp. 421-422).

5. *JGaM*, pp. 22-30.

with the so-called "new quest." At the same time, it must be asked of Pannenberg whether he does not overly de-emphasize the importance of the present experience of Christ for christology. He argues that the risen Jesus is not now present to the community in the event of proclamation but rather has been exalted to "heaven," where he remains "hidden" until his return in glory. Pannenberg deliberately chooses the understanding of the presence of Christ characteristic of the older dogmatics against Bultmann and existentialism in general.

> No one now has an experience of [Christ] as risen and exalted, at least not an experience that could be distinguished with certainty from illusion. In the Corinthian Gnosticism, Paul battled the illusion that one can *experience* the glory of the exalted Lord in the present. The *experience* of the presence of Christ is promised only for the end of time. Therefore, also, whatever concerns the certainty of the present life of the exalted Lord is based entirely on what happened in the past.[6]

Here Pannenberg's peculiar emphasis upon the future at the expense of the present in over-reaction to existentialism is evident. The stress on the future requires a corresponding stress upon the past, or at least upon certain events of the past where the future comes proleptically into view. Hence in Pannenberg's theology the danger exists that the present will be absorbed into its past basis or its future destiny, and that consequently the proper dialectic will not be maintained between the present Christ and the historical Jesus.

The necessity of this dialectic is the fundamental concern of the present chapter. On the one hand, we must maintain, with Ebeling and Pannenberg, that the task of christology is coterminous with the quest for the historical Jesus. On the other hand, we must insist that the present experience and agency of Christ is an equally constitutive theme of christology, and that inquiry concerning the historical Jesus inevitably takes its start from this experience (or lack of it). On the one hand, the critically recovered Jesus of history is the basis and criterion of the proclamation and mission that

6. *Ibid.*, p. 28; cf. pp. 21, 371, and the whole of Chapter 10.

give expression to his presence. On the other hand, our contemporary mode of participation in the Christ-event provides the hermeneutical context for raising in significant fashion the question about the historical Jesus. Christology must move between these two poles and in both directions simultaneously. In the remainder of this chapter I shall examine this claim more fully—first with reference to the structures of historical thinking as such (Sec. 2), then with the christological problematic more specifically in view (Secs. 3-4).

2. THE DIALECTIC OF HISTORICAL THINKING

Let us consider the following thesis: the hermeneutical "circle"[7] is constituted by the dialectical movement between critico-interpretive and practical-responsive thinking in the total process of historical understanding. Hermeneutic is to be identified with the process of historical understanding as a whole, to which are subordinated two reciprocal and mutually conditioning functions: the critico-interpretive movement from the interpreter (or historian) through the text (or author) to the subject matter of the text, and the practical-responsive movement from the subject matter through the text to the interpreter. The first movement is a back-

---

7. The circle metaphor is not an entirely happy one. It suggests that understanding always returns to the point where it began (hence a "vicious" circle), which is not the case if true understanding takes place. The circle metaphor originated with romanticism, which conceived the hermeneutical problematic in terms of the relation between the whole and its parts, and which sought ultimately a hidden identity between interpreter and subject matter. (See H.-G. Gadamer, *WM*, pp. 178-179.) For this reason it may be appropriate, as Ray L. Hart has suggested, to think of a "hermeneutical spiral" rather than a hermeneutical circle. There *is* a circularity of motion in understanding; but rather than returning to the *same* point, understanding ought to move forward towards a richer, more complex, and ever-changing relation between the knower and what is known—a process that does not come to an end at some hypothetical pinnacle but continues in an open-ended spiral. (See Ray L. Hart, *Unfinished Man and the Imagination* [New York, Herder and Herder, 1968], pp. 60-62.) For my part, what is important is not the image of a circle but rather the dialectical or reflexive movement between critical and practical thinking, a continuous movement in which each element serves as the presupposition of, yet is critically corrected by, the other.

ward, "questioning" movement from the interpreter to the
subject matter of history, which he constitutes as an "object"
of his critical scrutiny. The second is a forward, "responsive"
movement of historical *praxis* from the subject matter to the
interpreter and his future, a movement to which the interpreter himself belongs, in which he must actively participate,
and for which he must assume responsibility if he is to
achieve authentic understanding.

The critico-interpretive movement involves a filtering of
empirically observed and transmitted historical data through
the medium of consciousness and the critical categories of
the mind; categories that serve to illumine the relation
between subject matter and text, to correct critically the
prejudices or forejudgments of the interpreter himself, and
to establish both text and subject matter in their historical
distance from the present. The critical factor applies interpretive categories by which the subject matter can be discerned as an "object" confronting the knower. It represents
noetic initiative on the part of the knower, by which things
are constituted before him as objects of knowledge. It
involves a flow of meaning *from* the interpreter through the
text to the subject matter. In the language of idealism, critical thinking can be described as the *self-transposition* of the
interpreter into the phenomena of history. F. C. Baur said
that the task of the historian is to "transpose himself into
the objective reality of the subject matter itself," so that
"instead of making history a reflection of his own subjectivity, he may be simply a mirror for the perception of historical phenomena in their true and real form."[8] And Wilhelm
Dilthey wrote that the task of understanding is to discover
"a life-structure in the given," which is accomplished by a
"transposition" of our own life-structure into that of a his-

8. F. C. Baur, *The Epochs of Church Historiography*, in Peter C. Hodgson,
ed. and trans., *Ferdinand Christian Baur: On the Writing of Church History*
(New York, Oxford University Press, 1968), p. 241. For Baur's technical
terminology, see p. 20, n. 46, and p. 364, n. 45.

torical figure or work. In this respect "understanding is intrinsically an operation inverse to the dynamic course [of history] itself."[9]

In the midst of (indeed, as the essential condition of) critical interpretation, a reversal in the flow of meaning must occur so that now the subject matter, the given of history, is permitted to present itself on its own terms and by its own power, rather than having an alien meaning imposed upon it. The interpreter brings a set of critical, conceptual tools to bear upon the subject matter, which occasions a reversal in the flow of meaning—from the subject matter (which is no longer "objectified") through the text toward the interpreter and his future, rather than merely from interpreter to subject matter. In turn, the pre-understanding or forestructures given with this "forward" flow of meaning and historical *praxis* is the fundamental source of the conceptuality that makes critical thinking possible, so that a constant dialectical tension and movement must exist between critical thinking and practical thinking in the process of understanding. It is impossible to say which comes first: we stand in a circle and are *in media res* wherever we start.

Again, the idealists grasped this point well. Baur argued that the purpose of the historian's critical transposition into the subject matter is to enable him to "present" (*darstellen*) or "rethink" (*Nachdenken*) the inner, essential continuity of the given of history, a rethinking that follows or traces the objective course of history as it moves itself forward in such fashion that the historical phenomena are permitted to present themselves or to appear for what they really are.[10] He also recognized the legitimacy and hermeneutical function of "interest," or what he called "theological standpoint" or "dogmatic consciousness," in the process of historical presentation and rethinking on the part of the theologian. This

9. Wilhelm Dilthey, *Gesammelte Schriften*, 4th unaltered ed. (Stuttgart, B. G. Teubner Verlagsgesellschaft, 1957-58), Vol. 7, pp. 213-214.
10. Hodgson, *op. cit.*, pp. 18, 20, n. 46, 46-48, 241, 283, 305, 366.

was a central theme of his book, *The Epochs of Church Historiography*.[11] Instead of *Nachdenken,* Dilthey used the categories *Nacherleben* and *Nachbilden* to express the same process—a terminological shift that reflects his movement away from an idealist to a more broadly experiential or vitalistic framework. Historical understanding develops in terms of the dialectic between critical "transposition" and empathetic "reliving." "On the basis of this transposition there now emerges the highest art, in which the totality of the spiritual life is effective in understanding—reproducing [*Nachbilden*] or reliving [*Nacherleben*]. . . . A complete empathy is . . . dependent upon understanding proceeding along the line of events itself. It moves steadily and progressively forward with the course of life itself. . . . Reliving is a creating along the line of events."[12]

These themes have been developed in masterful fashion by Hans-Georg Gadamer in his philosophical hermeneutic, *Wahrheit und Methode*.[13] He defines the hermeneutical circle in contrast to the main stream of hermeneutical theory of the nineteenth century:

> The circle is . . . not formal in nature, nor is it either subjective or objective. Rather it describes understanding as the intertwining play of the movement of tradition and the movement of interpretation. The anticipation of meaning that guides our understanding of a text is not an act of subjectivity but rather is determined by the commonality that binds us to the tradition. . . . It is not simply a presupposition under which we always stand; rather, we produce it ourselves, in so far as we understand, take part in the event of tradition, and thereby further determine this event ourselves. The circle of understanding is thus not a "methodological" circle but describes an ontological structural moment of understanding.[14]

Understanding is accomplished through "the intertwining play of the movement of tradition and the movement of

---

11. *Ibid.,* pp. 12, 46-49, 270, 335-336.
12. Dilthey, *op. cit.,* Vol. VII, p. 214; see pp. 213-216.
13. I have been aided in my understanding of Gadamer by an unpublished doctoral dissertation by David E. Linge, "Historicity and Hermeneutic: A Study in Contemporary Hermeneutical Theory" (Vanderbilt University, 1969).
14. *WM,* p. 277.

interpretation." The "movement of tradition" is the medium of what Gadamer calls "forejudgments" or "prejudices," following Heidegger's analysis of the "forestructures" of interpretation and Bultmann's concept of "pre-understanding."[15] We are not to attempt to deny or escape our forejudgments, as was the case with historicism and rationalism, but rather to recognize "the essentially 'prejudicial' character of all understanding." The "fundamental prejudice of the Enlightenment is the prejudice against prejudice in general and thus the weakening of tradition." "Prejudice" (*Vorurteil*) does not simply mean "false judgment" (*falsches Urteil*); that is another of the prejudices of the Enlightenment. Rather there are also *préjugés légitimes*, and the task of interpretation is "to distinguish the *true* prejudices, by which we *understand*, from the *false* prejudices, by which we misunderstand."[16] This distinction requires, in turn, a recognition of the significance of temporal distance for understanding. Temporal distance is not something to be overcome by identification with the thoughts of the author, as was thought to be the case by romanticism and historicism. Rather, it represents a positive and productive possibility of understanding. Contemporaneity with an event means uncontrollable, misleading, and uncertain prejudices. Only when an event is far enough removed in time for its context to be closed and definable is it possible to achieve a degree of objectivity in understanding. Time is not the

15. On Bultmann's analysis of pre-understanding as the existential relation of the interpreter to the subject matter, which prompts the question he brings to the text and elicits the answer he obtains from the text, see "The Problem of Hermeneutics" in *Essays Philosophical and Theological* (London, SCM Press, 1955), pp. 234-261; and *Jesus Christ and Mythology* (New York, Charles Scribner's Sons, 1958), pp. 49-53. See also Pannenberg's criticism of Bultmann's "anthropological narrowing" of the pre-understanding in "Hermeneutics and Universal History," *JThC*, Vol. 4 (1967), p. 132; and Gadamer's criticism of Bultmann's conception of pre-understanding as the "self-understanding of faith" in *Kleine Schriften I* (Tübingen, J. C. B. Mohr [Paul Siebeck], 1967), pp. 70-81. On Heidegger's analysis of the function of the "forestructures" of interpretation in the hermeneutical circle, see *BT*, pp. 194-195.

16. *WM*, pp. 254-255, 279, 282.

great enemy of historical understanding but its indispensable asset.[17]

The recognition of temporal distance means that we can overcome false prejudices, not by eliminating *our own* prejudices through identification with those of the author (precisely this is to deny historical distance), but rather by bringing our prejudices *into play* in what Gadamer describes as the language game of conversation. Conversation with a text is conducted by the dialectic of question and answer. We understand the question posed to the text by its subject matter and likewise respond to the text's question directed to us by posing a new question to the subject matter of the text from our own perspective. The text thus comes alive by becoming the answer to a real question; the one retrieved or reconstructed in our questioning. In this process the meaning-horizons of the text and the interpreter "merge" or "fuse" in the common subject matter, which is brought to expression anew by the interpreter's questioning. Instead of separate, static, and closed horizons of meaning, there is accomplished in conversation a horizon-fusion, an encompassing horizon that is coterminous with the process of historical tradition as such. In this encompassing horizon our own prejudices are brought into play and contribute to the formation of tradition, but at the same time they are purified and corrected by the questions posed by the text.[18] Gadamer makes it clear that we *respond* to the question of the text (thus entering responsibly into the movement of tradition) by *questioning further* the subject matter of the text, which is thereby brought to light in a new way. In other words, our "backward" critical questioning of the text is precisely the way we move "forward" with the historically given. Here the critical-interpretive and practical-responsive elements of historical thinking are brought

17. *Ibid.*, pp. 279-282.
18. *Ibid.*, pp. 283, 286-290, 351-360, 365-366, 437-438.

together in the closest unity and are seen to be distinguishable aspects of the same process.

By emphasizing its character as a language game, Gadamer shows that understanding is something that occurs in the event of conversation itself and is not imposed by either the interpreter or the object. The interpreter is caught up in the game, which has its own movement and "buoyancy." Understanding is an event that "happens" to the interpreter rather than being accomplished by him.

> . . . the game itself plays, since it encompasses the player within itself and thus itself becomes the true *subjectum* of the movement of the game. Accordingly, we are not to speak here of a playing with language or with the contents of world experience or tradition that address us, but rather of the play of language itself, which addresses us, proposes and withdraws, questions and in the answer fulfills itself. Therefore, understanding is a game not in the sense that he who understands playfully holds himself back, denying binding participation in the claim that confronts him. The freedom of self-possession that belongs to the ability to hold oneself back is here not given at all, and this must be said in applying the game concept to understanding. Whoever understands is already incorporated into an event that validates itself through its own meaningfulness.[19]

In the dialectic of conversation there occurs "an action of the subject matter itself."[20] Hence Gadamer seeks to free understanding from the "methodicalness" of the modern sciences and to view it as an event transcending the interpreter. The task of hermeneutic "is not to develop a method of understanding but rather to clarify the conditions under which understanding happens."[21] Thus we must appreciate the somewhat ironic title of Gadamer's book, *Wahrheit und Methode*. "Truth" is not something accomplished by "method"; rather it gives itself in the game of understand-

19. *Ibid.*, pp. 464-465; see pp. 97-105, 461-465, and *Kleine Schriften I*, pp. 75-81.
20. *WM*, pp. 439-441; see also pp. 437-448. The words are Hegel's in describing the dialectical method: true method is "das Tun der Sache selbst" (*Logik*, Vol. II, p. 330).
21. *Ibid.*, p. 279.

ing, which corresponds to the structure and reality of history as such. The book as a whole represents an extended polemic against the "methodical" character of post-Cartesian scientific knowledge, which in Gadamer's view has obscured authentic hermeneutical experience, displacing the event of truth by the subjectivity of the knower.

Several of Gadamer's insights have been developed further by one of his students, the Frankfurt sociologist and philosopher Jürgen Habermas, in his recent book, *Erkenntnis und Interesse*.[22] In reaction to the traditional model of the "disinterested" pursuit of truth, as well as to the "pure methodology" of the modern positive sciences, Habermas attempts to develop the concept of *erkenntnisleitende Interessen*—"interests that guide knowledge"—as a legitimate and essential epistemological principle in its own right.[23] By means of critical self-reflection, interest guides knowledge toward a *praxis* that achieves liberation from pre-critical dogmatism (Kant, Fichte, Hegel); from the domination of nature, class society, and "ideology" (Marx); and from psychological self-delusion and cultural and institutional constraints (Freud).[24] In each instance the "interest" of reason moves towards the practical achievement of emancipation, enlightenment, and maturity. This interest is characterized by "spontaneity of hope, acts of participation, the experience of relevance or indifference above all, sensibility for suffering and suppression, passion for maturity, will to emancipation, and the joy of discovered identity."[25] Habermas traces the development of interest as an epistemological principle, and the concom-

22. Jürgen Habermas, *Erkenntnis und Interesse* (Frankfurt, Suhrkamp Verlag, 1968). See also his earlier collection of essays, *Theorie und Praxis: Sozialphilosophische Studien* (Neuwied am Rhein and Berlin, Hermann Luchterhand Verlag, 1963; 2nd ed., 1967), esp. "Dogmatismus, Vernunft und Entscheidung—Zu Theorie und Praxis in der verwissenschaftlichen Zivilisation," pp. 231-257.

23. Habermas, *Erkenntnis und Interesse*, pp. 9-14, 235, 242, 258, 364.

24. *Ibid.*, pp. 245-259, 261, 265-266, 348-350; *Theorie und Praxis*, pp. 231, 238-239.

25. Habermas, *Theorie und Praxis*, p. 239; cf. *Erkenntnis und Interesse*, pp. 286-290, where Habermas describes the characteristics of psychoanalytical knowledge as a form of self-reflection.

itant correlation of theory and practice, from its inception in Kant, Fichte, Hegel, and Marx, through the expulsion of interest from the court of knowledge by positivism, pragmatism, and historicism, to the attempted reconstruction of a theory of knowledge on the basis of scientific self-reflection by Freud.

It is now possible to explain more fully why I have described the "forward" movement of historical thinking as "practical" and "responsive" in character. Jürgen Moltmann rightly observes: "Hermeneutic falls into the danger of a formalism when it only inquires backward towards an understanding of the past under the conditions of the present. . . . Theological hermeneutic remains abstract so long as it does not become the theory of a practice, and sterile if it does not permit the 'access to future truth.' "[26] "Practice" here does not mean the pragmatic utilization of historical study for the purpose of furthering one's own subjective prejudices, as was the case with Enlightenment historiography. Rather, it means engagement with a process that transcends the interpreter and corrects his prejudices as he brings them into play. It means orientation toward the future, which is the common bond between past and present in the dialectic of understanding. It means the "interest" that guides knowledge in whatever form (scientific, historical, philosophical, theological) towards the achievement of liberation, maturity, identity, presence. Such "interest" involves both a receptive, responsive element—a being caught up in and responding to the givenness of history; and an active, practical element—a moving of history forward toward its goal, and thus an involvement in the dynamic course of history itself. Response and practice belong to the essence of the hermeneutical enterprise. They do not merely follow from understanding but enable it; truth is won only by *engagement*. The term "responsibility" may be taken to

---

26. Moltmann, "Toward a Political Hermeneutic of the Gospel," *RRF*, pp. 97-98. Translation mine; cf. *Perspektiven der Theologie* (München, Chr. Kaiser Verlag, 1968), p. 139.

embrace the elements of both response and practice.[27] Historical responsibility involves response to what is given by
tradition and engagement in the *praxis* by which the possibilities mediated through tradition are brought to realization anew. What this means concretely may be shown by
applying the concept of responsibility to the method of
christology.

3. CHRISTOLOGY AS PRESENT RESPONSIBILITY AND AS HISTORICAL QUEST

A vital christology must maintain the tension between the
present responsibility of faith, which seeks to bring the
Christ-event to expression anew in the contemporary situation, and the quest of the historical Jesus. It must maintain
the sense of historical distance between past and present
that Gadamer has shown to be essential for understanding.
In this respect christology, as a hermeneutical procedure,
reflects the dialectical movement that characterizes historical
thinking in general. The constant temptation of christology
is to avoid this tension by collapsing one of its two poles
into the other. Since both poles together are essential to its
genuine historicity, this temptation can be described as the
de-historicizing of christology. We may refer to a "Catholiciz-
ing" tendency on the one hand and to a "liberalizing" tendency on the other. According to the first, the temptation is
that of absorbing the historical Jesus into the present Christ
(and thus the Christian community) without remainder,
robbing christology of its critical-historical dimension.
According to the second, the temptation is that of absorbing the present Christ into the historical Jesus without
remainder, robbing christology of its practical-responsive

27. Ebeling has developed the theme of responsibility instructively. Theology,
he says, is both a critical and a responsible science. It involves critical exegesis
of the tradition, but also must "assume responsibility for that with which it is
confronted in history," answering it by bringing it to expression anew in
responsible fashion. (*ThP*, pp. 107-109.)

dimension. The great weakness of the "old," liberal quest of the historical Jesus was its lack of genuine interest in and sense of responsibility for the presence of the Christ-event, and thus it was hard put to account for the reconciling significance of Jesus. Christology became largely a biographical procedure (the *Leben-Jesu-Forschung*) into which contemporary prejudices nevertheless surreptitiously crept, as Schweitzer so devastatingly showed, because of the loss of hermeneutical distance. In reaction to the liberal quest, dialectical theology fell into the opposite danger. This is especially clear from Bultmann, who emphasizes again and again in his writings the contemporaneity of the "salvation-event" (the Christ-event), which can happen only "here and now," "in my particular present," and must always be laid hold of anew in the immediate situation.[28]

Against these two tendencies, the practical-responsive and the critical-historical dimensions of christology must be held in balance. The contemporary act of faith (the confession that Jesus is the Christ and the worldly mission based on this confession) is the "forestructure" of christological understanding in general and of the quest for the historical Jesus in particular. Participation in the contemporary occurrence of the Christ-event is the fundamental "prejudice" with which historical thinking about Jesus must begin. To paraphrase Heidegger, any critical interpretation of the historical Jesus that is to contribute to understanding of him must already have understood what is to be interpreted. The quest for the historical Jesus already operates in the forestructure of faith (or the lack of it). Our task is not to deny this forestructure either by attempting to achieve "contemporaneity" with Jesus or by restricting historical research to a purely positivistic method. Rather, we must allow our prejudices to be corrected and purified by bringing them "into play" through conversation with the tradition, by work-

28. Rudolf Bultmann, *Existence and Faith*, ed. and trans. by Schubert M. Ogden (New York, Meridian Books, 1960), pp. 73, 78-79; and *Jesus Christ and Mythology*, pp. 63-65, 79.

ing them out "in terms of the things themselves."[29] In this process, as Gadamer points out, the tradition comes alive by becoming the answer to a real question—the question posed by our responsible participation in the tradition and our questioning further with it. The task of christology in the first instance is not merely to *repeat* the faith of Jesus or the dogmatic norms of the tradition, but rather to bring this faith to expression anew in ways that determine and direct our own existence. The expression of this faith is to be understood not merely as *kerygma,* proclamation (although it is certainly that), but also as *mission,* responsibility for the world. This makes explicit what often remained unrecognized in kerygmatic theology, namely, that the word of faith is a word-*event,* issuing in the *praxis* by which a new world is constituted. Thus rather than speaking of "kerygmatic christology," I prefer to speak of "responsible christology"—a christology that moves forward with and participates in the event of salvation that Jesus of Nazareth *is.* Precisely this participation is not the denial of the historicity of christology but the fundamental expression of it, the expression of the practical-responsive element in its hermeneutical structure. The emasculation of this element in the nineteenth-century *Leben-Jesu-Forschung* led to the de-historicization of christology, its reduction to a merely biographical procedure, a preoccupation with dead and therefore meaningless facts of the historical past. Of course, acknowledgement of christology's responsible function does not permit the substitution of assertions of faith for the realities of history or the avoidance of pursuing historical questions to their limit. Rather faith is to be brought into hermeneutical play with the given of history, and thus is to be corrected and purified in the process of understanding, which it permits.

Christology that participates responsibly in the contemporary practice of faith maintains continuity with the tradition

29. *BT,* pp. 194-195.

often by means of the most radical discontinuity. We move backward only by moving forward. This paradox has been brought out forcefully by Ernst Käsemann:

> . . . the community bore (and still bears) witness to history as being living and contemporary. It interprets out of its own experience what for it has already become mere history and employs for this purpose the medium of preaching. It is precisely by this method that the community rescues the facts of the past from being regarded only as prodigies and wonders. And in so doing, it demonstrates that in its eyes Jesus is no mere miracle-worker, but the *Kyrios,* from whom it knows itself to receive both grace and obligation. To state the paradox as sharply as possible: the community takes so much trouble to maintain historical continuity with him who once trod this earth that it allows the historical events of this earthly life to pass for the most part into oblivion and replaces them by its own message. It is not only at this point in its history that the community does this. The same process is always being repeated in the course of Church history. Time and again, continuity with the past is preserved by shattering the received terminology, the received imagery, the received theology—in short, by shattering the tradition. . . . The truth is that it is this variation which makes continuity possible at all. For mere history becomes significant history not through tradition as such but through interpretation, not through the simple establishment of facts but through the understanding of events of the past which have become objectified and frozen into facts. . . . Mere history only takes on genuine historical significance in so far as it can address both a question and an answer to our contemporary situation; in other words, by finding interpreters who hear and utter this question and answer. For this purpose primitive Christianity allows mere history no vehicle of expression other than the kerygma.[30]

"Continuity with the past is preserved by shattering the received terminology": this means that we can say again what came to expression in Jesus only by saying it differently. Within the continuity of content must be acknowledged discontinuity of form of expression. Thus we can recognize the continuity of fifth-century Chalcedonian christology with the earliest New Testament christologies, despite the quite radical discontinuity of form; and likewise we can recognize the continuity of contemporary christology with that of the Greek and Latin Fathers, despite the fact that their mytho-

---

30. "The Problem of the Historical Jesus," *ENTT,* pp. 20-21.

logical world view and metaphysical concepts are no longer
viable for us. Christology in each epoch of the church's
history has had to exercise its responsibility in different
fashion, depending upon its philosophical, cultural, and
linguistic context. In each case it has had to engage in a
"coherent deformation" (Merleau-Ponty) of tradition in
order to maintain continuity with it.

But it is insufficient to start with our contemporary situation alone. Not only do we learn the meaning of Jesus' past
presence and identity from his contemporary presence, but
the reverse is also true: Jesus is now present in terms of the
qualities of his historical presence, and it is from the latter
that we learn to recognize the former. Only because he was
then presence can he now be present. Just as we move
backward only by moving forward, so also we move forward
only by moving backward. Each new *form* of christological
confession must be tested and interpreted by reference to
the common *content* of christology—God's redemptive deed
in the words, activity, and fate of Jesus. He is the criterion
of christology to whom we must always return in carrying
forward his cause. Hence, christology has a critical-interpretive, as well as a practical-responsive task. It must interpret
the confession and practice of faith by critical reference to
the ground of faith. It must move "behind" the kerygma
(both ancient and contemporary) to the historical Jesus.

Three points may be advanced in defense of this thesis:
(1) The quest for the historical Jesus is not a matter of the
"proof" or "legitimation" of faith but rather of its interpretation. (2) Christological tradition (both biblical and post-
biblical) itself expresses a relation to the historical Jesus.
(3) The present responsibility of faith can be interpreted
only by reference to the historical Jesus.[31]

(1) My analysis of the structures of historical thinking
demonstrated that the task of historical study is not merely

31. The extent to which I am dependent upon Chapter 3 of Ebeling's
Theology and Proclamation in developing these themes will be apparent. At
the same time, I have sought to systematize the argument in a way not found
in his chapter.

to ascertain objectively demonstrable "facts" but to under-
take the critical interpretation of events, and, furthermore,
that such interpretation engages the "forestructures" or "prejudices" of the interpreter. To be sure, the historian must concern himself with the establishment of facts and the critical
sifting of data, but that is at best preliminary to the more
fundamental exercise of historical understanding in the dialectical movement between critical and practical thinking.
The investigation of facts is at best "sub-history" rather than
history proper.[32] Or more precisely, there are no historical
"facts" that are not already interpreted events. Can we
properly speak of "proof" in reference to historical work at
all? What is it that the historian "proves"? It is certainly
possible to establish with a high degree of probability the
place and time of a large number of events of the historical
past. But understanding the causes, significance, and precise
nature of these events is a complex matter, involving a
reflexive or dialectical relation between event, text, and
interpreter. Historical knowledge in its full range cannot be
construed on the model of the natural or empirical sciences;
hence such concepts as "proof," "verification," "corroboration," do not properly apply to it. They are alien to the
process of historical judgment.

This is doubly true when it comes to the question of faith.
Faith by definition is not subject to proof or legitimation of
any sort. Faith is the gift of the word of God, empowering
man to a new mode of existence. Although intrinsically
related to historical events, it is not "caused" by such events.
Faith involves acknowledging as normatively true and constitutive for one's own existence what is precisely always
only probably certain in the historical mode. It involves a
recognition of the significance of certain events for salvation
that goes beyond any possibility of proof. We may be able
to argue historically that Jesus' speaking exhibited in definitive fashion the qualities of faithfulness (cf. Chapter 4),

32. I am indebted to Paul Schubert for this suggestion.

but that he was thereby *in fact* the word of God is a judgment of faith, not of historical reason. Ebeling has argued that when we speak of Jesus as the "ground" or "basis" of faith we do not mean that he is the cause of faith. Faith cannot occur as an effect within a causal sequence. As the gift of the word of God, faith is the quintessence of freedom. It can be "provoked" only in the sense of being "invited" and "called forth." As the ground of faith, Jesus is the "provocation" of our faith. At the same time, he is the criterion of faith, encouraging and requiring it to be pure faith, not founded in itself or in any human source but only in the gift of the word. Finally, he is the example of faith, the one in whom faith came fully to expression. He is the provocation, criterion, and example of faith because he is the witness of faith; and it is as witness that he becomes the ground of faith. The quest of the historical Jesus involves the *interpretation* of faith by critical reference to the ground of faith rather than its proof or legitimation.[33]

(2) Christological confession and practice itself expresses a relation to the historical Jesus. Above all, the primitive Christian kerygma concentrated attention on his name and person; he was its subject matter. Its purpose was to correspond to Jesus by functioning as an appropriate and relevant response in its own situation to the word that came to expression in him. "If the difference between Jesus and the kerygma should turn out to be in the nature of an absolute contradiction, and, as such, to be a startling misinterpreta-

---

33. *ThP*, pp. 36-39, 55-58, 68-69; and Lectures on Christology, University of Tübingen, Summer Semester 1967, pp. 184-185. Ebeling points out that Bultmann's strictures against the quest of the historical Jesus are motivated by his insistence that faith is not subject to historical "proof," combined with his tendency to reduce historical study to a positivistic model (the ascertainment of objectively demonstrable facts), which means in principle that the historian can describe only the bare *Dass* of Jesus. Faith, on the other hand, is concerned with the *Was* of Jesus, which is not accessible to objective scientific inquiry. Although Bultmann has combined historical and systematic interests in his own work as a New Testament theologian with great skill, nevertheless there lies at the heart of his epistemological reflections a dualism between *Historie* and *Geschichte*. On this question, see Heinrich Ott, *Geschichte und Heilsgeschichte in der Theologie Rudolf Bultmanns* (Tübingen, J. C. B. Mohr [Paul Siebeck], 1955), Chapter 1.

tion of Jesus, . . . then the kerygma would have cancelled itself out as a self-contradiction."[34] The ancient church, in proclaiming the presence of the risen Lord, declared him to be the same one who had taught among men and died on a cross. Hence the Evangelists found it necessary to bring narratives about Jesus' earthly ministry and passion together with their affirmations of his resurrection and present lordship once the living memories of his ministry had faded away. Now it was necessary to guard against Gnosticism, docetism, and the mythologization of the Gospel; for this purpose, the Pauline kerygma alone was insufficient. The tendency toward the historicizing of the kerygma was at work in all the Gospels, including the Johannine.[35] Furthermore, this tendency was exercised in not uncritical fashion, although obviously we cannot speak of a critical historiography in the modern sense. But already, a critical element was at work in the principle of selectivity by which both the 'Evangelists and the canon culled authentic traditions from apocryphal ones and riveted attention to what was absolutely essential about Jesus, excluding speculative biographical, psychological, and apocryphal factors, and many of the more blatant forms of miracle.

(3) The present responsibility of faith can be interpreted only by reference to the historical Jesus. Such interpretation is required because the meaning of traditional christological formulae is no longer self-evident. The titles by which Jesus was identified in the tradition—Christ, Lord, Son of God, Son of Man, Word of God—although intended to interpret the meaning of Jesus, are no longer directly intelligible and cannot interpret themselves. They presuppose a view of the world in which talk about God could be taken for granted. But this is no longer the case; we can learn to speak about God, if at all, only by turning to the historical Jesus. Thus

---

34. *ThP*, pp. 64-65; cf. pp. 71-72. See also *ENTT*, p. 25; and Günther Bornkamm, *Jesus of Nazareth*, trans. by Irene and Fraser McLuskey with J. M. Robinson (New York, Harper & Row, 1960), pp. 22-23.
35. *ENTT*, pp. 24-34; and *ThP*, pp. 130-133, 174.

the christological titles must be interpreted by reference to
him, to whom they refer in any case. This does not mean
that these titles must of necessity be abandoned; but it does
mean that if we are to continue to speak of Jesus as "son of
God" or "word of God" we must do so in a way that takes its
bearing from his historical life and avoids the mythological
context to which these titles originally belonged.[36] It is not
only traditional christological confession that must be interpreted by reference to Jesus; our own situation requires
such interpretation too. The language of our time offers of
itself no christological schemata. As suggested in Chapter 1,
it is precisely the experience of the absence of God rather
than his presence that characterizes our age. Thus, if we are
to speak of Jesus as the one in whom God and man are
definitively co-present, and by whom this co-presence is
rendered efficaciously present to us as well, then we cannot
take our bearings in the first instance from available definitions of divine-human presence but from the person of Jesus.
The requisite interpretation of christological confession can
only be carried out by a critical investigation of the person
and words of Jesus. This investigation involves bringing the
best available tools of literary, form-critical, and traditio-
historical analysis to bear upon the Synoptic traditions concerning Jesus—a task to which I shall address myself in
Chapter 4. Such analysis operates in the forestructure of
faith and christological *praxis* not in order to escape this
forestructure but precisely to interpret and correct it.

4. PERSON AND WORK: JESUS AS PRESENCE AND AS PRESENT

In summary, the faith that understands Jesus by exercising its present responsibility must, itself, be interpreted by
critical reference to its historical ground, criterion, and
example; in this process the hermeneutical structure of

36. *ThP*, pp. 49-52, 65.

christology is completed. Now a further step may be taken: a correspondence exists between the content of christology and its hermeneutical structure, provided that *what* we say about Jesus derives from the way we *know* him, and conversely that our *knowledge* of him corresponds to his *being*. Thus the classical distinctions in christology between person and work, humiliation and exaltation, earthly Jesus and risen Lord (but not between human and divine natures[37]) may be seen to correspond to the two poles of its hermeneutical structure that have been described—historical quest and present responsibility. They are, above all, hermeneutical distinctions, and that means they must be viewed as different moments in understanding the same subject matter. They must never be separated and can be distinguished only dialectically, as a means of understanding who the one man, Jesus of Nazareth, is in his self-manifestation.

The systematic foci of this essay—Jesus as presence and as present—represent an attempt at reformulating the classical distinction between the person and work of Christ in such a way as to bring out the dialectical relation between these two themes (a dialectic that follows from the hermeneutical structure of christology, i.e., from the way we know Jesus), and with the intent of focusing upon the problematic of the absence and presence of God. The doctrine of the *person* of Christ (the doctrine of the incarnation) may be understood to direct its attention to the historical Jesus, the one who *was presence* in virtue of God's self-presentation in word. The doctrine of the *work* of Christ

---

37. I do not intend to argue, in a fashion similar to Pannenberg, that the "humanity" of Jesus corresponds to the critically recovered Jesus of history, whereas the "divinity" corresponds to the risen Lord. I shall propose in Sec. 1, Chapter 3 that the impasses of the traditional doctrine of divine and human "natures" in Jesus must be avoided entirely. Needless to say, this does not amount to eliminating the distinction between God and man. But the concept of distinguishable "natures" in Jesus is a metaphysical abstraction that violates historical experience and does not correspond to the hermeneutical structure of christology, i.e., to the way that we *know* Jesus. Both as past historical figure and as one who is now present, we know him only in the unity of word of God and word of man, i.e., as the *homologia fidei.*

(the doctrine of atonement or soteriology) is properly concerned with the one who *is present*, the one who is risen
from the dead and "comes to stand" in the world as the
agent of reconciliation, in whose agency we are called to
share. "Resurrection" means the contemporary practice of
presence, which is reconciliation, atonement, salvation. It
means the making present of what Jesus *was*, namely,
"presence." Thus, the doctrine of the work of Christ and
the doctrine of the resurrection are ultimately one and
the same.

The association of the *work* of Christ with his *contemporary reconciling presence* represents a departure from classical theories of the atonement, justification for which must
now be provided. At the risk of over-simplification, three
basic types of atonement theory may be distinguished.
According to the first, the work of Christ is understood as
an objective, past fact, accomplished essentially without
human participation. Here two subtypes may be distinguished. The first subtype is what Aulén referred to as the
"classic" or *Christus victor* theory of atonement—the theory
that he hoped to rehabilitate. The work of Christ is understood as a victorious conflict with the powers that hold men
in thralldom. George S. Hendry has rightly designated three
basic difficulties with this theory. It is based on a dualism
and the notion of a cosmic struggle between God and Satan
that is no longer intelligible and in any case is intrinsically
alien to the Christian faith. Second, the objective transformation of the human situation accomplished by Christ's victory over Satan has no direct bearing on the subjective
human condition—man remains a spectator. Finally, no
essential significance is attached to the humanity of Christ,
for only a suprahuman person, the eternal Son of God, could
subdue suprahuman evil; on this theory it is not clear why
the incarnation should have been necessary.[38] The second subtype is the Anselmic "satisfaction" or "transaction"

38. George S. Hendry, *The Gospel of the Incarnation* (Philadelphia, The
Westminster Press, 1958), pp. 122-123.

theory, which became normative for Latin Christianity, including the Reformers. Here "Christ is held to have done something to God—either he discharged a debt or he paid a penalty or he performed an act of obedience or he made a confession or he offered a sacrifice—by means of which he procured forgiveness for man."[39] Thus atonement is the result of a transaction between the Son and the Father from which man is essentially excluded. Forgiveness seems to become "a matter of commutative justice, of *quid pro quo*," rather than being a free gift of God directed to man. "The questionable aspect of the theory is the assumption . . . that the root of the problem is in God and that it consists in his having to find an equation between his mercy and his justice, in virtue of which he can extend mercy without prejudice to his justice."[40] Hendry points out that Barth combines the "classic" and "transactional" theories in his understanding of the work of Christ as "the judge judged in our place."[41] Juridical concepts are given an ontological basis. Hence Barth stands as the major contemporary representative of "objective" theories of atonement.

According to the second major type of atonement theory, the work of Christ is understood as a subjective transformation in the believer. Salvation is effected by the moral influence that Jesus exerts as our example: the locus of redemption is the subjectivity of the believer, and the "work" of Christ can become synonymous with man's accomplishment of moral freedom and universality of intention. This theory is generally traced back to Abelard (although he stressed the priority of the love *of God* in atonement), and it received some impetus from the Reformers' interest in the *beneficii Christi* (although they held to a transactional theory of atonement), as well as from Socinianism and Arminianism. But it achieved fruition only in late eighteenth- and early nineteenth-century rationalism—above all in Kant, for whom

39. *Ibid.*, p. 116.
40. *Ibid.*, pp. 116-121.
41. *CD*, Vol. IV/1, Sec. 59.2. See Hendry, *op. cit.*, pp. 123-128.

"Christ" is really nothing more than the ideal of moral perfection. Accordingly, the whole process of atonement falls into the sphere of moral consciousness.

The shortcoming of the subjective theory in its boldest expression is self-evident for ultimately it locates redemption in a human action or ideal for which God is unnecessary, and it loses sight of the fact that reconciliation has to do with the relationship between God and man. On the other hand, the great weakness of objective theories of atonement is that they locate the work of Christ in some objective fact of the past, whether transcendent (the cosmic victory over Satan) or historical (the substitutionary death on the cross). Not only does this procedure remove man from the atonement process, so that reconciliation confronts him as an extrinsic magnitude to be appropriated or rejected. It also reduces the atoning work of Christ to certain isolated deeds and thus abstracts from his humanity as a whole. The distinction between the "person" and the "work" of Christ has usually been *misunderstood* as a distinction between what Jesus "was" and what he "did." His reconciling deed (his suffering and death on the cross) was something different from his human identity, his person. But this form of the distinction can only be regarded as an abstraction. A person *is* what he says and does: one's work is the expression of one's person, and one's person is manifest in one's work. Accordingly, Jesus' work was his person as a whole—his identity as the one in whom presence was definitively accomplished. We must not delimit his work to certain isolated elements in his life-history, such as his passion and death, or his proclamation of the kingdom of God, or his healing of the sick and afflicted, or his polemic against conventional religious piety. If we speak of Christ's "work" as a distinguishable theme, it can only refer to the making *present*, i.e., to the efficacious realization for us today, of what Jesus *was*, namely, "presence." My formula, "Jesus as presence and as present," suggests a third type of atonement theory, according to which the work of Christ is understood as the contemporary practice of presence—the making efficacious for us today of what came to speech (in deed as well as word) in Jesus. The point of transition (if we may refer to it as that) between the "person" and the "work" of Jesus is the transition from death to resurrection—for "resurrection" means the present reconciling action of Christ.[42]

Anticipations of this form of atonement theory are found in Schleiermacher. He begins with the thesis that "the peculiar activity and the exclusive dignity of the Redeemer imply each other, and are inseparably one in the self-consciousness of believers."[43] The "exclusive dignity" of the Redeemer refers to the person of Christ, whereas the "peculiar activity" refers to his work. The two themes of activity and dignity are dialectically related, and Schleier-macher notes that the whole doctrine of Christ could be developed from either of them.[44] Christ's "peculiar activity" is comprised of both "redemptive" and "reconciling" components: on the one hand, "he assumes believers into the power of his God-consciousness" (which is his "exclusive dignity")—his redemptive activity; on the other hand, he assumes them into "the fellowship of his unclouded blessed-ness" (which is the state of harmony or peace that accrues

---

42. Although Barth's treatment of the work of Christ belongs to the objective-transactional theory, in another context he acknowledges just this point. In turning from the death of Jesus to the resurrection, he says, we are concerned with "the transition from the understanding of the person and work of Christ to soteriology proper, to the question of the *applicatio salutis:* How does the atonement made then and there come to us and become our atonement? And at this supreme point the question is answered by the recognition that Jesus Christ as the Son who was once obedient to the Father and offered Himself and reconciled the world and us with God is in eternity and therefore to-day now, at this very hour, our active and effective Representative and Advocate before God, and therefore the real basis of our justification and hope. . . . All honour to the human and historical pragmatism of recollection, tradition and proclamation. But in relation to the divine history of this *repraesentatio* and *oblatio* it can be considered only as an epiphenomenon, with a significance which is only secondary, and indirect, that of an instrument and witness. The eternal action of Jesus Christ grounded in His resurrection is itself the true and direct bridge from once to always, from Himself in His time to us in our time." (*CD*, Vol. IV/1, pp. 314-315.)

43. *ChrG*, Sec. 92, thesis statement (Redeker ed., Vol. II, p. 31; Eng. tr., p. 374).

44. *Ibid.*, Sec. 92.3.

from the power of God-consciousness)—his reconciling
activity.[45] Redemption and reconciliation are accomplished
by "the living action of Christ" in "the corporate life he
founded."[46] Such action involves the dissemination and
internalization in the consciousness of humanity of the
God-consciousness and blessedness that Jesus of Nazareth *is*.
This is Christ's redemptive-reconciling *work*. It is important to stress that for Schleiermacher it is *his* work. For,
whereas reconciliation occurs as a fact of self-consciousness,
it remains, nevertheless, an act of the Redeemer. Reconciliation "is the act of the Redeemer become our own act. . . .
This . . . is the best way of describing the common element
in the Christian consciousness of the divine grace. . . . What
we have thus described is in every case an act both of the
Redeemer and of the redeemed."[47]

Schleiermacher argues that no *one* element in the life-
history of Jesus is to be identified with his redemptive and
reconciling activity. For example, he says that the suffering
and death of Christ are not to be viewed as primitive elements in his atoning activity, for then "no complete assumption into vital fellowship with Christ, such as makes
redemption and reconciliation completely intelligible, would
have been possible before the suffering and death of Christ."
They are, however, elements of secondary importance, for
they signify Jesus' overcoming of opposition and his sharing in
the misery of men: " . . . it is only, as it were, a magical
caricature, if we isolate this climax [Jesus' death], leave out
of account the foundation of the corporate life, and regard
this giving up of himself to suffering for suffering's sake as

45. *Ibid.*, Secs. 100, 101, thesis statements (Redeker ed., Vol. II, pp. 90, 97;
Eng. tr., pp. 425, 431). On "blessedness" and its association with the state
of "resurrection," see Sec. 163. Redemption is expressed in the consciousness
of believers as "regeneration"; reconciliation, as "sanctification" (Sec. 106).

46. *Ibid.*, Secs. 93.1, 100.2, 101.1, 106.1.

47. *Ibid.*, Sec. 100.1 (Redeker ed., Vol. II, p. 90; Eng. tr., p. 425). This point
is often overlooked by those who classify Schleiermacher among subjective
theories of the atonement. I return to this aspect of Schleiermacher's thought
below, pp. 224-225.

the real sum-total of Christ's redemptive activity."[48] It is possible to value the crucifixion of Jesus much more highly than Schleiermacher himself does without losing sight of his essential point. I shall argue that the cross is the event by which Jesus' being as presence is fully realized, since it is the final, although paradoxical, enactment of the word of faith. As the cry of God-forsakenness it is the word in which God fully identifies himself with the experience of the absence of God. But this does not mean that it can be abstracted from Jesus' words and deeds as a whole and regarded as the exclusive locus of his atoning work.[49]

I have argued that the "person" of Jesus refers to his historical existence as the one in whom presence was fully accomplished, and that his "work" signifies the making present—the efficacious realization for us today—of his being as presence. Although these two foci are essentially related to each other, they must not be reduced to an identity in one direction or the other. The constant temptation of christology has been to absorb Jesus' "work" (thus understood) into his "person," or his "person" into his "work." With the first, the danger is that of losing sight of the *significance* of Jesus' redemptive act, reducing it to a past historical *factum* rather than understanding it as a living

---

48. *Ibid.*, Sec. 101.4 (Redeker ed., Vol. II, p. 102; Eng. tr., p. 436). In Sec. 101.3 (Redeker ed., Vol. II, pp. 100-101; Eng. tr., pp. 434-435), Schleiermacher designates as "magical" those views of the atonement "which make the impartation of his blessedness independent of assumption into vital fellowship with him," and as "empirical" those "which [reduce] it altogether to the level of ordinary daily experience." Here, in other words, he rejects what I have described as "objective" and "subjective" theories of the atonement.

49. See below, Sec. 4b, Chapter 4. Among contemporary theologians, George Hendry has made a significant effort to understand the work of Christ as the making present of "forgiveness"—the transformation of the relationship between God and man—which was fully actualized in his life among men. Jesus' "presence among men as the Son of God, the man whose existence is for other men, is the presence of forgiveness. . . . We have forgiveness only in personal relation with God incarnate. Kierkegaard was right, therefore, when he said that in order to be Christians we have to become contemporaneous with Christ. We can have no personal relation with one who is separated from us in time or in space, and who is known to us only as a memory or a picture. His presence is essential." (*The Gospel of the Incarnation*, p. 148; see pp. 131-147, and the whole of Chapter 8, pp. 148-170.)

event in which we participate. Expressed in hermeneutical terms, this means the surrender of christology's *present responsibility*. Here I have in mind not only the so-called *Leben-Jesu-Forschung*, which found it difficult to account for the contemporary significance of the Christ-event, but also the recent work of Pannenberg. In line with his insistence that christology must have its basis in the historical Jesus and his identity as the Son of God, Pannenberg makes it clear that he considers soteriology to be a secondary theme in christology. Otherwise, he fears that we face "a reduction of Christology to soteriology, to the question of Jesus' existential significance"—a tendency he traces back to Melanchthon and Schleiermacher and sees currently exemplified in Bultmann and existentialist theology generally.[50]

The danger to which Pannenberg refers is a real one, and indeed the more common one in contemporary theology—namely, the reduction of the person of Jesus to his work. Here the tendency is to lose sight of the particular historical identity of Jesus and to allow the Christ figure to become the idea of redeemed, authentic humanity. Viewed from a hermeneutical perspective, this means giving up christology's task as *historical quest*. Bonhoeffer, for example, in his christology lectures, tries to answer the question about the identity of Christ (the so-called "who" question), not by reference to his past works in history, which are at best ambiguous, but from his personal presence *pro nobis*. He cites Melanchthon's famous statement in the *Loci: Hoc est Christum cognoscere, beneficia eius cognoscere* ("Who Christ is becomes known in his saving action").[51] Nevertheless, Bonhoeffer himself acknowledges that a person's identity cannot be inferred from his work, and in so far as he succeeds in answering the "who" question, he too is driven back to the historical Jesus for the concrete filling-out of his

---

50. *JGaM,* pp. 38, 47-48.

51. Dietrich Bonhoeffer, *Christ the Center,* trans. by John Bowden (New York, Harper & Row, 1966), pp. 37-40, 74-75. Cf. Philipp Melanchthon, *Loci communes* (1521) (*Corpus Reformatorum,* Vol. XXI, p. 85).

christology. But here his approach is entirely uncritical, remaining only with the community's portrait of Jesus.[52] In the final analysis, Bonhoeffer's tendency, as may be observed from the *Ethics* and the prison letters, is to absorb Jesus into the church and ultimately into the world, i.e., into the formation of authentic humanity. We must resist this tendency as well as the opposite one, insisting that the *identity* of the one who is now present can be learned only from the qualities of his past, historical presence, and conversely that the *significance* of the one who was presence can be learned only from the efficacious realization of his presence for us today.[53]

52. See Bonhoeffer's treatment of "Positive Christology" in *Christ the Center,* pp. 106-118.

53. Hans W. Frei has made a significant attempt to argue that the identity of Jesus *is* his presence—namely, his contemporary, living presence as the risen Lord: Jesus *is* the resurrection and the life. Frei believes this can be shown from the logic of the story of Jesus in the Gospels. As we move from the birth and infancy narratives, through the accounts of Jesus' teaching and journey to Jerusalem, to his passion and resurrection, his identity as a unique human being comes increasingly clearly into focus until it reaches a climax in the accounts of the post-resurrection appearances. See "Theological Reflections on the Gospel Accounts of Jesus' Death and Resurrection," *The Christian Scholar,* Vol. 49 (Winter 1966), pp. 263-306; and "The Mystery of the Presence of Jesus Christ," *Crossroads,* Vol. 17:2 (January-March 1967), pp. 69-96, and Vol. 17:3 (April-June 1967), pp. 69-96. Frei's analysis of the concepts of "identity" and "presence" is of great value. However, his conclusion remains problematical. If Jesus' identity is taken up into his contemporary, living presence, how can we ever be certain that it is a historical individual who confronts us and not merely the "idea" of presence? Symptomatic of this difficulty is the fact that Frei's biblical interpretation is, by intention, "literary" rather than critical. He wants to exhibit the novel-like structure of the Gospels and to uncover the internal logic of their portrait of Jesus. Whether Jesus in fact corresponded to this portrait is a question that does not come into view. It is unimportant for a novel that its hero is merely fictitious. But can the same be said for the Christian faith? Frei's argument for the "necessary existence" of Jesus, on the basis that in the resurrection he is identified as life itself, remains unconvincing for me.

PART TWO
JESUS AS PRESENCE

3

WORD AS THE MEDIUM OF PRESENCE

1. THE DIVINITY AND HUMANITY OF JESUS

a. Christology "From Above," "From Below," and "From Before"

In the history of christological tradition, the person of Jesus has been understood on the basis of a distinction between divine and human "natures," which enter into some sort of unique relationship or union in him. A christology that orients itself in the first instance to the "divinity" of Jesus can be characterized as "from above," whereas that which turns first to the humanity of Jesus can be described as "from below." Pannenberg writes: "For Christology that begins 'from above,' from the divinity of Jesus, the concept of the incarnation stands in the center. A Christology 'from below,' rising from the historical man Jesus to the recognition of his divinity, is concerned first of all with Jesus' message and fate and arrives only at the end at the concept of the incarnation."[1]

Christology "from above" had its roots in the New Testament christological traditions emerging from the Hellenistic-Gentile mission; here for the first time we find the theory of the incarnation of a pre-existent divine being—the Logos or

---

1. *JGaM*, p. 33. As far as I can tell, F. C. Baur was the first clearly to enunciate the distinction between a christology "from above" and "from below." See *Kritische Untersuchungen über die kanonischen Evangelien* (Tübingen, L. F. Fues, 1847), pp. 312-314; and *Ferdinand Christian Baur: On the Writing of Church History* (New York, Oxford University Press, 1968), p. 252.

the Son of God—in human flesh.[2] This theory was perpetuated by the second century Apologists and by the great
second- and early third-century theologians, Irenaeus, Ter-
tullian, and Origen, although with them the Logos-concept
did not yet exhibit the features it had acquired by the fourth
and fifth centuries. They insisted on the full humanity of
Christ, including a created soul or spirit, and they based
their theology on a world view (Stoic or Middle Platonist)
according to which the divine Logos is not a supernatural
person alien to man but rather that principle which is constitutive of his existence as a rational, spiritual creature, the
bond of union between God and man.[3] Christology "from
above" received its classical formulation in the Alexandrian
"Logos-flesh" doctrine, which had its beginnings with Apolli-
narius of Laodicea and was given the stamp of orthodoxy
by Athanasius in the fourth century and Cyril of Alexandria
in the fifth. The Logos-flesh christology, which entailed the
personification of the divine Logos and a concomitant
diminution of the human agency of Jesus, became the back-
bone of Catholic orthodoxy down to the present day. It was
given a Protestant variation by the "word of God" theology
of the dialectical theologians: Emil Brunner, Heinrich Vogel,[4]
and, above all, Karl Barth. Pannenberg points out that Barth
combines in his christology the classical doctrine of the two
natures with "the doctrine of the humiliation and exaltation
of the incarnate Son of God as two consecutive stages along

2. Reginald H. Fuller, *The Foundations of New Testament Christology* (New York, Charles Scribner's Sons, 1965), pp. 232-233, 245-257. The incarnational christology of the Hellenistic-Gentile milieu did not necessarily exclude the theme of adoption. What was pre-existent was the divine Spirit as impersonal power, not the Son as a hypostasis of the Trinity; Jesus was "adopted" *at birth* as the bearer of this power. In the formation of christological tradition, the time of adoption was moved progressively backward in the story of Jesus: from parousia, to ascension, to birth.

3. Aloys Grillmeier, *Christ in Christian Tradition: From the Apostolic Age to Chalcedon (451)*, trans. by J. S. Bowden (London, A. R. Mowbray & Co., Ltd., 1965), pp. 108, 125-126, 129-130, 132-133. My interpretation of christological developments down to Chalcedon is based primarily on this book. On the matter of the Apologists, I find myself at variance with Pannenberg; cf. *JGaM*, pp. 33, 160-163.

4. This pattern is found in Brunner's *The Mediator* but not in his *Dogmatics*. For Vogel see his *Christologie* and *Gott in Christo*. (See *JGaM*, p. 34.)

Jesus' path," which had its origin in seventeenth-century
Protestant scholasticism. Thus *Church Dogmatics*, Vol. IV/1,
Sec. 59, treats the "divinity" of Jesus under the theme of
humiliation ("The Obedience of the Son of God"), whereas
Vol. IV/2, Sec. 64, treats the "humanity" of Jesus under the
theme of exaltation ("The Exaltation of the Son of Man").
At the heart of Barth's christology stands the notion of the
descent and ascent of the Redeemer, bringing it into proximity with the structure of the Gnostic redeemer myth,
which is characteristic to a greater or lesser extent of incarnational christologies constructed "from above to below."
In all of these christologies, says Pannenberg, "the doctrine
of the Trinity is presupposed and the question posed is: How
has the Second Person of the Trinity (the Logos) assumed
a human nature?"[5]

Christology "from below," on the other hand, orients itself
in the first instance to the historical man Jesus, and it is precisely the doctrine of the Trinity that is not self-evident.
This christological pattern first appeared in the "adoptionist"
christologies of the earliest New Testament traditions, those
originating in the Palestinian Jewish-Christian church (adoption as Messiah or Son of Man at the parousia) and the
Hellenistic Jewish-Christian mission (adoption at the ascension, with the stress upon Christ's present lordship).[6] The
second-century adoptionist christology of Paul of Samosata,
which views the humanity of Jesus as the locus of the
indwelling of the Spirit of God, stands in continuity with
these traditions. However, this christology was given its
classic expression in the patristic period by the "conjunction"
christology and the *communicatio idiomatum* of the Antiochene school—above all, Theodore of Mopsuestia and Nes-
torius. Protestant christology from below had its roots in
Luther, who stressed—with a radicalism hitherto unparalleled—the humanity of Jesus (the crucified, God-forsaken

5. *JGaM*, pp. 33-34.
6. Fuller, *op. cit.*, pp. 173, 197, 243-245.

humanity of Jesus) as the locus of the being of God.[7] But
Luther himself did not work out systematically the implications of this position for christology. That remained the task
of nineteenth-century neo-Protestant theology and its intel-
lectual progenitor, the Enlightenment. The great watershed
in the history of christology was Schleiermacher. From him
we may trace the development of an anthropologically
oriented christology "from below" through idealism and the
Ritschlian school down to the present day in existentialism
and hermeneutical theology (Bultmann, Gogarten, Tillich,
Ebeling, Fuchs), the Pannenberg circle, and Catholic transcendental theology (Rahner and others).

Jürgen Moltmann has argued recently that it is no longer
possible to do christology either "from above" or "from
below." He believes christology "from above" to have presupposed either a universally valid God-concept or the
notion of God's self-revelation in the present reconciliation
of the world; whereas christology "from below" has started
with the general problematic of human existence. Neither
of these starting points speaks to the contemporary needs
and experience of men, and neither of them permits us to
reach Jesus of Nazareth, the Crucified One. Accordingly,
Moltmann proposes a christology "from before" or "from
ahead" *(von vorn)*, oriented to the question not about God
or man, but about the coming of the Messiah.[8] Such a

7. Friedrich Gogarten, *Jesus Christus, Wende der Welt* (Tübingen, J. C. B.
Mohr [Paul Siebeck], 1966), pp. 1-5; and "Theologie und Geschichte," *ZThK*,
Vol. 50 (1953), pp. 383-387. Gogarten cites the following texts as especially
characteristic: *WA*, 1, 362, 434; 3, 54, 347, 458; 4, 87; 10 I/1, 208; 34 I,
147; 40 I, 77; 56, 377. The radicalization of the doctrine of the *communicatio idiomatum* by Luther and Lutheran theology in the sixteenth and seven-
teenth centuries (Melanchthon, Osiander, Chemnitz, and others) opened up
the possibility of a more adequate understanding of the humanity of Jesus.
But the communication of attributes was from the divine nature to the human,
not vice versa, and the whole concept remained within the confines of the
two-natures doctrine, demonstrating its ultimate impasse. See Pannenberg,
JGaM, pp. 298-302; Eberhard Jüngel, "Vom Tod des lebendigen Gottes,"
ZThK, Vol. 65 (1968), pp. 100-104; and Theodor Mahlmann, *Das neue
Dogma der lutherischen Christologie* (Gütersloh, Gütersloher Verlagshaus
Gerd Mohn, 1969).

8. Moltmann, Lectures on Christology, University of Tübingen, Winter
Semester 1968-69.

christology assumes that God is not now present but is the
coming one, the one "with future as his essential nature."
The function of the messianic figure is to serve as the "mediator" of the qualitatively new future in the present. He is the
"representative" of the coming God (Dorothee Soelle), the
one who holds God's place in the old aeon (Ernst Käsemann).
Thus, the horizon in the context of which the Messiah must
be interpreted is that of the future rather than the present.
Jesus as the Messiah cannot be fixated or defined in respect
to present existence. He shatters all presently available
anthropological categories of interpretation, and his crucifixion shatters all traditional concepts of God. However,
christology "from before" poses the same general problems
as christology "from above." In both instances, we are
required to start with a claim about reality that lies "above"
or "before" presently accessible knowledge: either the doctrine of the Trinity and the incarnation of the Logos or the
doctrine of the qualitatively new future. Just as it is not
clear how a concept of the Son of God can be established
apart from the concrete historical figure of Jesus, so also we
must ask how the future can provide the hermeneutical
horizon for interpretation when access to the future is first
had through that which is to *be* interpreted, namely, Jesus
of Nazareth the Messiah. Christology "from below," on the
other hand, orients itself in the first instance to the historical
words and deeds of Jesus (not simply to a general doctrine
of man, as Moltmann supposes). It enables the formation
of concepts of God and the future on the basis of the one in
whom both God and future are present in virtue of his
definitively faithful human word. As the one who was
presence and is now present, Jesus defines not only human
existence but also the concepts of "God" and "future."

Although I am unable to accept Moltmann's alternative,
I am prepared to acknowledge, indeed insist upon, difficulties with the traditional "from above" and "from below"
formulations as well. The classical Logos-flesh christology
"from above" is no longer viable on at least three counts.

(1) It diminishes the humanity of Jesus, robbing him of personal agency as an historical figure. The Logos is conceived as an active, personal, suprahuman agent who incarnates himself in generic human flesh or nature (including, for orthodoxy, soul as well as body, being in that technical sense "complete"), and who constitutes the personal individual subjectivity of that flesh in lieu of a human subjectivity, while the flesh itself is merely instrumental to the action of the Logos. This position can be traced in part to the ancient distinction between "nature" and "person," which, by separating them, reduces each to an abstraction. A human nature that is something other than personal, i.e., conscious, temporal, linguistic, is an abstraction. And a "person" that exists apart from human nature is ultimately nothing other than a principle of individuation, not self-conscious subjectivity; as indeed was the case with the classical concepts of *persona* and *prosopon*. As Paul Tillich points out, in the Logos-flesh doctrine Jesus Christ really becomes a god disguised in human flesh. This, he says, is not the Christian doctrine of the incarnation but a pagan transmutation mythology, which is fundamentally anti-historical and docetic. In paganism, because the gods belong to the cosmos they can easily enter all forms of the universe and endless metamorphoses are possible.[9] Not only does this mythology represent a distortion of the Christian understanding of God, who is not a projection of man's nature or a part of the cosmos; it also denies the fundamental historicity and finitude of human experience. We simply can no longer believe in such mythological God-men who transcend the limits of the human. Karl Rahner puts it well:

> . . . mythology in this connexion could be defined as follows: The representation of a god's becoming man is mythological, when the 'human' element is merely the clothing, the livery, of which the god makes use in order to draw attention to his presence here with us, while it is not the case that the human element acquires its supreme initiative and control over its own actions by the very fact of being

9. Paul Tillich, *Systematic Theology*, Vol. II (Chicago, The University of Chicago Press, 1957), pp. 94, 149.

assumed by God. Looked at from this point of view a single basic
conception runs through the Christian heresies from Apollinarism
to Monothelitism, sustained by the same basic mythical feeling. . . .
[This conception] probably still lives on in the picture which countless Christians have of the 'Incarnation', whether they give it their
faith—or reject it.[10]

(2) The Logos-flesh christology is inadequate in terms
not only of what it does to the "flesh" (the human nature)
but also of what it does to the Logos, especially when carried
over into contemporary formulation. In essence, it personi-
fies or hypostatizes the Logos, regarding him as a personal agent. Personification of the Logos, which had already
been initiated in Hellenistic Judaism, was encouraged by
Arianism. When the Logos was considered a substitute for
the human soul of Jesus (the initial "Apollinarian" impulse
in Arianism[11]), then it, of necessity, in the Arian view,
became a subordinate, personal agent if the transcendence
of God was not to be compromised. However, the ancient
terms for person (*persona, prosopon, hypostasis*) did not
mean "person" in the modern sense of a conscious, self-
subsistent center of personal relationship. Rather *persona*
referred to the role played by an actor, symbolized by his
"mask" (*persona*), and *prosopon* meant "face" or "counte-
nance." In philosophical discussion, these terms came to signify "functioning entity," "individuating principle," highest
degree of concretion of a nature. Moreover, word is not
to be conceived as personal agency, rather, it is the power
or event that *constitutes* personhood by gathering into presence. Accordingly, the word or *logos* of God should not
itself be personified, regarded as a divine hypostasis, a distinguishable personal agent who assumes generic human
nature, *humanum*. Rather, as the one who *has word* absolutely, God subsists in three "modes of being" or "modes of
relationship,"[12] and exists in a twofold structure of self-

10. *ThI*, Vol. I, p. 156; cf. Vol. IV, pp. 117-118.
11. Grillmeier, *op. cit.*, pp. 178, 190-192, 220-221, 235.
12. Barth, *CD*, Vol. I/1, Sec. 9; Vol. II/1, Sec. 28.

distinction and self-relation, by which his being as perfect person is constituted.[13]

(3) Christology "from above" presupposes what we must seek to understand, namely, the "divinity" of Jesus. What is problematic for us in the "hypostatic union" is not the humanity, as with orthodox christology, but the divinity of Jesus. As Ebeling succinctly puts it: "Whereas traditional Christology assumed the fundamental truth of the *vere deus,* thus jeopardising the confession of faith in the *vere homo,* it is now the *vere deus* which raises the most acute problems for Christology."[14] Ancient christology was based on a world view that allowed for some sort of general belief in God, but for us, the meaningfulness of God-talk has evaporated. We cannot presuppose it but must seek an intelligible basis for it. We can learn to speak about God, if at all, only by turning to the historical man Jesus.[15]

The difficulties with a christology that starts "from below" may also be summarized under three points. (These difficulties stand in some degree of tension to each other and are not all exhibited equally in any given theologian.)

(1) As Moltmann suggests, christology "from below" can be construed to mean that christological reflection begins with a general doctrine of man or a general anthropology. Then it becomes (in Heideggerian terms) a form of subjectivistic or anthropocentric thinking. The God-man relation is defined in terms of man's self-transcending qualities (feeling, reason, spirit, consciousness), and God then appears to become a projection of human consciousness, as Strauss and Feuerbach argued was the case with idealist christologies. Ebeling contends that traditional christology "from above" did not intend, in the first instance at least, to describe an

13. See below, Secs. 3.a, d; 4.b.
14. *ThP,* p. 35; cf. pp. 38-39, 50-52, 65, 146-147.
15. For the third point, see also *JGaM,* p. 34. Pannenberg adduces two other reasons for rejecting a christology "from above": it makes it difficult to recognize the significance of the historical particularity of the man Jesus, especially his relationship to Judaism; and it requires us "to stand in the position of God himself in order to follow the way of God's Son in the world." (*JGaM,* pp. 34-35.)

epistemological direction but rather to reflect the direction of the event itself—from God to man. The real meaning of christology from above, he says, is the movement from God to man, in which God alone is the giver and man the receiver; in this respect, every christology must be "from above." Hence, the alternative "from above" or "from below" is insufficient. Christology from above is correct in giving expression to the fact that in christology we have to do with God and the primacy of his action, but it is wrong as an epistemological procedure that looks away from the human situation. Christology from below is correct in stating that all christological language must take its beginning with the appearance of Jesus and with the humanity of mankind generally, but it is wrong in its effort to mount up from humanity to divinity—to reverse, as it were, the flow of direction of the event itself by attempted proof of the divinity of Jesus from historical materials, as is apparently the case with Pannenberg.[16] On similar grounds, Rahner's definition of christology as "self-transcending anthropology"[17] can be criticized. This definition is misleading, because, according to Rahner, man's transcendental openness or *potentia oboedientialis* (the so-called "natural existential") is, in fact, fulfilled only by a free act or call "from above," namely, God's unexacted self-communication in word (the "supernatural existential").[18] The "power" by which man is enabled to enter into transcendental relationship with God is not his own, and hence strictly speaking this is not a question of *self*-transcendence.

(2) The concept of a christology "from below" tends to perpetuate the same dualism in which christology "from above" operates—the idea of vertically distinguishable dimensions of reality by which the difference between God

16. Ebeling, Lectures on Christology, University of Tübingen, Summer Semester 1967, pp. 177-182.
17. *ThI*, Vol. I, p. 164, n. 1; cf. also *STh*, Vol. VIII, p. 43.
18. See my chapter on Rahner in *The New Day: Catholic Theologians of the Renewal*, Wm. Jerry Boney and Lawrence E. Molumby, eds. (Richmond, Va., John Knox Press, 1968), pp. 46-61.

and man is defined, and the concomitant notion of divine and human "natures" as abstract essences that are conjoined in the person of the God-man. It merely reverses the direction of movement: not "from above below" (the descent of the divine Redeemer, the Logos, into human flesh) but "from below above" (as Pannenberg puts it, a "rising from the historical man Jesus to the recognition of his divinity"). For the Antiochene theologians, the unity of Christ is made up of a compenetration or exchange of moral and volitional qualities that belong to mutually disparate natures (divine and human). They differed from the Alexandrines by insisting upon the completeness of the human nature, but the unity of *prosopon* in Christ becomes an abstraction, a kind of hypothetical construct.[19] The same was true later of the *communicatio idiomatum* of sixteenth- and seventeenth-century Lutheranism and the nineteenth-century *kenosis* christologies (e.g., Thomasius): divinity takes on human properties, but the two-natures formulation remains intact. Protestant idealist christology in the nineteenth century, under the inspiration of Schleiermacher and Hegel, sought to break out of this impasse. Nevertheless, it too, for the most part, remained with an ultimate dualism between the archetypal and the historical, the universal and the particular, the divine idea and the human individual, which permits their mediation only either miraculously (Schleiermacher) or in terms of a negative dialectic that ultimately absorbs the finite into the infinite (Hegel).

(3) Because of either the residual dualism or the anthropocentric bias, christology "from below" has generally not succeeded in carrying through a christology that takes its orientation from the concrete historical figure of Jesus. It can readily start with a general anthropology, or with the idea of divine-human unity, or with the Easter traditions, but not with *Jesus*. For example, the Antiochene christology produced an abstract unity of *prosopon* that was only vaguely informed by the real person of Jesus. Even christolo-

19. Grillmeier, *op. cit.*, pp. 347-355, 358-360, 383, 433-439, 442-448.

gies that followed the emergence of modern historical
consciousness often displayed a curious indifference or even
hostility toward the concrete historical figure of Jesus, perhaps out of recognition of the theological embarrassment
that can be caused by historical research. This was true
(in quite different forms) of Schleiermacher, Hegel, Strauss;[20]
of Kähler and Herrmann; of Bultmann, Tillich, Rahner, and
even of Pannenberg. The latter affords an instructive example. He writes: ". . . while Christology must begin with
the man Jesus, its *first* question has to be that about his unity
with God. . . . The specific element in the Christological
question about Jesus is that it does not begin with some preliminary aspect of his words and deeds or of his effect on
men, but with his relation to God as it is expressed in the
whole of his activity on earth. Individual aspects of his work
and message as well as of his fate are *then* to be evaluated in
this context."[21] Jesus' unity with God (his divinity) comes
decisively into view only in the resurrection. It is not to be
discovered by an analysis of his "deeds and words." The
historical materials with which Pannenberg starts in his
effort to "prove" the divinity of Jesus are drawn from the
Easter traditions, not from the earthly ministry of Jesus. To
get to the "above," Pannenberg, in effect, starts from above:
the divine demonstration of the divinity (or divine sonship)
of Jesus by means of his resurrection from the dead. And

20. Just this criticism was brought against the christologies of these three
figures by F. C. Baur, who pursued the method of a christology oriented to
the historical man Jesus with a consistency and rigor not found in either his
mentors (Schleiermacher, Hegel) or his student (Strauss). See, e.g., the following against Schleiermacher: "Whether the person of Jesus of Nazareth
really possesses the attributes that belong to the established concept of the
Redeemer is in fact a purely historical question, which can be answered only
by a historical investigation of the literary sources of the Gospel stories, sources
that surely nowhere in the Introduction to this Christian *Glaubenslehre* are
brought forward as the proper sources of knowledge for Christianity."
(*Tübinger Zeitschrift für Theologie*, Vol. I [1828], p. 242.) Cf. a similar statement, relating to Hegel, in *Die christliche Lehre von der Dreieinigkeit und
Menschwerdung Gottes in ihrer geschichtlichen Entwicklung*, Vol. III (Tübingen, C. F. Osiander, 1843), p. 974. See also my book, *The Formation of
Historical Theology: A Study of Ferdinand Christian Baur* (New York, Harper
& Row, 1966), pp. 47-50, 58-66, 73-84, 100-121.
21. *JGaM*, p. 36 (italics mine).

that divinity is in no way problematic for Pannenberg for it is ultimately identical with Jesus' authentic humanity as the "other" in relation to which God becomes God; a "negative" identity, to be sure, for it entails Jesus' self-surrender in obedience unto death, whereby he becomes the true son of God. In starting "from below," Pannenberg really starts with the second moment in the dialectic of the divine life, and the historical life of Jesus is finally without decisive significance.[22]

The thesis advanced in this book has a closer affinity with the christological tradition that starts "from below" than with those prosecuted "from above" or "from before." But because of the difficulties just enumerated, I think it preferable to avoid this means of formulating the task of the doctrine of the person of Christ as well as the other two. What is needed is a way of avoiding the supernaturalism and docetism of the Logos-flesh christology, of overcoming the subjectivistic bias of a self-transcending anthropology, and of moving beyond the impasse of the doctrine of the two natures entirely, while at the same time holding radically to the historical man Jesus as the criterion of christology.

b. A Contemporary Word-Christology?

Such a way is provided by means of the concept of "word." Word is not a supernatural substance that invades from another sphere of reality, although it "transcends" man as an unexacted gift. Word is not a capacity at man's disposal, although it is the fundamental human act. The word of God does not infinitize human speech but deepens and perfects its finitude. The relation of the word of God and word of man is not like that of two qualitatively distinct substances or "natures"; rather, in Jesus of Nazareth they become *homologous* with each other. Word, finally, characterizes the distinctive quality of Jesus' mission and person;

22. *Ibid.*, pp. 181-182, 323, 334-337, 339-340, 342-343. See my review article, "Pannenberg on Jesus," *Journal of the American Academy of Religion*, Vol. 36 (Dec. 1968), pp. 373-384.

it does not tempt us to look away from the concrete historical figure.

But by what right can I propose to retain "word" as the
central christological category and indeed to develop a
contemporary word-christology, when I have just rejected
the classical Logos-flesh christology and its modern-day
equivalent in the "word of God" theologies of Brunner,
Vogel, Barth, even Bultmann? Have not the possibilities of
a word of God theology, with its tendency toward supernaturalism and authoritarianism, been pretty thoroughly
exhausted, as Pannenberg contends?[23]

In my view, the dialectical theologians never sufficiently
explored the concept of "word" to its roots, and, consequently, they remained with a concept of the word of God
that to some extent corresponded to the orthodox Logos-
christology, according to which the "word" is a transcendent
divine hypostasis, the miracle of divine salvation and revelation that shatters all human categories. Rather than being
viewed as a natural, historical phenomenon, "word" became
the chief weapon in the conflict with natural theology, and
"word of God" readily became an authoritarian concept. On
the other hand, by radicalizing the concept of "word" it may
be possible to understand it in such a way that it can
become the clue to the co-presence of God and man, overcoming the abstract distinction between divine and human
"natures" entirely, avoiding both the supernaturalism of the
traditional Logos-flesh christologies and the subjectivism of
modern anthropocentrically-oriented christologies, and preserving the finitude and historicity of human experience.
This radicalization of word has been carried out philosophically by Heidegger and recent phenomenology of language,
and theologically by Ebeling and the so-called "new
hermeneutic." I propose to build on the results of this
radicalization, attempting to carry it further and applying
it specifically to the christological problematic.

23. *JGaM*, pp. 166-168.

Word is the medium of presence. It is the power of the future by which man is gathered into presence both temporally and spatially. This word is what Christians mean by "word of God." Although it "transcends" man and confronts him as an unexacted gift, nevertheless, it comes to speech in finite, fully historical human words and actions, which, when conformed to the word of God, we call "faithful." Jesus was *the* word of faith. His definitively faithful words and acts were the "place" where God's word, as the power of the future, came to speech and thus where God himself was present. In virtue of his faithful word, Jesus *was presence,* which means both that humanity was "finished" in him and that God's word-presence in the world was "definitively" established in him. Both the finishing of humanity and the definitive presence of God in Jesus must be understood as "proleptic"—anticipatory of a final, universal, and perfect co-presence of God and the world in the return of all things created to their Creator. Nevertheless, where human presence is accomplished (in both temporal and spatial dimensions, as presence to oneself and presence to the world) "by faith," i.e., provisionally, there God himself is present; for his word is the source and power of human presence, just as man's enacted speech is the essential means by which God's future word becomes event here and now in the world. A word-christology can thus avoid the impasse of the two-natures doctrine entirely. Precisely where *vere homo* is radically accomplished, there *vere deus* is definitively present. As the *vere homo,* the one in whom humanity was finished, Jesus was also the *vere deus,* the one in whom the word of the future God came to speech.

God and man are not thereby to be confused, identified, or merged. Rather, their true difference is brought out when their relationship, their co-presence, is understood by means of word. Heidegger referred to this difference philosophically as the "ontological difference." We may describe it theologically by saying that God's word is *true* whereas man's word is *false* and sinful, that God's word is the *power* of the *future* whereas man's unaided word is rendered *powerless* by the burden of the *past,* that God's word is *grace* and *address* whereas man's word is *faith* and *response.* Where the word of man is empowered by the word of God to become a true, faithful, saving word, it is not thereby infinitized but deepened and perfected in its finitude. For it is set free from futile attempts at self-creation and self-salvation, and is allowed to be what it was created to be: the limited, fragile, fallible, though essential place of God's self-presentation in history.

2. RECOVERY OF AUTHENTIC ELEMENTS IN THE LOGOS
   TRADITION

a. Greek Logos and Hebrew Dabar

Originally and etymologically λόγος did not mean "thought," "reason," "logic," "calculation," or even "speech," "discourse," or "word." It derived from the verb λέγειν, whose most primitive meaning is "to gather" or "to glean" in the critical sense of gathering something selectively from a larger context. Λέγειν is related etymologically to the Latin *lego* (which also means "to gather," "to select"), to the Gothic *lisan* ("to gather," "to harvest"), and to the High German *lesen. Lesen* means "to read," but when used with prefixes it retains its more primitive meaning: e.g., *auflesen* ("to gather," "to glean"), *die Auslese* ("the cream of the crop"), *die Weinlese* ("the vintage").[24] "Reading," of course, involves a process of critical sifting, of gathering meaning from the page, of bringing together, so that it is only slightly removed from the original meaning of λέγειν. The same is more true of "speech" or "word," which involves fundamentally a process

24. On the etymology of λέγειν and λόγος, see Hjalmar Frisk, *Griechisches etymologisches Wörterbuch* (Heidelberg, Carl Winter Universitätsverlag, 1960 ff.), Vol. II, pp. 94-96; *TDNT,* Vol. IV, pp. 77-78; Martin Heidegger, *An Introduction to Metaphysics* (trans. Ralph Manheim; New Haven, Yale University Press, 1959), pp. 123-128, and "Logos (Heraklit, Fragment 50)," *Vorträge und Aufsätze* (paperback ed.; Pfullingen, Neske, 1967), Vol. III, pp. 3-25.

of collecting, of gathering, of gathering into presence and making manifest, of letting be seen. The spoken word represents a gathering of sound into coherent, structured units, by which a meaning is expressed, communication is established, and reality is unconcealed. In the process of speaking, man himself is gathered into presence, both in a temporal sense—for word is the means by which the modes of time are integrated—and in a spatial sense—for word is the means by which man transcends distance and establishes communication with other persons and the world at large. Thus, the spokenness of the word is its more primordial form, although the ability of the word to be written signifies its transcendence of the speaker and its capacity to integrate the past and the present, i.e., to establish contemporaneity: a past text is present in virtue of its writtenness. Reading is, in fact, a form of speaking: when we read (especially when we read out loud, as in a lecture) we bring to vital, living speech again the word of the text.

Heidegger has pointed to the original association of Logos and being, of λόγος and φύσις, δύναμις, or εἶναι, in the pre-Socratic philosophers, especially in Heraclitus and Parmenides, where being means "emergent power" (Heraclitus) or "entering into unconcealment," "disclosure" (Parmenides).[25] This association is one which Heidegger attempts to retrieve and revitalize in his own philosophy. Thus, it is misleading to state, as is often done, that a sharp contrast exists between Greek and Hebrew understandings of "word," according to which the Greek concept expresses the notion of "coherence," "rational meaning," or "logical structure," whereas the Hebrew concept stresses the spokenness of the word as living, historical, temporal power. For the pre-Socratics, λόγος had the character of *power* (the dynamic act of "gathering" and "unconcealing") just as clearly as did Hebrew *dābār*. It was only in later Greek thought that λόγος lost its original dynamic character. Two sides to the

25. Heidegger, *Introduction to Metaphysics*, pp. 125-139, and below, p. 90.

development of the λόγος concept in the Greek world may
be distinguished. On the one hand, λόγος was dissociated
from εἶναι and came to mean "logic," *ratio*, "assertion," the
meaning content of what is spoken, rather than the act of
speaking. At the same time, being was defined as εἶδος, ὄντος
ὄν, ἀεὶ ὄν—idea, paradigm, static essence, substance. Heidegger has pointed to the deleterious consequences of this
dissociation of Logos and being.[26] On the other hand, λόγος
was hypostatized and became a cosmological entity, the
cosmic principle (either immanent or supernatural) of the
world's rationality and order. As Divinity was increasingly
regarded as eternal, unchanging essence vis-à-vis the world,
the Logos assumed a mediatorial function since it belonged
both to God, whom it represented in the world, and to the
world, which had its reality and order through it. Hence
there developed a cosmic dualism in Plutarch, Plotinus, the
Corpus Hermeticum, Philo of Alexandria, and Gnosticism.
The Logos became a middle being between God and the
world—an emanation of God that was mythologized and
personified. It (or "he") assumed soteriological and revelatory functions. For the Hermes-Logos-theology, the Logos
was personified as the god Hermes, who was sent to men
from the gods as κῆρυξ and ἄγγελος. "The more radically the
knowledge that was attributed to the Logos was conceived
as supernatural, the more he himself must have been conceived as person, as the 'Son' and 'envoy' of the highest
God, who reigns over the world eternally in unknown
fashion."[27]

It is undoubtedly true that the original meaning of word
as dynamic event was better preserved in the Hebraic world
than in the Greek. *Dābār* ("word") is related to *dᵉbīr*, the
"holiest of all," the "back of the temple," which gives the
basic sense of "back," "the heart of the matter." In *dābār*

26. Heidegger, *Introduction to Metaphysics*, pp. 181-193. See also Bultmann,
GuV, Vol. I, pp. 274-276; and *TDNT*, Vol. IV, p. 80.
27. *GuV*, Vol. I, pp. 277-278; cf. *TDNT*, Vol. IV, pp. 81-89.

one is thus to seek the "back" or "background" of a matter.[28]
According to Otto Procksch, two main elements in the term
dābār derive from this basic meaning, a dianoetic and a
dynamic element.

(1) "Dianoetically, *dābār* always contains a νοῦς, a
thought. In it is displayed the meaning of a thing, so that
dābār always belongs to the field of knowledge. By its *dābār*
a thing is known and becomes subject to thought. To grasp
the *dābār* of a thing [i.e., to grasp its 'background' or 'meaning'] is to grasp the thing itself. It becomes clear and
transparent; its nature is brought to light."[29] Thus, very
much as for λόγος, the dianoetic function of *dābār* involves
a process of disclosure, unconcealment, making manifest—
not by gathering things into presence (as with λόγος), but
by uncovering their "background," their quintessence.
Dābār means "that in which a thing shows itself."[30] This
meaning is brought out by the association of the Hebrew
word for "fidelity" or "truth" (*'emeth*) with *dābār*.[31] As
Yahweh's words are *'emeth* (II Sam. 7:28), so human words
must be (Gen. 42:16, 20; I Kings 10:6; 17:24; Ps. 45:4;
119:43; II Chron. 9:5). If a word is to be valid, the one
concerned ratifies it with an *'āmēn* (Deut. 27:15 ff.; Num.
5:22).[32] "The sum of [Yahweh's] word is truth" (Ps. 119:
160).

(2) The dynamic element follows from the fact that
dābār is the manifestation of the "background" or quintessence of things. "Every *dābār* is filled with power which
can be manifested in the most diverse energies. This power
is felt by the one who receives the word and takes it to
himself. But it is present independently of this reception

28. *TDNT*, Vol. IV, p. 92.
29. *Ibid.*
30. *WF*, p. 326.
31. Cf. also the connection between λόγος and ἀλήθεια, which means truth in
the sense of "unconcealment." On the relation between word, truth, and faith,
see below, pp. 147-148.
32. *TDNT*, Vol. IV, p. 93.

in the objective effects which the word has in history."[33]
Indeed *dābār*, or the plural, *d^ebārīm*, is sometimes used as
a synonym for "history" or "acts." See I Kings 11:41: ". . . in
the books of the acts [or "history"; Heb. *d^ebārīm*, LXX
ῥημάτων] of Solomon"; or I Kings 14:29: ". . . the rest of the
acts [Heb. *d^ebārīm*, LXX λόγοι] of Rehoboam." The same
is found in Gen. 15:1, 22:1: "After these things [or "events";
Heb. *d^ebārīm*, LXX ῥήματα]. . . ." "History is the event
established and narrated in the word, so that the thing and
its meaning may both be seen, as expressed by the Hebrew
d^ebārīm in the plural."[34] Or, as Ebeling puts it, "word is,
taken strictly, happening word";[35] thus the expression "word-
event."

Both the dianoetic and more especially the dynamic
elements are present in the Old Testament concept of the
"word of God." According to Bultmann, "the word contains
power and thus signifies the expression of God's power." This
is the case, not only with a literal speaking by God (as is
implied in Ps. 29:3-9), but also when the notion of an
actual speaking has disappeared, as the metaphorical phrases
show: "Yahweh has 'sent' a word against Jacob, and it will
'light upon' Israel" (Is. 9:8; cf. Ps. 107:20). God's power
is designated as his "word" because it is of the essence of the
word that it is spoken, that it "happens as temporal event,"
rather than subsisting as eternal truth. Such a word is
address; it is spoken to man as the expression of God's
effective command or his power, which calls forth existence.

> For he spoke, and it came to be;
> he commanded, and it stood forth (Ps. 33:9).

Bultmann adds: "God's word is also 'word' in the proper
sense, as word spoken to men in human language, capable

33. *Ibid.*, p. 92.
34. *Ibid.*, p. 93.
35. *WF*, p. 326. This point is developed more fully in his essay, "Zeit und
Wort," in *Zeit und Geschichte: Dankesgabe an Rudolf Bultmann zum 80.
Geburtstag* (Tübingen, J. C. B. Mohr [Paul Siebeck], 1964), pp. 341-356, esp.
pp. 354-355.

of being heard and understood, namely, the word that is
'instruction' for man as the word of prophets or priests."
Finally, the Old Testament drew the closest connection
between God's being and his word: "God's word designates
God as he is there for man and is perceivable. *God's word
is God* in so far as it calls man into being, limits him, and
mysteriously surrounds him. . . . Further, God's word is
God in so far as it takes man into claim as the compre-
hensible demand under which man stands."[36] Or, as we
could also express it: God's word is God in so far as God is
present to man as the power of the future, gathering him
into presence.

The ensuing analysis of "word" and "word of God"
(Secs. 3-4) will be assisted by these Old Testament insights,
specifically, the concept of word as disclosure and as
dynamic, temporal-historical event, the insistence that God's
word is spoken in human language rather than occurring
as a supernatural voice from on high, and the connection
between God's being and his word.

b. *Logos in the New Testament*

In the New Testament usage of λόγος, the impact of the
Hebraic understanding of word—already felt in the shaping
of λόγος and ῥῆμα as translations of *dābār* in the Septuagint—
is clearly to be seen. The reference is always to a living,
spoken word, not to an independent entity or to a rational
principle. Speaking and hearing assume an enormous importance in the New Testament, both as the vehicle of human
activity and relationship and as the means of revelation.
This intensification of word may be observed from the
multiplicity of speech forms peculiar to the Gospel (dialogue, story, parable, poem), and from the great quantitative and qualitative expansion of the terms for speech in
the New Testament: λέγειν/λόγος and derivatives, ῥῆμα, λαλεῖν,

36. *GuV*, Vol. I, pp. 269-271.

ἀγγέλλειν, κηρύσσειν/κήρυγμα, μαρτυρεῖν, etc.[37] More highly spe-
cialized or technical usages are unable to displace the basic
meaning of spoken word.[38] That this is the case is confirmed
by the reference to Jesus as "word of life" (λόγος τῆς ζωῆς) in
I Jn. 1:1-3. Clearly no personification of λόγος occurs here;
the reference rather is to true and actual word—word that
gives, indeed *is*, life. The relative pronouns referring to λόγος
are neuter rather than masculine, despite the masculine gender of λόγος. Jesus *was* the word of life in the sense that his
words and deeds gave life.[39]

The passage in I Jn. 1 may serve as a clue to the Prologue
of the Fourth Gospel. Here the pre-existence of the word
is stressed. But we are not necessarily to conclude that
John hypostatized the word, regarding it as a cosmological
entity, a supernatural personal agency. The question, rather,
is what is *meant* by "pre-existence." Bultmann is correct in
arguing that the mythological form of expression has already
lost its mythological meaning for John.

> Jesus is not presented in literal seriousness as a pre-existent divine
> being who came in human form to earth to reveal unprecedented
> secrets. Rather, the mythological terminology is intended to express
> the absolute and decisive significance of his word—the mythological
> notion of pre-existence is made to serve the idea of Revelation. His
> word does not arise from the sphere of human observation and
> thought, but comes from beyond. It is a word free of all human
> motivation, a word determined from outside himself. . . . Therefore
> his word is not subject to men's scrutiny or control. It is an authori-
> tative word which confronts the hearer with a life-and-death
> decision.[40]

According to Kittel, the Johannine Prologue does not engage
in an abstract personification of the Logos but rather is
solely concerned with what has taken place in the person
of Jesus. The pre-existence language is an attempt to set

37. *TDNT*, Vol. IV, pp. 101-102; and Amos N. Wilder, *The Language of the
Gospel: Early Christian Rhetoric* (New York, Harper & Row, 1964), pp. 18-19,
48, 51.
38. *TDNT*, Vol. IV, p. 103.
39. *Ibid.*, pp. 127-128; *ThNT*, Vol. II, p. 64.
40. *ThNT*, Vol. II, p. 62. A similar case can be made for Paul's concept of the
pre-existence of the Son; see below, p. 201.

this event in its eternal, primordial framework, to pursue
the origin of the "glory" we have beheld in the son. This
origin is the eternal creative activity of the divine word.
The beginning of the Gospel harks back to the account of
God's creation through word in the first chapter of Genesis;
and the ἐν ἀρχῇ ("in the beginning") of Jn. 1:1 deliberately
adopts the first words of the Septuagint version of Gen.
1:1.[41] Thus, it is quite unfortunate that English translations
of Jn. 1:1-13 have customarily personified the word by
translating the pronouns that refer to it as masculine rather
than neuter ("he" rather than "it"). In Greek, λόγος is
masculine in a grammatical, rather than a conceptual sense.
Beginning with Jn. 1:14, the subject of the predicates becomes the historical man Jesus, and here it is correct to
translate the pronouns as masculine.[42]

With these reflections in mind it is of value to raise the
difficult question of the background of the Logos-concept
in the Fourth Gospel. Of four possible sources—the Hellenistic Gnostic λόγος, the oriental primal man (*Enos*), the
Hellenistic Jewish σοφία/*chokma*, and the Palestinian Jewish
Torah—Kittel argues for the latter. The Prologue is not a
hymn to wisdom or to primal man, for this would require
the supposition that an original and different form of the
Prologue preceded the Fourth Gospel and was only later
attached to it. The influence of Gnosticism is ruled out,
despite the formal parallels, if we are correct in arguing
that the Johannine λόγος is not the metaphysical personification of a mythical concept.[43] In defense of the Palestinian
Jewish Torah, several scholars (A. Schlatter, P. Billerbeck,
K. Bornhäuser, and E. Hirsch) have pointed out that the

41. *TDNT*, Vol. IV, pp. 130-132. Kittel himself is the author of this section
of the article on λόγος.
42. *WF*, p. 325: ". . . when John 1:14 says that the word became flesh, that
surely means . . . that here word became event in a sense so complete that
being word and being man became one. . . . When the Bible speaks of God's
word, then it means here unreservedly word as word—word that as far as its
word-character is concerned is completely normal, let us not hesitate to say:
natural, oral word taking place between man and man." See below, pp.
138-147.
43. *TDNT*, Vol. IV, pp. 132-134.

contrast between λόγος and νόμος, between Christ and the
law, is one of the central themes of the Prologue (see 1:14,
17), indeed of the Gospel as a whole. Of course the Torah
too is a word, so that John presents a conflict between word
and word—the word of Jesus versus the word of the Torah.
John's choice of λόγος as the central christological concept
thus is not accidental. It represents his way both of challenging and of appropriating the Old Testament conception
of revelation.

> . . . the statements concerning the pre-existence and majesty of the
> Torah [in rabbinic speculation] are now intentionally heaped upon
> the λόγος. It was in the beginning. It was with God. It was God,
> or divine. All things were made by it. In it was life. It was the light
> of men. In the Rabbis these are all sayings about the Torah. But
> they are now statements about Christ. In him the eternal word of
> God, the word of creation, the word of the law, is not just passed
> on (ἐδόθη) but enacted (ἐγένετο). Christ is not just a teacher and
> transmitter of the Torah. He is himself the Torah, the new Torah.[44]

If this analysis is correct, then the Fourth Gospel, like
the rest of the New Testament, understands word in its
fundamental sense as living, spoken word; the word by
which human existence is constituted and God's revelation
is mediated. Throughout the Gospel of John, the words of
Jesus are identified with his works, his deeds (see 8:28, 38;
14:10; 15:22, 24; 17:4, 8, 14). His work *is* his word, the
word that bestows eternal life and truth (5:24; 6:63, 68;
17:17). "Whatever Jesus does is a speaking, whatever he
says is a doing. His actions speak, his words act."[45] In this
sense, Jesus himself *is* the word of God, not as the incarnation of a pre-existent divine Person but as the one whose
word is the power that brings life, whose word is the coming-
to-speech of God himself. The use of "word" as a christological title does not violate its fundamental sense of living,
spoken event but is rather its fullest exemplification.

44. *Ibid.*, pp. 134-135. Kittel points out that the Rabbis identified wisdom
and Torah, and he believes it was in this fashion that wisdom speculation
indirectly influenced the Fourth Gospel (pp. 133, 136).
45. *ThNT*, Vol. II, pp. 60-61, 63; and *GuV*, Vol. I, pp. 290-291.

Nevertheless, the original New Testament understanding of word, and the way in which word was used as a christological title in the Johannine literature, were soon lost or distorted in the development of christological dogma. The second- and early third-century theologians, relying upon a Stoic or Middle Platonist conception of Logos, preserved a sense of the original word-character of Logos, understanding it as a person-constituting principle rather than as personal agency itself. But the personification of the Logos and the concomitant depersonification of the humanity of Jesus began to develop after the middle of the third century, came to classic expression in the Alexandrian Logos-flesh christology, and remained the orthodox doctrine of both Catholic and Protestant traditions until the beginning of the nineteenth century.

3. WORD AND THE HORIZONS OF PRESENCE

a. Word and Temporality

Not only is a contemporary word-christology required to go back to the classical and biblical roots, it must also direct its attention to contemporary philosophical and theological discussion of the phenomenon of "word," a discussion that has sought in many respects to retrieve the radical meaning of word. My intention is not to provide a survey of the extensive current discussion of language in its various facets, but rather to develop certain themes that will prove important for the systematic and historical efforts in Chapters 4 and 5. My orientation, broadly speaking, will be to phenomenology of language as it is represented in the work of Martin Heidegger, Hans-Georg Gadamer, Maurice Merleau-Ponty, and William J. Ong. Regrettably, it is beyond the scope of this project to bring to bear upon the themes under consideration the perspectives of analytical philosophy, structural linguistics, and communications theory. Whether a synthesis of the analytical and linguistic

approaches with that of the phenomenological and hermeneutical tradition can be effectively accomplished, and what
this would imply for the work of theology, are questions
that lie beyond my present competence.[46]

Word is an event or a power—the power of the future—
that gathers into presence (or unconceals) both temporally
and spatially, transcending human speech while coming to
expression precisely there. As such, word is the event of
being itself. The first question that must be addressed,
then, concerns the nature of being. The basic failure of
metaphysical thinking, according to Heidegger, was that
it conceived being as a static, unchanging, eternal *ground*—
the *causa sui*, the unmoved mover—or as "permanent presence," the "standing now" (*nunc stans*). This was the God
of metaphysics or of "onto-theo-logic."[47] But being is not a
cause or eternal ground. It is an event (*Ereignis*); *the*
event, which "grants" or "gives forth" more than any cause

46. In Secs. 3-4 of this chapter I am drawing on material first published in
my article, "Heidegger, Revelation, and the Word of God," *JRel*, Vol. 49 (July
1969), pp. 228-252. Used by permission.

   My argument in this section presupposes the view, now widely accepted in
modern linguistics, that language is an original and unique human phenomenon, constituting the essence of the human species. See especially Susanne
Langer, *Philosophy in a New Key* (New York, Mentor Books, 1948), Chapters 3, 5; also works by Ernst Cassirer, Edward Sapir, and Wilbur Marshall
Urban. After completing this manuscript, I read Eugen Rosenstock-Huessy's
Speech and Reality (Norwich, Vt., Argo Books, 1970), a collection of essays
written between 1935 and 1955, but published now for the first time. I have
discovered some remarkable similarities between my analysis and the central
themes of Rosenstock-Huessy—e.g., his understanding of speech as the power
that unifies and sustains the temporal and spatial axes of human existence,
thus constituting a social world, a "cross of reality"; the potentiality of speech
for concealment and disintegration as well as disclosure and unification; a con-
centration on "peace" (what I have called "presence") as the a priori datum
of the social sciences; a definition of God as "the power which urges us to
speak" or "the power to speak the truth." Although it differs in many details,
I believe my own analysis is generally supported by Rosenstock-Huessy's work,
and I wish I had had the benefit of his unique insights when writing this
chapter.

47. Heidegger, *An Introduction to Metaphysics*, pp. 180-182, 193; "Die onto-
theo-logische Verfassung der Metaphysik," in *Identität und Differenz*, 4th ed.
(Pfullingen, Neske, 1957), pp. 31-67, esp. pp. 64-65. See Otto Pöggeler,
Der Denkweg Martin Heideggers (Pfullingen, Neske, 1963), pp. 41-42, 269.
This is the conception of "eternal presence" against which Jürgen Moltmann
polemicizes in *Theology of Hope* (New York, Harper & Row, 1967), pp. 26-32
—a polemic that is misdirected because it does not apply to the Heideggerian
and post-Heideggerian discussion of presence.

or ground. As event, it is "the most unapparent of the unapparent, the simplest of the simple, the nearest of the near, and the farthest of the far, in which we mortals have our temporal lives."[48]

What sort of event is being? According to Heidegger, it is the event of unconcealment, of unveiling, of revelation.[49] Being is not a thing, "a being," which itself could be revealed. Rather it is the event of "lighting" that illumines or unconceals *beings*—the finite entities of the world, including, above all, man.[50] As such being remains invisible, unseen, "the most unapparent of the unapparent." To unconceal beings means to lay them open, to "free" them, to "lighten" them, to bring them to presence, to *let them be*. As "letting-be," "unconcealing," "presencing," being assumes a creative, dynamic, spontaneous character that it seemingly lacked as "horizon" in *Being and Time*.

Among the several names used by Heidegger for the event of unconcealment, one, according to Otto Pöggeler,[51] is especially important: "world." It figures prominently in *Being and Time* and returns for fresh consideration in later essays. Unconcealment, thought of in terms of a "frame" or "structure," is the world—the structure in which unconcealment establishes itself. In "Bauen Wohnen Denken,"[52] Heidegger thinks of the structure of the world as a "quadrate" made up of four "regions": earth and heaven, divinities and mortals. The world is the unity of these regions, a unified event of unconcealment. Each of the four regions can be thought of only in terms of its relation to the others; they exist together, in the dance of the four, in the world game. Earth and heaven describe man's spatio-temporal environment. The term "divinities" apparently refers to the

---

48. *US*, pp. 258-259; and *Identität und Differenz*, pp. 24-27.
49. Cf. the Latin root of "reveal": *re*, take back + *velo*, to veil.
50. I shall follow the now rather widely-accepted convention of translating *Sein* as "being" and *das Seiende* as "beings" or "a being."
51. Pöggeler, *op. cit.*, pp. 247-250.
52. Heidegger, *Vorträge und Aufsätze* (paperback ed.), Vol. II, pp. 23-25; see Pöggeler, *op. cit.*, p. 268.

"means" or the "messengers" by which unconcealment comes
to pass; it is a mythological expression for the hermeneutical
function of language. And men of course are the mortals.
They dwell *within* the quadrate as one of its regions. The
world is not a self-enclosed "natural" process vis-à-vis man,
but the event of unconcealment in which man is included
and to which he belongs in his essence. This is what
Heidegger earlier means in *Being and Time* when he introduces "being-in-the-world" as the constitutive state or
fundamental existential of Dasein.[53] Later, in *Über den
Humanismus*, he describes the world as "the clearing of
being" or "the openness of being" in which man stands
exposed to "an openness that is being itself, that has projected the essence of man into 'care.' " In this openness,
man "stands out" (ek-sists) from his thrown essence, projecting himself upon his own possibilities in anticipatory
resoluteness; the openness of being is what makes this
projection possible. The world, then, is a kind of finite
transcendence within which man's existence (ek-sistence)
can come to pass. Hence to refer to man's being-in-the-
world "is not to claim that man is simply a 'secular' being
in the Christian sense, and so turned away from God and
devoid of 'transcendence.' "[54]

As world-constituting *event*, being is fundamentally *temporal* in character. Temporality is Heidegger's most direct
or unpoetic, nonmetaphorical way of naming being: in its
essence being *is* time. By making this equation Heidegger
fundamentally shatters, according to Gadamer, the "transcendental schema" of post-Cartesian and Kantian philosophy, according to which time is a function of subjective
consciousness, the pure a priori form of intuition by which

53. *BT*, pp. 78 ff.

54. Heidegger, *Über den Humanismus* (Frankfurt, Vittorio Klostermann,
1947), pp. 16, 35, 42. This understanding of "world" will be of value for
subsequent discussion of the kingdom of God as the "new world" constituted
by God's word (Sec. 3.c, Chapter 4), and of world as a "mode" of the presence of the risen Christ (Secs. 2.a and 3.c, Chapter 5).

the world is experienced.[55] Again, the great mistake of the metaphysical tradition was to regard being as a non- or supratemporal, static, "eternal" ground of the temporal-historical world order, and as such an "object" of human cognition, a "ground" posited by the transcendental consciousness. Even those theologians and philosophers who made time their basic theme—Augustine, Hegel, Schelling, Nietzsche—were unable to think of time in its inmost essence as being itself. The breakthrough for Heidegger came with *Being and Time*. There he says quite explicitly:

> If being is to be conceived in terms of time, . . . then being itself (and not merely beings, let us say, as beings "in time") is thus made visible in its "temporal" character. But in that case, "temporal" can no longer mean simply "being in time." Even the "non-temporal" and the "supratemporal" are "temporal" with regard to their being, and not just privately by contrast with something "temporal" as a being "in time," but in a *positive* sense, though it is one which we must first explain. . . . Thus the fundamental ontological task of interpreting being as such includes working out the *temporality of being*. In the exposition of the problematic of temporality the question of the meaning of being will first be concretely answered.[56]

Being as temporality is the unified event of "a future which makes present in the process of having been [*gewesende-gegenwärtigende Zukunft*]."[57] From this structure it is evident that the foremost of the temporal modes is the *future*. Being is the power of the future that calls men forward[58] through the process of having been (the past), gathering into presence and unconcealing by its call. In his

55. *WM*, p. 243. Immanuel Kant, *Critique of Pure Reason*, trans. by Norman Kemp Smith (London, Macmillan, 1933), pp. 76-78, 80.
56. *BT*, pp. 38-40, 488; quotation from p. 40. Translation slightly altered; cf. *Sein und Zeit*, 11th ed. (Tübingen, Max Niemeyer, 1967), pp. 18-19. See Pöggeler, *op. cit.*, p. 42.
57. *BT*, pp. 374, 401 (citation from latter page). Cf. *Sein und Zeit*, p. 350.
58. This expression is borrowed from John B. Cobb, *God and the World* (Philadelphia, Westminster Press, 1969), Chapter 2. But Cobb never explains why it is that the future should *call* us or what the means of this call are. One suspects that "calling" is to be taken metaphorically because Cobb never develops the theme of language. It is my contention that Heidegger offers a more adequate philosophical basis for Cobb's definition of God as "the one who calls us forward" than Whitehead.

study of Hegel, Heidegger advances as a basic thesis that being (Hegel's Absolute Spirit), in and for itself, wills to be with us, to be present to us. "This being-present-to-us, this *parousia*, this Advent, is part and parcel of the Absolute in and for itself." The "presence" of being is its *parousia*, advent, coming. Being is "arriving presence." Accordingly, history is not driven forward by the impulse of past possibilities but is pulled forward by the power of this arriving presence (a pull mediated, to be sure, through past possibilities). "The progression in the history of consciousness' formation is not driven forward by the given shape of consciousness into a still undetermined future, but is drawn by the pull of the goal which is already set. In that pull, the goal that pulls brings itself forth in appearance, and brings the course of consciousness from the start to the plenitude of its full status." The forward pull of being accounts for the fact that the dialectic of historical process is characterized by diastasis, discontinuity, leaps or breakthroughs, violence, death, and resurrection. It is "the irresistible pull by which consciousness is violently carried beyond itself." Thus human existence requires a fundamental openness to the future—to the surprising advent of being in unconcealment, by which the present state of consciousness is uprooted and violated.[59]

At the same time, the fulcrum or center of history is the *present*, for being comes *into the present* as that which gathers into presence. In Merleau-Ponty's words: "History according to Hegel is [the] maturation of a future in the present, not the sacrifice of the present to an unknown future."[60] Finally, human existence is oriented to the *past*, for in projection toward the future that calls him, man takes over his heritage by handing it down, thus making those

59. Heidegger, *Hegel's Concept of Experience* (New York, Harper & Row, 1970), pp. 30, 40, 45, 48-49, 69, 77-80, 146-149 et passim; quotations from pp. 30, 69, 79-80.

60. Maurice Merleau-Ponty, *Signs*, trans. by Richard C. McCleary (Evanston, Northwestern University Press, 1964), p. 72. See also his discussion of temporality as "field of presence" in *Phenomenology of Perception*, trans. by Colin Smith (London, Routledge & Kegan Paul, 1962), pp. 416 ff.

possibilities that have-been his own in the present moment
of vision. Man responds to the forward call of being in
the process of coming back to himself; thus he exists in the
present moment as his own possibility. The power of the
future comes *through the past* into the present. Historical
"retrieve" is the handing down or traditioning of past possibilities (both actualized and unactualized) that thereby
become the basis of a present, anticipatory project in which
being comes anew. The past alone is not "historical." Rather,
"history" is the total, unified structure of future-past-present
(or, more precisely, of "future-making-present-what-has-
been"). Thus history is the event of time by which the
future comes, gathering into presence by its call.[61]

In the latter writings Heidegger increasingly understands
the being-event as language event. Language (*Sprache*)
or word (λόγος) is the "means" by which the future calls us
forward; it is the instrument by which history "happens," by
which being is "power" or "event."[62] In *Über den Humanismus* (1947), Heidegger described language metaphorically
as "the house of being."[63] He now regards this metaphor as
misleading, in so far as it suggests that being is some sort
of transportable "object" that can be contained "in" language
as a "house." Language, rather, is identified with the event
or power of being in the sense that it is its most proper
"way," "means," or "manner." "The event *is* an act of
saying" (*das Ereignis ist sagend*).[64] "Saying" (*die Sage*)
controls and ordains the freedom of the event of unconcealment, which in turn rests in the act of saying that is
language.[65] Although Heidegger does not directly acknowledge it, the association of language and the event of being

61. *BT*, pp. 371-379, 384-388, 434-438.
62. *US*, pp. 200-214; see Pöggeler, *op. cit.*, pp. 279-280.
63. Heidegger, *Über den Humanismus*, pp. 5, 20.
64. *US*, pp. 262-263; cf. pp. 261-266.
65. *Ibid.*, p. 257; see Pöggeler, *op. cit.*, p. 279. In ordinary German, *die Sage*
means "legend," "myth," "fable," but Heidegger clearly takes it in the more
primitive sense of "saying" or "utterance." Cf. the verb *sagen*, "to say."

harks back to the biblical insight that word is the means of
the event of creation, of letting-be: "God *said*, 'Let there be
light' . . ." (Gen. 1:3 ff.).

This understanding of language is based on the root
meaning of λόγος—to which I have already referred—as the
process of gathering or collecting, a meaning Heidegger
discovered in his studies of Heraclitus and Parmenides.
The association of λόγος, gathering into presence, and being
(as temporal event) is brought out in the following passage:
"The word ὁ λόγος names that which gathers all things that
are present [beings] into presence [being] and thereby lets
them lie forth. Ὁ Λόγος names that by which the presencing
of that which comes to presence [*das Anwesen des Anwes-
enden*] is brought to pass. The presencing of that which
comes to presence is named by the Greeks τὸ ἐόν, i.e., τὸ εἶναι
τῶν ὄντων. The Romans called it *esse entium*. We say: the
being of beings [*das Sein des Seienden*]."[66] Λόγος, then, *is*
being; for it is the power that unconceals by gathering into
presence, by "presencing." Being itself is pure presence,
presence as such (*Anwesen, Anwesenheit*), so long as presence is understood in a dynamic and temporal sense rather
than as static presence at hand (*stete Vorhandenheit*).[67]

Heidegger has not, however, availed himself of the root
meaning of the Hebrew term for word, *dābār*, which, as
we have seen, suggests the idea of uncovering the "background" or quintessence of a thing, making it manifest in
power. This etymology supports my proposal to understand
"word" as temporal power by which the modes of time are
gathered into presence. It is solely through word, says
Gerhard Ebeling, "that I can have a relation to past and
future, that past and future are present to me, that I can go

66. Heidegger, *Vorträge und Aufsätze* (paperback ed.), Vol. III, p. 23. See
William J. Richardson, *Heidegger: Through Phenomenology to Thought* (The
Hague, Martinus Nijhoff, 1963), pp. 491-493.

67. On Heidegger's definition of being as "presence," "arriving presence,"
"the presencing of what is present," see especially *Hegel's Concept of Experience*, pp. 27, 69, 105-107; also *Identität und Differenz*, p. 19.

back behind my present and stretch out ahead of it."[68] The reason is that "it is the business of word to make present what is not at hand, what is absent"—or, in the sense of *dābār*, to go back into the background of things, to uncover and bring to light what is hidden, to make it present. This can also be accomplished to some degree by pictures, symbols, mementoes, or relics. But here, says Ebeling, the making present of what is past or distant is imperfect and subject to illusion, i.e., to the confusion of mediated presence with immediacy. The word is infinitely more potent as a means of making present what is absent, although of course it is not all-powerful for many things lie beyond even its reach.[69] Historical reality is deeply hidden in space and time. Only by language are we able to retrieve the past (to make it present by bringing it to speech anew) and to grant the future (to open ourselves for it and to let it come near). It is by means of word that man's existence as historical is opened up for him.

> Although the hiddenness of the future is more oppressing, and the desire for a word that grants a future more burning than the need to lighten the darkness of the past and to become free from it, we ultimately have here a single interwoven mystery that embraces past and future and knocks at the door of the present. The word that makes us true and makes us free and therefore grants us a future will in no case lead us on a flight into illusion; but from the truth of what has happened in the past, it will invest us with an assurance for that future which is superior to all dwindling and disappointing futures.[70]

Not only does word *grant* time or constitute history; it also happens *as* time, as temporal event. The word as spoken in sentences runs through time; it "takes" time.[71] Its temporality is a function of its basic character as *sound*—an aspect of word that has been made the subject of some

68. Ebeling, *God and Word*, trans. by James W. Leitch (Philadelphia, Fortress Press, 1967), p. 19.
69. *Ibid.*, pp. 24-25.
70. *Ibid.*, pp. 25-26; see p. 21. See also Ebeling's discussion in "Zeit und Wort," *Zeit und Geschichte*, pp. 353-355.
71. *Ibid.*, p. 18; and "Zeit und Wort," *op. cit.*, p. 354.

interesting reflections by Walter J. Ong in his recent book,
The Presence of the Word. Speech as sound, he points out,
"is irrevocably committed to time. . . . Words come into
being through time and exist only so long as they are going
out of existence. It is impossible, as Augustine notes in his
Confessions (iv. 1) to have all of an utterance present to
us at once, or even all of a word. . . . A moving object in a
visual field can be arrested. It is, however, impossible to
arrest sound and have it still present. If I halt a sound it
no longer makes any noise. I am left only with its opposite,
silence."[72] From this, Ong concludes that the purest, most
natural form of the word is sound. The alphabet, consequently, represents "denatured word"; it transposes the
spoken word into space, gives it temporal permanence and
ordered consistency. Something of the dynamic power of
the word is lost when it is written down, whereas contemporary electronic culture has enabled word to live again as
sound. Ong believes that the media in their succession—
spoken word, writing, printing, electronically reproduced
sound (telegraph, telephone, radio, television)—do not
cancel one another out but build on one another, permitting
a progressive enrichment of the possibilities of word.[73]

b. Word and Spatiality

That word consists of sound, points immediately to the
second of its aspects with which we are here concerned—
its physical quality or embodiedness, and its function as a
power that gathers into presence spatially as well as temporally. This is an aspect of word to which Heidegger has
devoted little if any attention. He seems to think of man
as a speaker without a body. Consequently he has over-

72. Walter J. Ong, S. J., *The Presence of the Word: Some Prolegomena for
Cultural and Religious History* (New Haven, Yale University Press, 1967),
pp. 40-41.
73. *Ibid.,* pp. 42-45, 88-89, 92, 111-112. Although Ong is correct in his
assumption, shared with modern linguistics, that the basic form of the word
is spoken, thus bringing out its original quality as sound, I think it is probably
even more correct to say that the word transcends *all* its forms, including that
of speech.

looked the capacity of word to overcome spatial distance as
well as temporal and to establish "horizontal" relationships
among men. In verbal communication two or more persons
are brought together spatially and in this sense are made
present to each other.[74] We are not to think of communication as the transmission of objective content, as though the
basic purpose of word were statement or assertion. Rather,
as communication, word is an event of encounter. It gathers
spatially as well as temporally; word constitutes space as
well as time.

Again, Ong has pointed out that the ability of word to
integrate space is a function of its quality as sound. Word
as sound establishes personal presence. The human voice
conveys presence as nothing else does; indeed, we could
say that voice *is* presence. The reason, suggests Ong, is that
sound is a unique "sensory key to interiority." Sound has
to do with the self-manifestation of interiors. Sight presents
surfaces for it is based on reflected light. We are unable to
penetrate "into" a person when we see him. Touch helps
to form the concepts of exteriority and interiority (which
are to be understood "existentially" rather than mathemat-
ically). "We feel ourselves inside our own bodies, and the
world as outside. . . . But to explore an interior, touch must
violate the interior, invade it, even break it open. Kinesthesia, it is true, gives me access to my own interior without
violation—I feel myself somehow inside my own body and
feel my body inside my own skin—but kinesthesia gives me
direct access to nothing but myself. . . . Sound, on the other
hand, reveals the interior without the necessity of physical

74. Electronic communication (telephone, radio, television) has made it possible to transmit presence spatially without physical immediacy. Television is
a good example of the fact that without sound there is very little presence.
When the sound fails, the picture loses its communicative potential and is
generally cut off. The reciprocal dependence of sound upon picture is less
important, as radio demonstrates. Of course television is a much more adequate communications medium for it conveys the embodiedness of speech and
makes unmistakably concrete the mutuality of word and body. The distinction between spatial presence and physical immediacy will prove important
in another context for our discussion of the "presence" of the risen Christ
(see below, pp. 266-267).

invasion."[75] This is the clue. Sound moves from interior to
interior and thus is able to open up interiors to each other
without destroying their interiority. It is the means by
which man lays himself open to the world, discloses himself,
enters into relationships with others, without annihilating
his own autonomy and discreteness. Or, as Ong also puts
it, sound establishes "communication without collision."
"Because the spoken word moves from interior to interior,
encounter between man and man is achieved largely through
voice. The modes of encounter are innumerable—a glance,
a gesture, a touch, even an odor—but among these the
spoken word is paramount. Encounters with others in which
no words are ever exchanged are hardly encounters at all."[76]
Because of the intimate connection between sound and
communication, thought-processes and conceptualization are
unable to develop apart from words. Children learn to think
only as they learn to speak and are caught up in the objective
universe of language. Consequently, the congenitally deaf
are far more intellectually retarded than the congenitally
blind, unless they are introduced into the oral-aural world
by pedagogical techniques.[77] Finally, sound and the spoken
word are able to constitute presence so fully because they
convey simultaneity. Vision presents (or reflects) surfaces
sequentially, whereas we hear all there is to hear simultaneously. Sound surrounds us and thus situates us in the midst
of a world. We find ourselves *in* the presence of a person
rather than "in front of" his presence. "Being in is what we
experience in a world of sound."[78] In this sense, word
constitutes space as well as time.[79]

75. Ong, *op. cit.*, pp. 117-118; see also pp. 113-114.
76. *Ibid.*, pp. 124-125.
77. *Ibid.*, pp. 141-142; see pp. 140-146.
78. *Ibid.*, pp. 128-130.
79. The beginnings of an ontological reformulation of the category of space,
overcoming the Kantian treatment of it as an a priori form of consciousness,
are found in Heidegger's *Being and Time*, pp. 134-148. But the discussion is
not as fully developed as Heidegger's reformulation of the category of time;
and, as far as I can understand it, it is not based on an analysis of word as
spoken.

The fact that word is sound means, of necessity, that it is
embodied: it is a bodily "gesture." This is one of the central
themes in recent French phenomenology of language (above
all, Maurice Merleau-Ponty, Paul Ricoeur, and Gabriel
Marcel). The relation between consciousness (or mind),
body, and world has been the dominant interest in Merleau-
Ponty's work.[80] He set out to overcome the antithesis between idealism and empiricism, which is merely a prolongation of the Cartesian subject-object, mind-body dichotomy.
"Our century has wiped out the dividing line between 'body'
and 'mind,' and sees human life as through and through
mental and corporeal, always based upon the body and
always (even in its most carnal modes) interested in relationships between persons. . . . The twentieth century has
restored and deepened the notion of flesh, that is, of animate
body"—or, as we might also put it, of "incarnate spirit."[81]
The body stands, as it were, between consciousness and the
world, both constituting and being constituted. It is by
means of my body that I constitute the world in which
I live, establishing it in my perception of it; but at the same
time I know myself as body to be constituted by the world,
a place in the world, an object of perception: ". . . my body
must itself be meshed into the visible world; its power
depends precisely on the fact that it has a place *from which*
it sees. Thus it is a thing, but a thing I dwell in. It is . . .
on the side of the subject; but it is not a stranger to the
locality of things." "This subject which experiences itself
as constituted at the moment it functions as constituting is
my body." Hence the body is what Merleau-Ponty calls
"the *vinculum* of the self and things," or what Husserl
described as a "perceiving thing," a "subject-object."[82] The
body represents the possibility of communication between
persons for it enables each of us to be perceived, constituted,

80. See the fundamental analyses contained in *Phenomenology of Perception*.
81. Merleau-Ponty, *Signs*, pp. 226-227. See also *Phenomenology of Perception*, pp. 198-199, 428-433.
82. Merleau-Ponty, *Signs*, pp. 93-94, 166-172.

or signified at the same moment that we engage in an act
of perception or signification. It enables us to be both
subject and object in the act of communication, thus overcoming the theoretical impossibility of communication in a
pure idealism.[83]

Now, the body functions as the *vinculum* of self and
things above all in virtue of its capacity to speak. Speech
is the fundamental and unique bodily expression of man.
"The spoken word is a [bodily] gesture, and its meaning, a
world." Speech is at once an operation of intelligence and
a motor phenomenon. Its "inherence in the body" can be
established clearly by studies in speech pathology, which
show that motor disturbances impinge upon the ability of
speech to signify, and conversely that mental disturbances
manifest themselves in the motility of speech. The body
itself speaks rather than another, inner power, the "soul."
The body must become the thought or intention it expresses.[84]
Language conveys and constitutes the world in which we
live by "stylizing" it, very much like the painter stylizes
reality. "There is signification when we submit the data of
the world to a 'coherent deformation.' "[85] The close connection between speech and body, and the "stylizing" function
of language, which brings it into proximity with non-verbal
forms of expression, means that we must understand language as an event of the whole man. The linguisticality of
man's existence includes all the acts by which he unconceals
or "opens" his world: not just spoken words, but also written
texts, physical gestures (which always accompany speech),
painting and other non-verbal arts, music, moral and political
action, cultic acts of celebration, and the like. Conduct is
"acted word," a "sounding board" for word.[86] A human

83. Cf. the logical conundrum of Sartre's *No Exit:* I can know the other person
only by reducing him to an object in my world, whereas his very nature as
person is to resist objectification. Hence in knowing him I destroy him.

84. Merleau-Ponty, *Phenomenology of Perception*, pp. 183-184, 194-198; see
the entire chapter, "The Body as Expression and Speech," pp. 174-199.

85. Merleau-Ponty, *Signs*, pp. 54-55, 77-78. The expression is Malraux's.

86. Ebeling, *God and Word*, p. 19.

action that is not a form of "speaking" is meaningless; and a word that is not embodied in act—physical, moral, political, artistic, literary, cultic—is an abstraction. Thus we must insist that word is *event* not only in a temporal-historical but also in a spatial-bodily sense.

c. Word and Transcendence

A third aspect of word must now be considered—one that is most important for my constructive purposes, yet is perhaps the most difficult to understand. The word that gathers into presence both temporally and spatially is not simply identical with human speaking; it is rather that which comes to expression or "happens" in human speech. This is the distinction Heidegger draws between the power of unconcealment as such (being as language-event) and the instrumentality by which this power occurs—human speaking and thinking. He refers to this distinction as the "ontological difference."[87] According to Richardson, it is the fundamental theme of his philosophy.[88] It is rooted in the ambivalence of the Greek word for "being," ὄν. Grammatically, ὄν is a participle and may be used either as a noun (ὄντος) or as a verbal adjective (εἶναι). When taken as a noun, ὄν means that which is, "a being" (*Seiendes*); when taken as a verbal adjective, it designates that event or power by which a being "is," namely, "being" (*Sein*).[89] Hence the word for being is intrinsically ambivalent, pointing both to the difference between being and beings and their inseparable unity.

The same ambivalence and unity applies to the term λόγος, which as we have seen is another name for the being-event in Heidegger's later thought. Word (λόγος) can refer either to language (*die Sprache*) as the creative power by which man is gathered into presence and in which speech is

87. For the first time in *Vom Wesen des Grundes* (1st ed., 1929; 3rd ed., Frankfurt, Klostermann, 1949), p. 15.
88. *Heidegger: Through Phenomenology to Thought,* pp. 10-15.
89. See *Hegel's Concept of Experience,* pp. 105-107.

founded, or to the speaking (*das Sprechen*) by which word comes concretely to expression. In the later writings, a series of parallel terms is used to delineate this fundamental distinction-in-unity: language—*die Sprache, die Sage, die Zeige, die Rede* (all are feminine in gender and end in *-e*); speech—*das Sprechen, das Sagen, das Zeigen, das Reden* (all are neuter, all end in *-en*). Thinking (*das Denken*) is correlative with speaking (*das Sprechen*); the two together are the fundamental human "instruments" by which man responds to the creative address of language; as instruments, they belong not really to man but to language itself.[90]

The distinction between language and speech has long been noted. Schleiermacher called attention to it by distinguishing between grammatical and psychological interpretation in his hermeneutics. Modern structural linguistics (Ferdinand de Saussure, Louis Hjelmslev, and their followers) is concerned with language as an internally related structure of signs, which has an existence independent of the speaker and is the condition for the possibility of any meaningful speech, although in itself it is purely formal, empty of content. Language becomes an event, an episode of communication, in the act of speech—in sentences, whereby signs acquire a specific semantic value by pointing to something in the world.[91] For Heidegger language is not merely a formal sign-structure but the power of being by which things are called into being, constituted as what they are in a spatio-temporal network. Language does not *point to* a world but *constitutes* the world of man's experience. Finally, the similarity should be noted between Ludwig Wittgenstein's theory of the "language game" in his later work (the *Philosophical Investigations* and *The Blue and Brown Books*) and that of H.-G. Gadamer referred to in the next paragraph. It is not possible here to attempt an adjudication of the similarities and differences between

90. *US*, pp. 30-31, 243-245, 252-254; see Pöggeler, *op. cit.*, pp. 277-278.
91. Cf. Paul Ricoeur, "New Developments in Phenomenology in France: the Phenomenology of Language," *Social Research*, Vol. 34 (1967), pp. 14-27.

structural linguistics, Heideggerian phenomenology, and the later Wittgenstein; my concern rather is to point to an interest in the phenomenon of the transcendence of language from several different and possibly converging perspectives.

The "transcendence" of language vis-à-vis human speech is one of the central themes in Gadamer's philosophical hermeneutic. As we have noted from our earlier discussion of his work, he seeks to understand language as a "game" with its own freedom and buoyancy—a game of conversation in which the conversation partners are caught up and moved along by a process that seems to possess its own inner teleology.

> The back and forth of a movement which takes place within a given field of play is derived so little from the human game and from the playing attitude of subjectivity that, wholly, to the contrary, the real experience of the game consists, for human subjectivity as well, in the fact that something comes to dominate here that obeys its own set of laws. . . . The consciousness of the player is determined by the fact that the back and forth movement of the game has a peculiar freedom and buoyancy. . . . The game is not so much the subjective attitude of the two men who confront each other as it is the formation of the movement itself, which, as in an unconscious teleology, subordinates the attitude of the individuals to itself. . . . The self of the individuals, their activity and their understanding of themselves, is absorbed as it were into a higher determination which is the real determinant.[92]

Or as Gadamer also puts it, in the dialectic of conversation there occurs "an action of the subject matter itself."[93] The stress on the "game" character of language and its transcendence of the speaker is a way of saying that, although language comes to expression only in human speech, nevertheless, it is not a subjectivistic or anthropocentric phenomenon: language gives itself rather than being the product of human conceptualization. Thus, in the very process of speaking we have an experience of "finite" transcendence, of something that confronts us and draws us into its movement while at the same time it has no existence independent

92. H.-G. Gadamer, *Kleine Schriften I* (Tübingen, J. C. B. Mohr [Paul Siebeck], 1967), p. 77; see pp. 75-81, and *WM*, pp. 97-105, 461-465.
93. *WM*, pp. 439-441.

of us. Gadamer also refers to the "speculative" or "mirror-like" structure of the word. "The word is intangible in its own being and yet throws back the image that is offered to it." Human words are intrinsically limited and finite, yet in virtue of their speculative structure are transparent to the totality of being, which they bring to speech in ever-new configurations.[94]

Gadamer's concept of the "writtenness" of language is also important for this theme. The ability of language to be written down marks its transcendence vis-à-vis the speaker or writer. It is not bound to the act of speaking and writing, i.e., to its original production. Once a text is written, the author surrenders it to the community. It bears a "pure ideality of meaning," for in a written text the meaning of what was once said exists for itself, freed of the emotional and subjective elements in expression. At the same time, writing exists only to be transformed back into spoken, living words when it is read again and discussed. Thus, language enjoys transcendence over the written text as well as spoken words.[95] Indeed, it is probably accurate to say that word as language transcends all its forms, including the spoken, the written, and the electronically reproduced. The writtenness of language signifies its transcendence of the speaker; conversely, the reading of a text frees language from its written form. The manifold forms of word are proof of its transcendence of any one of them and of its objectivity vis-à-vis man as speaker and writer.

The transcendence of language helps define man's place or function in the event of unconcealment, which is the most central and basic of Heidegger's concerns, from the earliest of his writings to the latest. Here we stand at the crux of his thought. On the one hand, human essence rests in language. The ability to speak is not just one of man's capacities, equivalent to the others; rather it designates man

94. *Ibid.*, pp. 432-449.
95. On the writtenness of language, see *WM,* pp. 367-370, and the unpublished essay, "Image and Word," pp. 4-8.

as such. Man is the speaking animal, or more precisely, "that living thing whose being is essentially determined by the ability to speak"—ζῷον λόγον ἔχον.[96] On the other hand, language "needs" man and binds itself unequivocally to his speech; it "makes use of" man in his very essence, his speaking ability. The relation between language and man is a necessary one from both sides, a relation in which man is at the "disposal" of language and is "appropriated" by it, a relation in which language itself speaks—in so far as it is equipped with the tools of speech, namely, man as speaker and thinker.[97] Or, as Heidegger expresses it metaphorically, the relation of language to human speaking is that of a stream to its banks—it forms the banks, yet is forever dependent upon them.[98]

In this relation, human speaking is an answer that corresponds to the address of language, bringing its silent saying to sounded word by "re-saying" it.[99] Man is the sounding board for the silent saying of being. He is the place (*da*) where the power of the future, the power of being (*Sein*), takes place; he is the "there" of being (*Da-Sein*). As the "there," man in his speaking (answering) corresponds to the word of being. This correspondence or re-saying is not to be understood as an analogy. Analogy (ἀνά, up + λόγος, word) suggests a relation of proportionality between words or things that are otherwise different (e.g., exist at different levels of the ontological scale). It is rather a relation of homology (ὁμός, same + λόγος, word), a relation of correspondence rather than of proportionality. The word (λόγος) that comes to expression in human speaking as the power of being is not some sort of supernatural word that resides in another sphere of reality and is miraculously inserted into

---

96. *BT*, p. 47 (translation altered); cf. *Sein und Zeit*, p. 25. Cf. *US*, p. 241; *Introduction to Metaphysics*, p. 175.

97. *US*, pp. 122-126, 254, 256-257, 260, 266. Cf. also *Identität und Differenz*, pp. 13-20, where the same point is made in describing the "belonging together" of being and man.

98. *US*, p. 255.

99. *Ibid.*, pp. 254-255, 260; see Pöggeler, *op. cit.*, p. 278.

or between human words. It is the *same* word as human
words—when these words signify an authentic hearing,
re-saying, and answering of the creative, unconcealing,
gathering word. Richardson summarizes the point well:
"Such a λέγειν as this *oc*curs when human language *con*curs
(ὁμολογεῖν) completely with the aboriginal utterance of being.
. . . By letting beings lie-forth in the Open as what they are,
There-being [*Dasein*] concurs with the process of Λόγος,
which is the process that gathers these beings at once unto
themselves and unto itself as aboriginal Utterance. In concurrence, authentic language comes-to-pass."[100] Human
words are the "instruments" of the original word. It has no
other "means." It does not transpire in some realm or world
other than that constituted by man himself in his speaking.
Of course it is true that man's speech often, indeed most of
the time, falls into "everydayness," inauthenticity, "idle talk"
(*Gerede*), and thus fails to correspond to or re-say the
word of being. But the point is that this correspondence
does not involve a "supernaturalizing" of word but rather
a restoration of human speech to its own most proper
function. This point is essential for a proper understanding
of the relation between the word of God and the word of
man. When the latter is brought to authenticity by the
former, i.e., when it becomes word of faith, then it exists
in a relation of homology to the word of God, serving as
the appropriate instrument or means for the coming to
speech of God's creative, redemptive, and unconcealing
word. Rather than referring to the *analogia fidei,* as Karl
Barth does (thus suggesting the suprahistorical character
of the word of God), we may refer to the *homologia fidei.*
Faith means precisely homologous speaking.[101]

100. Richardson, *op. cit.,* p. 497; Heidegger, *Vorträge und Aufsätze* (paperback ed.), Vol. III, pp. 11, 13-14.
101. The insistence upon homology in this context is not intended to deny
the valid use of analogy in second-order language *about* God. *We* can speak
about God only analogically and metaphorically; yet God, when he speaks,
does so homologically. E.g., in Sec. 4.b, I shall have recourse to what Rahner
describes as the "analogy of having being" in defining God as the one who
has word absolutely. On homology, see further below, pp. 143-147.

In attempting to delineate the "difference" between word as language and as speech, and thus in arguing for the "transcendence" of word vis-à-vis man as speaker—as a means of developing a conceptual basis for understanding the transcendence of the word of God—I must beware of the danger of falling back into a hypostatization of word. A tendency in this direction haunts the later work of Heidegger himself. He says, for example, that language itself speaks, that there can only be a speaking *by* language, not *about* language[102]—as though language were an active, speaking subject and man only the inert instrumentality of this speaking by language itself. Hints occur of a word-mysticism in which poetic meditation remains the only authentic form of thinking.[103] But it is precisely the hypostatization of the word that I have sought to escape and avoid all along. The conception of word as hypostasis—as active, personal, divine agent—is what rendered the old Logos-flesh christology no longer tenable, for it robbed Jesus of his full humanity and required a mythologization of word. This danger may be guarded against in two ways. First, the word that is the power of the future has no "metaphysical" or "metahistorical" existence in another "world," apart from the words of man in which it comes to speech. It has its "being" only "there." This was the substance of my argument in the preceding paragraph. The result is a form of "finite" transcendence—a transcendence that takes place or happens only in the finitude of human experience, not violating that finitude but rather deepening and preserving it. Gadamer has pointed to the intrinsic finitude of word: in virtue of its "speculative" structure, it is always open to more than is said. Indeed, the finitude of human experience has its focus in man's linguisticality. In speaking man is not infinitized or supernaturalized; he is not annulled in the being of God, as was the danger in Hegel's infinite dialectic of Spirit. Rather, he becomes man in the true and proper

102. *US,* pp. 149-152.
103. *Ibid.,* p. 267.

sense. Word is the means by which man becomes "person";
it is not personal agency itself. The second point is related
to the first, namely, that human speaking must not be
thought to collapse into an *idipsum*, a mystical identity, with
the word of the being-event, which would thereby become
the true *subjectum* of human speech. A genuine *correspondence* between the λόγος of being and the word of man
would require a dialectical or reflexive movement in which
an element of non-identity is preserved. A true answer
must also become a question; a true hearing is also a
speaking; a true response must take up responsibility. Thus,
just at the point where man seems to be most radically
dependent upon the word that transcends him, he finds his
own true freedom and subjectivity.

d. Word as the Medium of Presence

I shall now attempt to draw the strands of the analysis of
word together by reflecting upon the threefold sense in
which word is the medium of presence. Word gathers into
presence temporally and spatially, and it transcends human
speech as the power of the future that gathers by its coming.

To say that word gathers into presence temporally, that
word is temporal power (Sec. 3.a), means that word constitutes presence to oneself. For presence to oneself means
that the temporal modes of existence—future, past, present
—are integrated, achieve mutual coinherence. Without
temporal integration human life would disintegrate into an
irredeemable past, an unachievable future, and a meaningless present. Such disintegration is the essence of schizophrenia—the loss of the center. Recent experiments on the
causes of schizophrenia sought to induce schizophrenic
symptoms artificially by submitting healthy persons to
hypnosis in which various dimensions of temporal experience
were momentarily blocked out. First, the patient was robbed
of his sense of the future. He continued to function but in
a totally listless, purposeless, "Epicurean" fashion. Then he
was robbed of all sense of the past; memory was obliterated.

He seemed to wilt into a mere vegetable, unable to speak (for of course speech belongs to past heritage) or to perform any routine human functions. It was the deep withdrawal characteristic of advanced schizophrenia.[104] These experiments serve as dramatic confirmation of Ray L. Hart's insight that we understand out of the past and live out of the future.[105] Without understanding and without life existence in the present is impossible. Word is the means by which understanding is gained from the past for word is the medium of memory and tradition; and word is the means by which the future out of which we live is opened, for being "comes" as the power of the future, gathering beings into presence, through word. Word retrieves the past and grants the future.

The expression "presence to oneself" is borrowed from Karl Rahner. Rahner defines the essence of being as "knowing and being known in an original unity, which we have chosen to call the presence to itself [*Bei-sich-sein*] or the lucidity . . . of the being of beings."[106] According to Rahner, the *Bei-sich-sein* of being is fundamentally an intellective act, involving a pre-reflexive self-possession, a pre-linguistic auto-lucidity; accordingly, being itself is "cognitivity" (*Erkennbarkeit*), and man in his "seminal person" is present to himself in a primordial act of knowing. Against these

104. The experiments (which were demonstrated on television) were an effort to determine whether certain disturbances in the body chemistry induce schizophrenia. If this hypothesis should prove correct, it is tempting to think that such disturbances might have something to do with a fundamental impairment of the speech processes.

105. Ray L. Hart, *Unfinished Man and the Imagination* (New York, Herder and Herder, 1968), pp. 11, 272, 307-309. Hart points out that this formula may not be reversed: "*Understanding* out of the past and its potency may indeed open the future out of which we are to live; but *living* out of the past on the basis of an understanding putatively won from the future (say, the imminent end of an age), the end-run tried by those moderns who hanker for pre-critical naïveté, is quite impossible" (pp. 272-273). Hart's discussion of the coinherence of the modes of historical time and of the relation between imagination and temporality has been helpful for my own formulations (see esp. pp. 97, 188-227, 287).

106. Rahner, *Hörer des Wortes: Zur Grundlegung einer Religionsphilosophie*, 2nd ed., J. B. Metz, ed. (München, Kösel-Verlag, 1963), p. 55 (see the whole of Chapter 3); *ThI*, Vol. I, pp. 168-170; Vol. V, pp. 200-201, 205, 207-209, 211.

Thomistic assumptions, I am arguing that presence to oneself is constituted by *word*; such presence is not a pre-linguistic but precisely a linguistic accomplishment. Presence to oneself is not an intellective but a temporal-historical phenomenon, a coinherence of the modes of time through word. Similarly, being is not cognitivity (*Erkennbarkeit*) but event (*Ereignis*) or power (*dynamis*), the power of which language is the "means." Hence, to locate a man's presence to himself, we must not seek to go "behind" his historical-temporal, verbal existence but rather to focus precisely there. Man has access to himself only when he *speaks*. His speaking does not, of course, need to be audible or visible (written); it can just as well be the silent speaking of thinking. But the point is that without access to words, man has no access to himself and thus no presence. Man's speaking (whether audible or silent) brings him into living relation not merely with his own private past and future but with the past and the future of the total history in which he is embodied. Presence to oneself (temporal presence) is not merely a personalizing but also a socializing event.

To say that word gathers into presence spatially, that word is embodied (Sec. 3.b, Chapter 3), means that word constitutes presence to the world. By "world" I mean the political and social nexus constituted by the relations between men (both as individuals and in greater and smaller groups), and the natural environment that embodies these relations. Word as sound and as bodily gesture moves across spatial distance and establishes horizontal relationships among men, thus constituting a world. Man has his being-in-the-world through the word, which enables him to constitute the world (making it the object of his speech and encounter, establishing the horizons by which he "has" a world) at the same time he is constituted by it (being made the object of someone else's speech, becoming part of the *Umwelt* because of his objective availability as embodied speaker). Only by passing out of his interiority and becoming an object to himself in the otherness of the

world does man achieve full presence to himself. Karl
Rahner devotes profound attention to this second form of
presence in his analysis of the "intermediary person" or the
"historicity" of human spirit. Man is capable of presence to
himself (*Bei-sich-sein*) only in so far as he is present to
another (*Bei-einem-anderen-sein*); "turning back to oneself" (*Rückkehr in sich*) is only possible through "turning
out to the world" (*Auskehr in Welt*). This is the case because being, by which man's self-presence is constituted, is
revealed only through the concrete phenomena, the *materia,*
of the world. Human spirit is precisely *spirit in the world.*[107]
Again, I differ from Rahner in wanting to make more explicit
than he himself does that the means by which spirit objectifies itself in the world is speech,[108] and by arguing that
word is the medium of spatial presence, not a "representative
sign" of non-linguistic reality.

It should be evident from what has been said thus far
that presence to oneself and presence to the world are
dialectically related: each is essential to the other, neither
can be had without the other. On the one hand, man has
full access to himself only by means of a circuit through
the otherness of the world, by which he is constituted as
an object in the world and (if Rahner is correct) being
enters into unconcealment for him. In this sense, spatial
presence constitutes the conditions of temporal presence
and indeed is the horizon on which the temporal presence
of an individual becomes historically visible. On the other
hand, temporal presence constitutes the conditions of the
possibility of spatial presence. For the very language by
which we have intercourse with the world is a heritage of
the past, which must be "retrieved" and "projected" anew
resolutely toward the future in the present "moment of

107. *ThI,* Vol. II, pp. 272-273; *Hörer des Wortes,* pp. 147-148, 151-159, 173-
175. This is a central thesis of *Hörer des Wortes,* Chapters 10-13, and of
Rahner's seminal study of St. Thomas' epistemology, *Geist in Welt,* 2nd ed.,
J. B. Metz, ed. (München, Kösel-Verlag, 1957).
108. This is rather obscurely hinted in *ThI,* Vol. II, p. 272. In general, Rahner
understands man's relation with the world in terms of his sensible *cognition.*
See *Hörer des Wortes,* Chapters 5, 10.

vision."[109] Authentic being-in-the-world (spatial presence) is
a function of authentic temporality, of the coinherence of
past and future in the present. Furthermore, the past and the
future to which man is present are not merely his private
history but the public history of the world in which he is
embodied; in this sense, presence to oneself already implies
presence to the world. In summary: space and time are
co-constitutive horizons of human existence, and full *personal*
presence is accomplished by the dialectical movement
between presence to oneself and presence to the world. "Personhood" means presence realized simultaneously in these
two horizons—the *An-und-für-sich-sein* of Spirit, expressed in
Hegelian terms,[110] or the "achieved person" or "historical
spirit" of Rahner's anthropology. As the medium of presence,
word constitutes personhood.[111]

Hans Frei has described the mutuality of presence to
oneself and what he calls the "sharing" of one's presence or
"communion." Communion is the normative situation of
being human, whereas alienation means a disruption in the
normal state of affairs. Man's fundamental or primordial
condition, according to Frei, is to exist as fellow man, in
friendship and communication rather than in estrangement
and isolation. Sharing means that "a person can give himself
in public and personal communication without losing himself

109. *BT*, pp. 387-388.

110. The concept of "presence" is central to Hegel's dialectic of Spirit. Unfortunately, I cannot pursue the analysis of this concept in Hegel without unduly
extending the discussion. Essentially, presence for him is a function of consciousness rather than of word. In the absolute self-consciousness of Spirit,
presence (or self-reconciliation) is fully realized; but this is an intrinsically
infinite, transhistorical moment in Hegel's dialectic. Rather than constituting
man's historical being, it annuls and absorbs it. See Heidegger's analysis of
the theme of "presence" in *Hegel's Concept of Experience*, pp. 27 ff.

111. The argument that word constitutes presence to the world as well as to
oneself, and the insistence that personhood is realized only in the dialectic
between these two horizons of presence, find support in Johannes Metz's concern to develop a hermeneutic of public word—a mode of speech that is
neither metaphysical nor existential but political. Language does not occur
merely within the private, transcendental domain of the person but must be
objectified in the world and become socially effective precisely to enable the
full realization of the person. See "Theological Aspects of the Word in Relation to Society," *Theology of the World*, trans. by William Glen-Doepel (New
York, Herder and Herder, 1969), pp. 125-130.

and that he can be received." "It is the word, the look, the gesture that passes between friends and lovers, indicating that to regard the self as encased within walls and communicating with others as though by code-tapping on the wall is not always correct." Because acts of sharing are self-initiated, it follows that one cannot be present to others without being present to oneself and vice versa. The loss of this mutuality leads to an increasingly destructive oscillation between acute presence to oneself and the dissolution of the self in intensive relationships with others. The end result is madness. Frei suggests that such an oscillation is portrayed in unforgettably powerful fashion in Thomas Mann's novel, *Doctor Faustus,* where the descent into madness of the composer-hero, Adrian Leverkühn, is apparently modeled on the final insanity of Nietzsche.

> This madness possesses a particularly haunting quality and is characterized first by a maniacal concentration of personal presence, or a power exercising itself with exhilarating and yet paralyzing and destructive effectiveness upon others as well as itself. This is followed by the collapse of the person, leaving an empty shell of quiescence and passivity, which is in frightful and complete contrast to the previous maniacal and fierce concentration of presence, and is underscored all the more by an occasional dumb and menacing look. . . .
>
> When we find a shell where there had been acute presence to self and charismatic presence to others, we sense how much in the case of human beings their presence is the equivalent of their whole being. We sense also the inescapable mutuality of presence to oneself with presence to others. In the collapse of presence we grasp as its contrary not absence but loss of everything—the loss of sheer being, of the cohesion of presence with identity that makes up personal being.[112]

According to Frei, we have no direct experience of the complete unity of presence to oneself and presence to another person. Such a unity can be found only in the Triune God, and proleptically, we might add, in the person of Jesus of Nazareth, whose self-presence is really identical with his being for others in word and deed.

112. Hans W. Frei, "The Mystery of the Presence of Jesus Christ," *Crossroads,* Vol. 17:2 (January-March 1967), pp. 76-77.

The transcendence of word vis-à-vis human speech, as the power of the future that gathers into presence by its coming (Sec. 3.c, Chapter 3), constitutes the third horizon of presence, in which the first two are founded. Human speech is based upon a power, a gracious word, not its own. At the point where word comes authentically to speech, a reality, a power, a word is experienced that transcends man, yet has no independent subsistence as a metahistorical entity apart from him. I have described this experience as "finite transcendence." Such transcendence may not be located by looking away from or above man but precisely toward him. Expressed theologically, the word that founds presence and exists in a homologous relation to human speech is the word of God. The explication of word as the word of God, and the relation between the word of God and God, is the substance of the discussion in the next section. Following that, we shall be in a position to understand how God himself is present as the power of presence wherever authentic human speech is accomplished.

4. WORD, WORD OF GOD, AND GOD[113]

a. *Word as the Word of God*

The word that gathers into presence both temporally and spatially, and that transcends human speech precisely as it comes to expression by means of it, is what Christian faith *means* by the word *of God.* This thesis is suggested by the analysis of word and the horizons of presence offered in the preceding section. Word, according to this analysis, is a world-constituting event: it establishes the "open horizon" in which man is able to "exist" by projecting himself on his own possibilities. It is a temporal event: indeed, it is time itself, understood as the power of the future that calls man

113. In Sec. 4, I continue to draw upon material first published in my article, "Heidegger, Revelation, and the Word of God," *JRel,* Vol. 49 (July 1969), pp. 228-252.

forward, laying open new, incalculable possibilities, but
which always come through a past that must be handed
down explicitly ("traditioned") and be made the basis of a
fresh possibility of existence through historical retrieve. It
is a word that comes to expression in homology with human
speech and activity—a homology in which man functions as
the indispensable instrument of word and yet experiences its
transcendence. Word is not an "anthropological" product
or a "subjectivistic" concept, although it is the fundamental
human act. It unconceals by gathering into presence both
temporally and spatially. According to Heidegger, this
"presencing" accomplishes an integration of the temporal
modes, so that man is brought back from preoccupation with
the merely present-at-hand and is directed instead to a
resolute projection toward the future, a projection in which
past possibilities are retrieved and presence is accomplished
as a dynamic "moment of vision." I have argued that word
must also be understood to constitute presence in a spatial
sense for as bodily gesture it is the means of communication
with the world and of horizontal social relations. In its
temporal and spatial dimensions, word as unconcealment has
both a creative and a "salvific" or "healing" (integrating)
function. What is unconcealed (and hence saved or healed)
is not being as such but human existence in its secular-
temporal-linguistic authenticity.

We have here the basic *formal* structures for a theological
understanding of the word of God. According to Christian
faith (to give it expression for the moment in a Heideggerian terminology), the word of God is a word by which
the world is constituted as God's "kingdom" or "city"; a
word that comes upon man as the power of the future
mediated through certain normative events of the historical
past, hence, in this fundamental sense is temporal; a word
that comes to expression in human speech and activity when
such speech and activity are redeemed from everydayness
and restored to faithfulness; a word that can only be understood as a gift, for it lies beyond man's capacity to produce

it and his worthiness to have it (in this sense he remains
always at its disposal, a recipient rather than an initiator); a
word, finally, that functions as the inmost, abiding existential of human nature. Without such a word, man could not
exist. Precisely at the point where he is most characteristically human—his ability to speak—man is dependent upon
the word that is the word of God. The claim that it is *God's*
word is one that follows from the peculiar message and
experience of Christian faith, not one that can be advanced
by formal analysis itself. It is a claim that has its roots ultimately in the definitive word-event, Jesus Christ. But we
have at least available the tools for a description of the *possibility* of God's word as a power that constitutes the world
by unconcealing and gathering it, should it in fact occur.

That the real significance of Heidegger's analysis of being
and word is to be found theologically at the point of a doctrine of the *word of God* seems to have been sensed by the
philosopher himself. In meditating upon his theological
background as a student in the Jesuit seminary at Freiburg,
Heidegger says he first confronted the problem of hermeneutic in his theological studies and was struck by the following
parallel: as the word of Scripture (i.e., the word of God) is
related to theological-speculative thinking, so being is related
to language.[114] Otto Pöggeler comments on this analogy in
illuminating fashion. The claim of the word of Scripture is
not that of a static permanence, a being ready-to-hand; rather
it is an event, an historical event, which is not closed but is
the way into an open future. In this claim, truth is presented,
although at the same time it remains a mystery, referring
to a future revelation. As salvific, this word calls man to
decision; it guides the believer into that truth in which he
finds freedom and his future place of abode, the house in

---

114. Heidegger, "Aus einem Gespräch von der Sprache," *US*, p. 96: "At that
time I was especially agitated by the question of the relation between the
word of Scripture and theological-speculative thinking. It was, if you will,
the same relation, namely, that between language and being [with which this
Gespräch has been concerned], although concealed and inaccessible to me.
. . ." That "being" is here intended to correspond with "word of Scripture" is
confirmed by Pöggeler in the passage cited below.

which he dwells (cf. Jn. 8:31-32). "This claim bestows a new being, although historically and in time. . . . Speculative thinking seeks to display this being as the being of beings. However, in this attempt the traditional thinking about being must be shattered, for here being is not static presence but the event that communicates itself at the same time it withdraws. If language is to refer to this being—the historical claim—then it can no longer be thought of 'metaphysically' as a *verum*, which is convertible with a static presence."[115]

Interpreted in this way, the analogy corresponds to one introduced by Heidegger into the discussion at the 1960 meeting of old Marburgers, just a year after the publication of the essay mentioned above: "As philosophical thinking is related to being, when being speaks to thinking, so faith's thinking is related to God, when God is revealed in his word."[116] According to Heinrich Ott, because the analogy is between the relations *A* (philosophical thinking) : *B* (being) and *C* (faith's thinking) : *D* (God), nothing may be learned from it about a possible correspondence between being *(B)* and God *(D)*. We rather learn how to think theologically in analogy to the meditative thinking of being by philosophy.[117] But if the relations *A : B* and *C : D* are analogous to each other, then it may be argued that the respective terms of the relations, *A* and *C*, and *B* and *D*, are also analogous, at least in respect of their relational functions. If philosophical and theological thinking are related to their respective subject matters analogously, then there would seem also to be an analogy between the subjects themselves. In this sense, the terms *B* (being) and *D* (God) function analogously; they stand in similar relations of disposal or evocation to the thinking they call forth, and hence they enjoy similar powers and qualities. But more

---

115. Pöggeler, *op. cit.*, p. 270.

116. James M. Robinson, *The Later Heidegger and Theology*, J. M. Robinson and J. B. Cobb, Jr., eds. (New York, Harper & Row, 1963), p. 43.

117. Heinrich Ott, "What Is Systematic Theology?", *ibid.*, pp. 106 ff.

important is the fact that it is not simply God who stands
in correspondence with being in this analogy but God as
he is *revealed in his word*—a subtlety that appears to have
been overlooked by Ott. Thus, what Heidegger is really
proposing is an analogy between the *functions* of being as
event of unconcealment and the *word* of God.

b. Word of God and God

We may conclude, then, that the *word* which unconceals
by gathering into presence temporally and spatially, and
which transcends man as it comes to expression in his speaking and activity, is what theology means by the *word of God.*
But we must now address the question of the relation between the *word* of God and *God.* Is God identical with his
word? Or must a distinction here be drawn that prevents us from identifying God and word? The relation
between word of God and God may be understood as a
dialectical one.[118]

In the first place, God is not to be thought of as some
"thing" or "being" behind his word. Such a view would
imply a return to a pre-Heideggerian understanding of both
God and word. Word is not the outward statement or
expression of a more fundamental, pre-linguistic reality.
God is not "a being" who exists, as it were, on the other
side of being, the power of unconcealment. To think of God
as a being would be to reduce him to the status of worldly
entities, even if he were regarded as the supreme being,
the metaphysical first cause. It is against such a notion of

118. This dialectical relation is suggested by Ebeling in reflecting upon the
subject of his lectures under the title "God and Word." "Between the two
principal terms there stands the word 'and,' simultaneously joining and separating those terms. . . . What if the 'and' which links them breaks down, so
that God is left without word and our word without God, a wordless God and
godless word—and thus the place of God is taken by a silence that renders us
speechless, smothering every sound and even every thought, while our word
ultimately fails and falls silent? Or what if an all too close contact between
God and word results in a melting of the 'and' which separates them, so that
we read, 'the word was God' (John 1:1), and consequently what is to be
expected of the word is no less than God?" (*God and Word,* pp. 1-2.)

God, which has held sway in the Western metaphysical and theological tradition, that Heidegger argues in the following passage: "The just and proper name for God in philosophy [is *causa sui*]. To such a God man can neither pray nor offer sacrifice. Before the *causa sui* man cannot fall on his knees in awe; in the presence of a God like this he cannot make music and dance. So it is that a god-less thinking which must forfeit the God of philosophy, God as *causa sui*, is perhaps closer to the God who is divine. Here this says only: such a thinking is freer for the divine God than onto-theo-logic would care to admit."[119] By a "god-less thinking" Heidegger seems to have in mind, according to Richardson, an essential or foundational thinking that does not pose the question of God "metaphysically" but rather thinks the event of unconcealment. Here the objection Heidegger has brought against the metaphysical conception of being as a static ground, a first cause, applies with equal force against the theistic conception of God. God is neither an infinite, supreme being situated "beyond" being, nor a finite being existing at the disposal of the power of being.

If God is not a being behind his word, then it would seem logical to identify word (or being) with God, and to state, presumably on the grounds of the Johannine Prologue, that "the word *is* God." However, this alternative must be rejected too. Biblical language about God ordinarily resists the temptation of reversing the relation between subject and predicate and of making the divine attributes the subject of statements about God. For example, in I Jn. 4:7-8 we read that "God is love" (ὁ θεὸς ἀγάπη ἐστίν), and that "love is *of* God" (ἡ ἀγάπη ἐκ τοῦ θεοῦ ἐστιν), but not that "love is God." A reversal of the predicates tends to lead to the hypostatization of the divine attributes ("word," "wisdom," "love," "being," etc.). Whether a hypostatization of the word actu-

119. Heidegger, "Die onto-theo-logische Verfassung der Metaphysik," *Identität und Differenz*, pp. 64-65. Translation from William J. Richardson, S. J., "Heidegger and God—and Professor Jonas," *Thought*, Vol. 15 (Spring 1965), p. 27.

ally occurs in the Johannine Prologue is too complex a question to be pursued here. I have already argued that, despite the tendency of the language, the notion of the pre-existence of the word, and the clear influence of mythological concepts, the basic thrust of the Fourth Gospel is not in the direction of hypostatization. The mythological form of expression has already been demythologized as to content. Nevertheless, the classical Logos-christology clearly reversed the predicates and thought of the Incarnate Word as a divine agent, the Second Person of the Trinity, a substitute for the human agency of Jesus. But hypostatization must be resisted since word itself is not a personal agent, although it is the medium or power that constitutes personhood. Belief in a supernatural word that functions as a divine agent requires a mythological world view and is certainly alien to Heidegger's understanding of being.

Against these first two positions I offer the following proposition as a way of identifying God and word dialectically: *God is the one who has word absolutely and in this sense is the primordial word-event, the event of being.* If God is not *a* being, and if being (as the unconcealing power of the future) is not to be hypostatized into a god, then this proposition seems necessary—unless at the critical juncture in developing a doctrine of God we are to step outside philosophical categories entirely.[120] To be sure, Heidegger him-

---

120. I am not willing to accept the Lutheran dogma of the law-gospel distinction as a basis for distinguishing between the tasks of philosophy and theology. When this distinction is applied to Heidegger's philosophy, it is taken to mean that, as an interpretation of the law, his philosophy is not really able to think unmetaphysically about God, or that any theological attempt to utilize Heidegger would fall back into metaphysics. Unmetaphysical thinking about God is claimed to be possible only on the basis of Christian revelation. See Eberhard Jüngel, "Der Schritt zurück. Eine Auseinandersetzung mit der Heidegger-Deutung Heinrich Otts," *ZThK*, Vol. 58 (1961), pp. 104-122; Helmut Franz, "Das Denken Heideggers und die Theologie," *ZThK*, Beiheft 2 (Sept. 1961), pp. 81-117; and Gerhard Ebeling, "Verantworten des Glaubens in Begegnung mit dem Denken M. Heideggers: Thesen zum Verhältnis von Philosophie und Theologie," *ZThK*, Beiheft 2 (Sept. 1961), pp. 119-124, esp. 122. This way of distinguishing theology and philosophy has also been an important theme in the work of Barth and Bultmann. See Barth's essay in which Heidegger among others is mentioned, "Philosophie und Theologie," in *Philosophie und christliche Existenz: Festschrift für Heinrich Barth*, G. Huber, ed. (Basel, 1960), pp. 93-106; and Bultmann's essay on Heidegger

self seems to have warned against an identification of **God** and being.[121] However, regardless of how such warnings are to be interpreted, it is not a dogma that we must follow Heidegger himself in determining the way his philosophy is most properly related to theology; our criterion rather should be consistency with the fundamental structures of his thinking as well as loyalty to the biblical and theological tradition as we understand it.

My thesis that "God is the one who has word absolutely" has been suggested by Karl Rahner's intriguing formula that God is "the being that 'has being' absolutely [*das Seiende absoluter 'Seinshabe'*]."[122] Of course the being that has being

---

and Gogarten, "The Historicity of Man and Faith," in *Existence and Faith*, trans. and ed. by Schubert M. Ogden (New York, Meridian Books, 1960), pp. 92-110. On the question of the formal relation between philosophy and theology, I am in agreement with Heinrich Ott: immediate application of the law-gospel dualism rules out in principle any *positive* significance of philosophy for the contents of theology. See Ott, "Response to the American Discussion," *The Later Heidegger and Theology*, pp. 198-199.

121. In *Über den Humanismus* he writes: "Being, indeed—what is being? . . . being is neither God nor some ground of the world. Being is broader than all beings—and yet is nearer to man than all beings, whether they be rocks, animals, works of art, machines, angels, or God. Being is what is nearest [to man]. Yet this nearness remains farthest removed from him." *Über den Humanismus*, pp. 19-20; translation from Richardson, *Heidegger: Through Phenomenology to Thought*, p. 6. The intention of this passage is not clear. First, Heidegger seems to think of God as something like a "ground of the world." Then he classifies him with other "beings" of the world—rocks, animals, works of art, machines, angels. In other words, the "God" described in this passage is either a metaphysical supreme deity or a god—an entity belonging to the world like the other gods. With such a God, to be sure, being is not to be identified. But both concepts of God are alien to the Christian faith and so also, it would seem, to Heidegger's own basic intuition. Is it possible that in this passage he intends to dissociate being from the corrupted God of Western theism—the God who either becomes a metaphysical first cause or is reduced to the status of a worldly, demonic power? In any case, according to Christian faith it is precisely God who is "nearest to man" and is also "farthest removed from him." That which Heidegger describes as being in this passage is what the Christian understands as God, not the "God" or gods to which being is here contrasted.

122. Karl Rahner, *Hörer des Wortes*, pp. 66, 69. This formula is based in turn on Rahner's concept of an "analogy of having being" (*Analogie der Seinshabe*)—not an "analogy of being" (the classical *analogia entis*). Being itself is not analogous but the emergence of the difference between being and beings and the degree to which or the mode in which beings "have" being. This modification is intended to avoid the objectivistic-hypostatizing misunderstanding of being and of the ontological difference. *Ibid.*, pp. 65-66. My thesis also reflects the Old Testament view of the relation between God's being and his word; see above, pp. 78-79.

absolutely is no longer "a being" (*ein Seiendes*) in Heidegger's sense but *is* being (*Sein*). Here the "ontological difference" between being and beings is taken up and completed in an "ontological identity." Rahner himself recognizes this fact[123] and speaks therefore of God as "pure being," "absolute being," etc. Nevertheless, if we say that God is "pure being," it is useful to understand this in the sense that he is "the being that has being absolutely." For being is always the being of some being or beings; we cannot think of being *in abstracto*, as though it were some sort of objective substance. This way of putting it discourages, furthermore, a reversal of the equation to state that "being is God," resulting in a hypostatization of being. Such a formula also enables us to speak of God as personal, whereas being as such is not personal but the means of personhood. To say that God is "the being that has being absolutely" means that in this one instance being and a being absolutely cohere. It is from the coherence of being and a being in God that the true ontological difference may be recognized.[124]

I have modified Rahner's formula to read: "God is the one who has word absolutely," for I am seeking a way of formulating the relation between God and his word, understood as the power of the future by which beings are unconcealed and gathered. I am proposing "the one who has word" rather than "the being that has being," because the distinction between "a being" (*ein Seiendes*) and "being" (*Sein*) is not

123. *Ibid.*, pp. 66, 69, 96.

124. The proposal that in God the ontological difference between being and beings becomes an ontological identity can perhaps find some basis in Heidegger himself. He writes: "First philosophy does not only contemplate beings in their beingness; it also contemplates that being which corresponds to beingness in all purity: the supreme being. This being, τὸ θεῖον, the divine, is also with a curious ambiguity called 'being' [*Sein*]." (*Hegel's Concept of Experience*, p. 135.) Heidegger's phrase, "that being which corresponds to beingness in all purity" is similar to Rahner's "the being that 'has being' absolutely." Such a being (*ein Seiendes*) is also being (*Sein*), but only with ambiguity, because being is not to be hypostatized and God is not to be directly and undialectically equated with the power that lets things be. He is the one who *has* that power absolutely, the being which *corresponds* to beingness in all purity.

very successfully conveyed in English, and because I want
to affirm the personhood of God. As *the one who* has word
absolutely, God is the one true and perfect person for word
is the constitutive power of personhood. As the one who
has word *absolutely,* God is distinguished qualitatively from
all other beings, which exist only at the disposal of word,
serving as the "place" where it comes to speech. My formula proposes a dialectical identification of God and word
in such a way as to discourage the hypostatization of word
and to designate the unique personal being of God vis-à-vis
all creatures.

The substance of this thesis is not entirely without precedent in contemporary theology. Gerhard Ebeling, for example, writes that we must not understand God "in the usual
sense of a content distinct from the word itself—a sort of
speechless thing that has to be brought into language by
being named, that is, designated by a vocable. On the contrary, it is here a question of God himself as word. That is
to say, the vocable 'God' points to a word event that is
always already in full swing." This statement, he says, can
be based on the trinitarian understanding of word as the
Second Person of the Godhead, so that "God himself is . . .
intrinsically word and not something which, in itself wordless, must first be placed by external means in the field of
language in order to become an object of word."[125] Similarly,
Eberhard Jüngel suggests that God's being is "verbal" *(wört-
lich)* in relation to himself because he says "yes" to himself.
"This 'yes' of God to himself constitutes his being as God
the Father, God the Son, and God the Holy Spirit. And it
constitutes equiprimordially the historicity of the being of
God, in which all history has its ground. This 'yes' of God
to himself is the *mystery* of the being of God and as such
is not to be inquired behind. For in this 'yes-saying' of God
to himself God's being *corresponds* to itself as Father, as
Son, and as Holy Spirit. This correspondence is absolute

125. Ebeling, *God and Word,* p. 28.

mystery, not to be outdone by any paradox."[126] Finally, Karl
Rahner has stated with increasing clarity that God *is* his
self-communication *ad intra* and *ad extra*,[127] although the
word-character of this self-communication is not made sufficiently explicit in his thought.

My proposition that "God is the one who has word absolutely" holds at least three fundamental implications for an
understanding of the being of God: God is presence, God is
personal, God is revelation.[128]

(1) As the one who has word *absolutely*, God is the
primordial unity of time.[129] He is not merely gathered into
presence by the power of the word, as finite beings are;
rather his being *is* presence. "Presence" signifies the dynamic
unity (not identity) of future-past-present accomplished by
word. To say that God is "presence" is a way of affirming
that God's being in its essence is being-as-temporality.
Heidegger saw the implications of his radicalization of the
temporality of being for an understanding of "eternity" and
of God's "temporality": "The fact that the traditional conception of eternity as signifying the 'standing now' (*nunc
stans*), has been drawn from the ordinary way of under-

126. Eberhard Jüngel, *Gottes Sein ist im Werden: Verantwortliche Rede vom
Sein Gottes bei Karl Barth, Eine Paraphrase*, 2nd ed. (Tübingen, J. C. B. Mohr
[Paul Siebeck], 1967), p. 110 (italics his).
127. Karl Rahner, "Der dreifaltige Gott als transzendenter Urgrund der
Heilsgeschichte," *Mysterium Salutis: Grundriss heilsgeschichtlicher Dogmatik*,
Vol. II, Johannes Feiner and Magnus Löhrer, eds. (Einsiedeln, Benziger
Verlag, 1967), pp. 371-382, 384; *ThI*, Vol. IV, p. 115.
128. What is offered here are only very brief hints at how a doctrine of God
might be developed from the dialectical identity of God and word. The theme
of this book is christology, not the doctrine of God, and hence I am unable to
pursue here the analysis required to develop these themes adequately. A fuller
argument could, in particular, show that God's being as presence, as personal,
and as revelation is intrinsically triune or trinitarian in structure.
129. He is also the primordial unity of space, because word gathers spatially
as well as temporally. A full analysis of God's being as presence would involve
consideration of the category of space, as well as of time. God is not non-
spatial, spaceless, but the one who creates, possesses, and *is* space, the one
who has "his own proper spatiality", *CD*, Vol. II/1, Sec. 31.1, esp. pp. 461-
478)—a quality not very satisfactorily expressed by the traditional attribute
of omnipresence. An adequate development of this theme would require an
ontological reformulation of the category of space similar to what Heidegger
has done for time.

standing time and has been defined with an orientation towards the idea of 'constant' presence-at-hand, does not need to be discussed in detail. If God's eternity can be 'construed' philosophically, then it may be understood only as a more primordial and 'infinite' temporality."[130] Thus to define God as "presence" is not to think of him as timeless eternity in the traditional sense, but as the most "primordial and infinite temporality."

Such a definition does not exclude God's futurity. Rather it demands it as the most appropriate model of his transcendence. Earlier I noted that the foremost of the modes of time is the future: time is the event constituted by the coming of the future through the past towards the present, gathering into presence or making manifest. Word may be defined as the power of the future, which gathers or unconceals by its coming. Because he has word absolutely, God has the power of the future absolutely. He *transcends* us as the future because he communicates himself to us or is present to us by his *word*, which is the power of the future. We experience him as future power because the proper mode of relationship with him is that of word. In this sense he is "before us" rather than "in us" or "above us." Of course, precisely because his presence is the dynamic unity of time, the God who is "before us" is also "with us" and "behind us"; he is not simply our future but also our present and our past. He is Alpha as well as Omega (Rev. 1:8), the beginning as well as the end. We must resist the temptation of identifying God and the future, in a manner similar to Ernst Bloch and theologians who have been influenced by him. As is the case with "being," "word," "love," or any other of the divine attributes, the sheer identification of "God" and "future" would result in an hypostatizing of the future or its apotheosis—

130. *BT*, p. 499 (translation altered slightly; cf. *Sein und Zeit*, p. 427). For a full discussion of this footnoted statement, see Schubert Ogden, "The Temporality of God," *The Reality of God* (New York, Harper & Row, 1966), pp. 144-163.

the "God hope," *Deus spes,* as Bloch himself wants to say.[131] Rather, as the one who *has* the power of the future absolutely, God *is* presence. Thus futurity can serve as an appropriate model of God's transcendence, but it is not to be equated with his essential being, which is presence.

Futurity is appropriate as a model of divine transcendence not only because God's word is the power of the future but also because the future has certain advantages as a limiting metaphor. Edward Farley argues that the transcendence of God has traditionally been conceived in terms of four types of limiting experience: the beginning, the end, the depth, and the height.[132] The first two follow temporal imagery, the second two, spatial. However, it is clear that space as an image of transcendence must be construed more metaphorically than time.[133] The reason is that time *is* transcendence in a way that space is not. Men have always been

131. At the root of the apotheosis of the future lies a very sophisticated atheism. This is evident from a careful study of Bloch and perhaps also of Karl Jaspers. If "God" is the religious hypostatization of the unknown human essence (Bloch), if the *Deus absconditus* must be converted into the *homo absconditus,* then the *absconditus,* the unknown human essence, must be located in the future rather than the present. Only *God,* not the ideal human essence, could be both present and presence. If the *homo absconditus* were present, it would prove to be either utterly trivial or more than man could bear. The human core (Bloch), the Comprehensive, the oneness of humanity (Jaspers), is not sufficiently transcendent to be present without collapsing into immanence; it must be reserved for the future, the *novum,* the goal. Thus a philosophy that preserves the dimension of depth, unity, and mystery as the secret of human existence must of necessity be eschatological, future-oriented. It can lead to the deification of the future and the apotheosis of the human core. Just this is the danger in defining God as "the power of the future." Moltmann recognizes the danger but succeeds in overcoming it only by constructing a horizontal dualism. Pannenberg's theology threatens to become a pantheism of the future, which could be converted into an atheism of the future. See Ernst Bloch, *Man on His Own,* trans. by E. B. Ashton (New York, Herder and Herder, 1970), pp. 172-173, 202-240; Karl Jaspers, *The Origin and Goal of History,* trans. by Michael Bullock (London, Routledge & Kegan Paul, 1953), esp. pp. 247-265, 272-276; *RRF,* pp. 61 ff., 153-159; Wolfhart Pannenberg, *Theology and the Kingdom of God* (Philadelphia, Westminster Press, 1969), p. 56-70, and "Der Gott der Hoffnung," *Grundfragen systematischer Theologie* (Göttingen, Vandenhoeck & Ruprecht, 1967), pp. 393 ff.

132. Edward Farley, *The Transcendence of God: A Study in Contemporary Philosophical Theology* (Philadelphia, Westminster Press, 1960), pp. 193-202.

133. Farley himself does not point this out, but it is evident from his language. "The depth" is a metaphor for the "power" of being, and "the height" is a metaphor for the "alien," the "strange," the "awesome"; whereas Farley is able to speak more directly of the transcendent as the beginning and the end. Cf. *ibid.,* pp. 199-200.

able to control and master space more successfully than time. Hence the descriptions of God's transcendence that operate in spatial metaphors have proved less satisfying than the temporal descriptions. The God whose locus of transcendence was "heaven" disappeared once men's spatial boundaries had extended far enough to render him either superfluous or inconceivable. As for temporal transcendence, the future is more satisfying than the beginning because the future enters into the constitution and dynamics of time in a way that the beginning does not. The beginning is to be distinguished from the past; it is a timeless, wordless void, and a God conceived *only* as the primal origin would be absolutely remote, inaccessible, incapable of revelation. Hence the transcendence of the one who *is* presence is most appropriately construed in terms of his futurity.

(2) As the one who has word absolutely, God is preeminently personal, for personhood consists of the event— the temporal, historical event—that happens by gathering and being gathered into presence through the word. To be personal means to exist in presence. As *the* word-event, God *is* presence. Human beings are personal in so far as the primordial word comes to expression in their speech and activity. They are *created* as personal by the word; hence their personhood is a continual gift and their creaturely existence radically contingent. God on the other hand *is* person, uncreated person, for he has word absolutely. Word as such is not personal agency but the "means" by which personal event happens. It is misleading to speak of three "persons" of the Trinity in the modern sense of the word "person." Rather the one person (God) exists in three "modes of being" (Barth) or "modes of subsistence" (Rahner), which are named in traditional trinitarian theology Father, Son, and Holy Spirit. Here "word" is not to be understood as *one* of the modes of subsistence (the Logos or "Second Person") of a divine being that in itself is more than or different from word. Rather God *as word* exists triunely

in three modes of being and in a twofold structure of self-communication (self-distinction and self-relation).

The conception of God as personal helps to resolve a problem to which Schubert Ogden points in his effort to understand "the reality of God" as the ground of the secular affirmation of "the ultimate worth or significance of our life in the world."

> First, God must be conceived as a reality which is genuinely related to our life in the world and to which, therefore, both we ourselves and our various actions all make a difference as to its actual being. To speak of a ground of significance or worth except as involving such relatedness is logically impossible. . . . Of necessity, therefore, the ground of the significance of our life has to be a supremely relative reality. God must enjoy real internal relations to all our actions and so be affected by them in his own actual being.
>
> But, second, we can think of God only as a reality whose relatedness to our life is itself relative to nothing and to which, therefore, neither our own being and actions nor any others can ever make a difference as to its existence. . . . Unless the ground of our life's significance exists absolutely, relative to no cause or condition whatever, that significance itself could not be truly ultimate or permanent, and so could not be the object of an unshakable confidence.
>
> Thus the only conception of God more or less clearly implied in a secular affirmation is intrinsically two-sided or dipolar. . . .[134]

Ogden's problem is to maintain the two poles of dipolar theism without allowing either to collapse into the other. But this is a difficult requirement without a concept of God's being that conjoins or subsumes these two poles. Such a concept is provided by the proposition that, as the one who has word absolutely, God is pre-eminently *personal*. In personhood alone do we find the peculiar juxtaposition of relativity and absoluteness that is required by the experience of God as the ground of the ultimate meaning of life. Personhood is not one of the poles in dipolar theism, as Ogden sometimes suggests, but is that mode of being in which the poles of relativity and absoluteness cohere. The question is not that of the personal *versus* the absolute in the concept of God,[135]

134. Ogden, *op. cit.*, pp. 47-48.
135. Cf. Karl Barth, "Der Glaube an den persönlichen Gott," *ZThK*, Vol. 24 (1914), pp. 21-32, 65-95; and Paul Tillich, *Systematic Theology*, Vol. I (Chicago, The University of Chicago Press, 1951), pp. 241-249.

but of the personal transcending and incorporating both relativity *and* absoluteness. This follows from our earlier discussion of the dialectic between presence to oneself (temporal presence) and presence to the world (spatial presence). Presence to oneself refers to a person's "absoluteness" —his self-integration or internal, temporal self-relatedness, his resistance to being assimilated into the horizon of another person. As the one true and perfect person, God is "supremely absolute." Presence to the world refers to a person's "relativity," his dependence on the otherness of the world to become a self-related self, his external, spatial relations that depend upon his embodiment and verbal communication with others. As the one true and perfect person, God is "supremely relative."

There is, however, one essential difference between God's personhood and ours, if indeed God is *uncreated* person, whereas we are *created* as personal. In virtue of our finitude and our creaturely status, we are dependent upon others to become persons. We must become an object to ourselves in the otherness of the world to achieve full presence to ourselves. But if God is uncreated person, he cannot be dependent upon that which is other than himself—the creature— to become personal. In the first instance, at least, he must be his *own* other. In perfect, uncreated personhood, no tension or conflict exists between absoluteness and relativity, presence to oneself and presence to others. As finite persons, we experience this conflict constantly. In order to become present to ourselves, we must risk being assimilated into the horizon of another person. But if in the first instance God is his *own* other (as uncreated person), then in his being the two poles of absoluteness and relativity merge into one and the same internal, dynamic process of becoming in self-divestment (self-distinction) and self-relation. God's "relativity" is in the first instance vis-à-vis *himself*; but precisely because of that he is able to enter into relation with the *world* in an unparalleled *freedom*. He does not *need* the world to be God (as we need the world to be men); thus

he is *free* to be for us, to live and act for us and in relation
to us, in a quite radical and unparalleled fashion.

Eberhard Jüngel grasps this point quite well. God's being
is a *double* relational being, he says. God is related to himself precisely in order to enter into relation with the world,
to *become* God *for another*. He chooses to be God not for
himself alone but for others, whom he constitutes in relation to himself by speaking his primordial word *ad extra*.
He can become God for another because the power of
becoming belongs to his own being in his original act of
self-distinction (self-divestment) and self-relation. Because
God is in the first instance his own other, he is able to enter
into relation with the otherness of the world without giving
himself up.

> God can enter into relation with the other (*ad extra*)—and pre-
> cisely in this relation his being can exist ontically *without* thereby
> being ontologically dependent on this other—because God's being
> (*ad intra*) is a *self-relating* being. The doctrine of the Trinity is
> concerned with the self-relatedness of the being of God. It under-
> stands the self-relatedness of the being of God as Father, Son, and
> Spirit appropriately only if it understands the self-relatedness of
> God in his modes of being, not as some sort of ontological egoism
> on the part of God, but rather as the *power* of the being of God
> *to become* God for another. . . . God's self-relatedness must be
> understood as a *becoming* of his *own* being, which allows us to
> conceive God's being as a "being in act." God's self-relatedness
> (εἶναι πρὸς ἑαυτόν) would then be the power of his being πρὸς
> ἕτερον. God's eternal love . . . would then be the ground of his . . .
> groundless mercy. God's being πρὸς ἕτερον is therefore no departure
> from himself. God's being-for-us is just as little a departure from
> himself as it is a coming-to-himself of God.[136]

Karl Rahner wants to say that God himself can "become"
something *in the other*, but that in himself he remains
"unchangeable," "immutable."[137] He draws back from intro-
ducing "becoming" into the being of God himself. But we
can conceive of God's "becoming" or "changing" in dynamic
and perfect presence to himself without becoming, in the

136. Eberhard Jüngel, *Gottes Sein ist im Werden*, pp. 113-115; see pp. 106-
109, 116-120 (italics his).
137. *ThI*, Vol. IV, pp. 112-114; Vol. V, p. 164.

first instance at least, something *other* or something *more* than what he already is in his perfection, his primordial temporality. For example, Schubert Ogden writes: "If God is the *eminently* temporal and changing One, to whose time and change there can be neither beginning nor end, then he must be just as surely the One who is also eternal and unchangeable. *That* he is ever-changing is itself the product or effect of no change whatever, but is in the strictest sense changeless, the immutable ground of change as such, both his own and all others."[138] God's ever-becoming or ever-changing may be understood as the constant coming of his future by which his being-as-temporality is constituted, or as the original and continuing dialectic between self-distinction and self-relation that is his perfect personhood.

Without an immanent becoming in the being of God, it is difficult to understand, as Jüngel points out, how God's becoming for another is his *own* becoming, or why his becoming *ad extra* should not in fact be a departure from himself. Precisely because God's being is in becoming *ad intra,* he is able to enter into a relationship of becoming *ad extra*—a relationship that adds something "existentially" but not "structurally" to the being of God. Structurally, we may affirm the perfection of the divine being: God is his own other and does not need to enter into external relations to become a fully personal God. But God has in fact entered into such external relations with a world that he has created, sustains, and will redeem. He adopts the world and man as his own other in addition to the otherness of his own being. The interior divine life is thereby affected existentially but not structurally. We participate in the divine life *ad intra* as well as *ad extra*; God has a "stake" in us whom he has adopted into eternal sonship; his personal being is enriched or depleted by the character of our relationship with him. He wills to be God not for himself alone but also for us, and this primordial divine decision to create and redeem permanently affects God's own being. God will not be the same

138. Schubert Ogden, *The Reality of God,* pp. 59-60.

God upon the consummation of all things and their return to the Father as he was prior to the act of creation. In this sense he will have undergone "actual" or "existential" change *within* the divine life; in this sense he will have "become" something "other" and will have experienced something "more" than was the case when God was God for himself alone. The divine "objectivity" now includes not only God's own being-in-otherness but the whole of creation as well. But this "becoming" is to be understood as a *donum superadditum* to a structure of divine life already complete in its interior vitality.

(3) As the one who has word absolutely, God is revelation. There is no God other than the revealing, unconcealing, self-communicating God, the God who speaks and *is* in his speaking. God cannot be seen but he may be heard. Visual images have never been permitted of the biblical God. The reason derives from a fact discussed earlier, namely, that sight reflects surfaces but sound communicates interiors without violating their interiority. Since God is not a body, he has no "surface" and cannot be seen (except metaphorically). But as word he is pure interiority and thus can be heard. Visually, he is non-objective. The only medium of relationship with God is that of word, which allows him to remain hidden at the same time he unconceals himself. But if God is not a body how can he speak, if speech is of necessity embodied? Here I must hazard the proposal that the world and man function as God's "body." To put it in Heideggerian terms, man is the "sounding board" by means of which God's word comes to speech. In this sense, God is dependent upon man for his unconcealing word to be spoken in the world.

But have I not thereby endangered God's transcendence, threatening to dissolve him into the world or to identify him with the process by which the world is? I have sought to lay a basis for avoiding this danger in two ways. (a) I have insisted, in connection with Heidegger's analysis of the "ontological difference" and Gadamer's theory of the "language game," that the word which gathers into presence transcends the world by founding it and thus is not a "part" of it, although at the same time it comes to speech by means of the world. The word remains free in its relation to the world: it puts man at its disposal and can never be institutionalized or localized; it remains always the initiator of the relation, that which addresses rather than responds; its coming is a matter of grace, not of necessity. Hence precisely *as* the constitutive existential of man's being-in-the-world, the word transcends man and is not at his disposal. (b) A distinction can be drawn between God's "outward" word—his revelation in the world, by which he is present to that which is other than himself—and his "internal" word, by which he is present to himself in an interior act of unconcealment. This distinction corresponds to that between God's internal and external relations, his absoluteness and relativity, analyzed above. God's being is a double relational being. Revelation is the outward "repetition"[139] of God's internal self-relatedness to which it perfectly corresponds because it is God's *self*-communication. In brief: God "is" the word of revelation both *ad intra* and *ad extra*. Only his revelation *ad extra* is dependent upon embodiment in the world for its coming to speech. But precisely in this dependence it transcends the world in a twofold sense. It is the outward "repetition" of God's internal act of unconcealment, which is purely self-constituted; and as the word that calls the world into being, it remains always free and unexacted, the disposer rather than the disposed.

What is unconcealed or laid open in the event of revelation *ad extra* is not God as such but the possibility of authentic human existence in the world, which is "gathered into presence" by this event. Revelation "refers to" ("discloses") the world, not God. It is difficult to escape the notion of revelation as the transmission of information about divine things

---

139. Jüngel, *op. cit.*, pp. 117-118.

by God himself.[140] But revelation is not a body of truths
from another world; it is an event of unconcealment in this
world. God himself is not the "object" of disclosure (as the
one who has being absolutely he cannot be an object);
rather he makes himself known or communicates himself
in the event by which the world is unconcealed as the one
who speaks (and therefore *is*) the primordial word that
lightens beings, brings them to presence. The light that
lightens, the word that gathers, remains the means of revelation rather than becoming its object. Revelation does not
reveal itself. Thus it is misleading to speak of God's revelation as *self*-revelation—as though there were a divine self to
be revealed prior to and apart from the event of revelation
itself. It is better to speak of God's *indirect* self-*communication* in his unconcealment of the world. I say "indirect"[141]
because God himself is not the object but the "power" of disclosure; and I say "self-*communication*" rather than "self-
revelation" because God does not reveal some "thing" about
himself but rather communicates or presents himself in the
word of revelation by which the *world* is brought into
unconcealment.

5. FAILURE OF WORD AND LOSS OF PRESENCE

I have argued that the *word* analyzed as an event of
worldly unconcealment is what Christians *mean* by the
word *of God*, and furthermore that God himself is the one
who "has word" absolutely. But how can we be certain
that what Christians *mean* by the word of God is *in fact*

---

140. Paul Tillich, *Systematic Theology*, Vol. II (Chicago, The University of
Chicago Press, 1957), pp. 166-167.
141. The concept of "indirectness" is indebted to Wolfhart Pannenberg.
Pannenberg holds to the notion of God's *self*-revelation while insisting, nevertheless, that such self-revelation is not a theophany but occurs indirectly
through God's acts in history. He infers this position in part from the structure
of personhood: a person can reveal himself only indirectly because he is one
with himself only in terms of his relations with others. See *Revelation as
History*, W. Pannenberg, ed., trans. by David Granskou (New York, Macmillan, 1968), pp. 13-19, 125-131; and *Theology as History*, J. M. Robinson
and J. B. Cobb, Jr., ed. (New York, Harper & Row, 1967), pp. 119-123, 233-236.

the word of God, or that such a word belongs to, and in a dialectical sense "is," God? How can we be certain that this word—by which man's existence is determined and disclosed—is not simply a matter of sheer fate, of demonic power, or of inexplicable, impenetrable mystery? This is not a certainty that can be established by a formal analysis of word as such. Rather, it is based on the confession of Christian faith that the event of revelation is patterned in certain specific ways; a patterning with its focus upon Jesus of Nazareth as the one in whom the word came definitively to speech. Not all that happens in the world is revelation; indeed, most of it is the opposite. Language is more often used to tear apart, to conceal, to destroy than it is to gather, to open, to create. Heidegger in his later writings has strangely neglected this problem, to which he once directed such forceful attention—the problem of the failure, the sinfulness, the "everydayness" of language, and the consequent loss of presence and corruption of world. Revelation is not omnipresent. It is rather discrete and patterned; a patterning by which criteria are constituted for discerning the true from the false, the upbuilding from the destructive, the divine from the demonic. The loss of the pattern and the consequent failure in discernment are perhaps part of Heidegger's personal tragedy. This discernment, for the Christian, is based on a patterning of revelation that comes to focus at certain nodal points possessing a peculiar and unrepeatable lucidity—points that serve as the norm for discerning when and where unconcealment in fact occurs and as the basis of the confession that revelation does not just happen by accident and at random, as a blind fate or demonic force that comes upon us, but that it is the word of the one whose name is "God"—the God of Abraham, Isaac, and Jacob, God the Father of Jesus Christ. A doctrine of God as word remains incomplete without a doctrine of Christ as *the* word of faith. It is Jesus who gives validity to our claim that the word which unconceals is the word *of God*.

It is just the failure of word and loss of presence to which we must now direct attention. The fact that word fails, that it can be used to destructive rather than creative and salvific ends, means that neither the existence of God as the one who has word absolutely nor an anthropology oriented to the horizons of presence is self-evident. Neither can be established apart from Jesus Christ. Man's essential structure of presence is in fact fundamentally impaired. Word does not gather into presence automatically at all times and in all places. Men resist and abuse the gift of word with its gathering power. The horizons of presence are not totally obliterated, for then man would cease to be man; but they are broken, shattered, impaired. Existence in broken presence is the condition described in religious terminology as "sin."

Sin may be defined, formally, as the loss of presence due to failure of word. It is not a positive quality but a negative one, a deficiency. Sin is *absence*. The ultimate state of absence is death: "the wages of sin is death" (Rom. 6:23); "the sting of death is sin" (I Cor. 15:56).[142] The ontological structure of sin corresponds negatively to the three horizons of presence: sin means loss of presence to oneself, loss of presence to the world, and loss of presence to God (whose word is the power of presence). Under the condition of sin, the structures of time, space, and transcendence are distorted because of the abuse of speech.

This abstract, formal definition of sin can be given concreteness and specificity when we learn what faith means, when we know what human existence is really like when it is gathered into presence by the power of the word. According to Christian faith, the definitive exemplification of human presence is found in Jesus of Nazareth. Both faith *and* sin, as ontic concretions of the ontological structures of human existence, can be fully described only with reference to Jesus Christ. An analysis of sin properly both

142. On the connection of sin and death in Paul, see Rudolf Bultmann in *TDNT*, Vol. III, pp. 15-16. See also below, pp. 211-212.

precedes and follows christology. It precedes christology in a threefold sense. (a) A *formal* definition of sin can be devised along the lines here proposed without any specific reference to Christ. (b) Sin is more widespread than faith and obviously does not depend upon faith for its origin, even though it may be impossible to describe sin concretely apart from the perspective of the law and the gospel: "sin indeed was in the world before the law was given, but sin is not counted where there is no law" (Rom. 5:13). (c) Although the grace of God is not occasioned by the human plight (God's primordial word of grace calls man into being), nevertheless the effective operation of grace is determined by the facticity of sin: "law came in, to increase the trespass; but where sin increased, grace abounded all the more, so that, as sin reigned in death, grace also might reign through righteousness to eternal life through Jesus Christ our Lord" (Rom. 5:20-21). Because of sin, Jesus Christ is necessary for the finishing and redemption of mankind; but this fact must not in any way be construed to diminish the actual contingency of the Christ-event and its unexacted character as grace.

An analysis of sin must follow christology in the sense that the concrete qualities of sin can be described only with reference to the definitive actualization of presence in Jesus of Nazareth. He is both the "finisher" of human existence (as *the* word of faith) and the "redeemer" of mankind from sin (by means of his resurrection from the dead, as Paul makes clear in Rom. 4:25; 5:18-21; and elsewhere). The concrete qualities of sin are first fully disclosed by the finishing of human existence in the person of Jesus; and the soteriological, redemptive efficacy of his resurrection from the dead becomes fully intelligible only with reference to the staggering facticity of sin, whose ultimate form and consequence is death. Thus the doctrine of sin and the doctrine of Christ are dialectically related themes that can only be discussed in relation to each other.

Defined formally, sin is loss of presence due to failure of

word. Described christologically, sin is *unfaith*, faithless
speech. The concrete qualities of sin correspond negatively
to the concrete qualities of faith exhibited in Jesus' being
as the word of faith. Contrasted with the authoritative,
truthful, and homologous structure of his speech, sinful language is uncertain, deceitful,[143] and despairing. Contrasted
with faith as a power that gathers life into wholeness by
means of present participation in the coming kingdom of
God, sin is a mode of existence characterized by powerlessness (anxiety, sloth), estrangement, and a peculiarly
debilitating oscillation between immediacy and absence
(i.e., possession and loss of the kingdom). Contrasted with
freedom, responsibility, and obedience as the new *praxis*
engendered by faith, the life of sin is one of bondage,
indifference, and disobedience (pride). These matters will
be discussed more fully in the next chapter.

We are living in an age of the experienced loss of presence, not only of God but also of ourselves and our world.[144]
As such our age bears certain analogies to that of Jesus. He
came at a time when Israel had lost a sense of God's presence

---

143. On the basis of the story of the fall in Gen. 3:1-6, I believe it can be
argued that deceit is the "original" form of sin. The serpent is a symbol of
man's fundamental deceitfulness: "the serpent was more subtle [or cunning]
than any other wild creature" (Gen. 3:1). The deceit—*spoken* by the serpent
—consisted in the presumption that man could be like God, knowing good and
evil; it was the falsehood that the creature, without penalty to himself, could
become his own creator. Such deceit led to the original act of rebellion or
disobedience against God, which according to the Bible is the highest form
of sin. The "cause" of sin must be located in man's fundamental abuse of the
power that makes him both man and *imago Dei*, namely, language, which is
the gift of God. Sin consists in forgetting that it is a gift; it is man's claim
of autonomy and omnipotence for his speech. But by that act, language loses
the capacity to unconceal and becomes instead an instrument of deceit.
Language enables man to enter into a relationship with God and the world
and thus also with himself; but it also gives him the capacity to destroy or
distort those relationships. Language gives the *possibility* of both sinful and
faithful existence. But the actual occurrence of sin has no cause other than
itself. Sin posits itself; deceit deceives itself. On the connection between sin
and deceit, see also Rom. 1:18, 25; 7:11; I Cor. 3:18; II Cor. 11:3; Col. 2:8;
Heb. 3:13; I Tim. 2:14. Among contemporary theologians, as far as I can tell
only Dietrich Bonhoeffer and Karl Barth have analyzed deceit as a fundamental form of sin; cf. Bonhoeffer, *Ethics*, Eberhard Bethge, ed. (New York,
Macmillan, 1955), pp. 326-334; and Barth, *CD*, Vol. IV/3:1, Sec. 70, "The
Falsehood and Condemnation of Man."

144. See Chapter 1.

by holding to an institutionalized mode of divine presence (Torah, cult, and temple) and to a dualistic-futuristic concept of history (apocalyptic). Günther Bornkamm's description of the contrast between Jesus and the "world" in which he appeared makes this point well. The Jewish people, he writes, "finds its God and itself in the past, in which its life and character were given to it; and in the future, in which its life and its character are to be restored to it. . . . It knows its sole task as that of guarding faithfully this past and this future. Thus the world in which Jesus appears is a world between past and future; it is so strongly identified with the one and with the other that, according to the Jewish faith, the immediate present is practically non-existent." The loss of the present, he says, and the tendency to oscillate between "torpidity and convulsion, petrifaction and blazing eruption," are the result of "a faith in a God who is beyond the world and history." By contrast, "the immediate present is the hallmark of all the words of Jesus," because of the remarkable authority and directness of his teaching.[145] This theme is the subject of the next chapter.

145. Günther Bornkamm, *Jesus of Nazareth*, trans. by Irene and Fraser McLuskey with James M. Robinson (New York, Harper & Row, 1960), pp. 55-56, 58.

4

JESUS AS THE WORD OF FAITH

1. JESUS, WORD, AND PRESENCE

a. Jesus' Person and His Word

On both philosophical and historical grounds, the "person" of Jesus is not to be located in an interior "messianic" self-consciousness behind or apart from his historical words and deeds. The philosophical grounds have been advanced in the preceding chapter, where I argued for the dialectical interpenetration of presence to oneself and presence to the world. Human speaking is, of necessity, embodied and thus enjoys a worldly objectivity. Man both constitutes the world in his cognitive-linguistic activity and is constituted by it. Only by passing out of his interiority and becoming an object to himself in the otherness of the world does he achieve full presence to himself. The "essence" of the person is found not in interior self-consciousness or cognition but in the reflexive movement between self and world, a movement mediated by language. A man *is* what he says and does in the world; he *is* his words and deeds. This statement is not meant to imply that personhood consists merely of *external* relations. Rather it means that man is present to himself precisely and only where such self-presence is fully realized, namely, in relationship with the world. Language is the instrument by which internal and external relations cohere, the medium where self and world dialectically interpenetrate. There is no person "behind" the word; word is the event by which the person "happens."

The historical grounds for this argument are found in the nature of the New Testament documents, which offer no

4
136

access to the interior life of Jesus. In this respect they are not unusual but like historical documents generally, which can concern themselves only with what objectifies or expresses itself outwardly in historical actions and words. Furthermore, it seems quite clear from these documents that Jesus advanced no direct messianic claims on his behalf. Even if he had advanced such claims, they would not be as significant as what he in fact said and did in other contexts. For a person reveals himself, not by what he states about himself objectively, but by the "style" of his words and actions. To be sure, Jesus awakened messianic expectations (or fears) on the part of his followers and opponents because of the unique authority of his teaching, his attitude towards the law, and his claim that the kingdom of God had come near. But he did not certify this authority and claim by assuming for himself a messianic title. Jesus lived the messianic life but made no messianic claims.[1] In Günther Bornkamm's words: "In all this the question of this [messianic] claim is only posed and not as yet answered. For what astonishes us most is that Jesus does not directly make this claim, but lets it be absorbed in his words and works without justifying either in virtue of some office well known to his hearers, and without confirming the authority which the people are willing to acknowledge in him. As little as he fulfills the demands of his opponents for proof of his claim, so little does he fulfill the expectations of his followers."[2] To be sure, Jesus may have spoken of the "Son of Man," a messianic figure to whom he himself was in some sense related. The Synoptic evidence for Jesus' actually having spoken of the Son of Man is strong but not unchallengeable. As recent investigations have shown— including those by H. E. Tödt, Eduard Schweizer, Philip

1. I am indebted to Paul Schubert for this phrasing.
2. Bornkamm, *Jesus of Nazareth*, trans. by Irene and Fraser McLusky, with James M. Robinson (New York, Harper & Row, 1960), pp. 170-171; cf. also Käsemann, *ENTT*, p. 44.

Vielhauer, Ferdinand Hahn, Nils Dahl, John Knox, Norman
Perrin, and others—it is not at all clear in *what* sense Jesus
spoke of the Son of Man, if at all, and the nature of the data
may be such as to render a certain judgment impossible.
Jesus may have referred to a future, apocalyptic figure, of
whom he was a forerunner but with whom he was not to be
expressly identified. Or he may have used the title in an
enigmatic sense to reflect his own earthly mission as the
one who proclaimed the kingdom of God, yet was rejected
and misunderstood by men.[3] But in neither case does the
use of the title reveal much about Jesus' identity and self-
understanding, and the criteria by which one argues for the
authenticity of one group of sayings concerning the Son of
Man versus another derive from the way one interprets other
aspects of Jesus' teaching—his proclamation of the coming of the kingdom, his parables, his conception of the
future, etc.

Thus a christological interpretation of the person of Jesus
cannot be based on what Jesus may have said or thought
about himself. The Synoptic Gospels do not point in this
direction either. They show little disposition to put messianic titles (other than "Son of Man," which Jesus himself
probably used) on the lips of Jesus.[4] Rather, as a means of
understanding the person of Jesus, they point consistently
and unambiguously to the acts of Jesus, and more especially
his *verbal* acts.[5] As Gerhard Kittel puts it, "Since the work

3. Or possibly none of the Son of Man sayings can be attributed to Jesus (the
position of Vielhauer and Käsemann). For a brief review of the issues, see
Norman Perrin, *Rediscovering the Teaching of Jesus* (New York, Harper &
Row, 1967), pp. 164-199, 259-260.

4. For example, the title *Christos* is found on the lips of Jesus as a *self*-refer-
ence in only three places, all of which are clearly secondary: Peter's confession
at Caesarea Philippi (Matt. 16:16-20 par.), Mark's version of Jesus' appearance before the high priest (Mk. 14:61-62), and Mk. 9:41. There are no
instances where "Son of God" appears on the lips of Jesus as a self-reference.
The title is attributed to Jesus by *others* (the devil, Peter, the high priest, etc.).
In Matt. 11:27 Jesus speaks of "the Son," presumably in the sense of "the Son
of God," but this saying must be attributed to the Evangelist.

5. This is acknowledged by Karl Barth. The distinctiveness of Jesus' existence
and his likeness to God are to be found in his *act*, his "life-act." Furthermore,
"his life-act was his word in the concrete but comprehensive sense, the comprehensive but also the concrete. We are not to say that Jesus did not only

of Jesus consisted to a large extent in the proclamation of the message, i.e., the spoken word, it is natural that there should be countless references to his λέγειν or λόγοι or ῥήματα."[6] From a christological point of view, just this is the most characteristic and significant aspect of Jesus' person: that he spoke, that he spoke a liberating, truthful, and salvific word, that his speaking was his work, and that what he said was essential to the primitive church, which maintained the oral traditions concerning his teaching and eventually committed them to writing.[7] The fact that the church exercised a remarkable freedom in citing and referring to the words of Jesus indicates that it regarded these words, not as supernatural, ecstatic, esoteric words, requiring preservation of the *ipsissima verba,* but as ordinary human speech—speech that was not of itself inviolate but could be repeated, handed on, and interpreted. The significance of Jesus' speaking for the church may be seen in the fact that the first Christians were conscious of a new endowment of

---

speak, but also acted and healed and did good and instituted a community of Spirit, word and act, and finally suffered: as though he did not also speak in all these things; as though their totality was not the word which he spoke; as though his concrete speaking was not the culmination or light of this totality; and above all, conversely, as though his concrete speaking was not also action or act, his decisive and effective act. If we are to think of the speaking of Jesus as understood in the Gospel tradition, we must abandon completely the current distinctions between *logos* and *ethos,* or speaking and action. . . ." (*CD,* Vol. IV/2, pp. 193-194.) There follows a lengthy excursus on the words used by the Synoptic tradition to denote and characterize the speech of Jesus: εὐαγγελίζεσθαι, διδάσκειν, and κηρύσσειν (*CD,* Vol. IV/2, pp. 195-209)—but not, unfortunately, an analysis of Jesus' own speech. The latter omission may reflect Barth's conviction (p. 194) that it is not so much the content of Jesus' words that is important but the fact that it was he who spoke them. Nevertheless, Barth recognizes and affirms the fundamentally verbal character of Jesus' life-act. On the other hand, Paul Tillich's tendency to separate the being of Jesus as the Christ from his words must be criticized. "His being, which is called 'the Word,' expresses itself *also* in his words. But, as the Word, he is more than all the words he has spoken." Tillich intends to hold to the principle that "being precedes speaking." (*Systematic Theology,* Vol. II [Chicago, The University of Chicago Press, 1957], pp. 121-122.) This means that Tillich's christology is oriented not to the historical words and deeds of Jesus but to the pictorial representation of essential manhood or New Being found in the biblical materials (*Ibid.,* pp. 101-107, 113-117, 121-135).

6. *TDNT,* Vol. IV, p. 105.

7. Herbert Braun, "The Meaning of New Testament Christology," *JThC,* Vol. 5 (1968), pp. 93-94.

language, as Amos Wilder has put it. Jesus spoke a new word that required new modes of discourse or new speech forms: the dialogue (the situation of address and response characteristic of the sayings of Jesus) and the story (above all the parable). These speech forms have remained characteristic of Christian language and have now become part of the Western cultural heritage.[8] Here we are reminded of Schleiermacher's insight that Christianity is a language-forming agency.[9] That this is the case can be traced to Jesus himself, who created a new rhetoric out of quite ordinary speech. It is no wonder that the early Christians concluded that Jesus himself *was* the word, the word of God, a conclusion drawn with especial clarity by the Johannine author (Jn. 1:14, Rev. 19:13).[10]

Some of the Synoptic evidence for the identification of Jesus' person and his word may be examined more closely. The theme of Jesus' ministry is summed up in Matt. 4:23-25 (par. Mk. 1:39): "And he went about all Galilee, teaching [διδάσκων] in their synagogues and preaching the gospel [κηρύσσων τὸ εὐαγγέλιον] of the kingdom and healing [θεραπεύων] every disease and every infirmity among the people." A similar formula is found in Matt. 9:35 and Mk. 1:14-15. The verbs διδάσκειν and κηρύσσειν each occur thirty-two times in the Synoptic Gospels in reference to Jesus, and the phrase κηρύσσων τὸ εὐαγγέλιον occurs eight times. This frequency of usage indicates, according to Bultmann, that although the community first described Jesus' preaching as εὐαγγέλιον and placed the verb εὐαγγελίζεσθαι ("to proclaim the good news") on his lips, "there is no doubt that he himself was conscious of being the proclaimer of the word" and of being commissioned by God for this purpose. "He comes with the word,

8. Amos Wilder, *The Language of the Gospel* (New York, Harper & Row, 1964), pp. 11-13, 17-18, 26-28. For his analysis of the dialogue and the story forms, see Chapters 3-5.

9. Schleiermacher, *Hermeneutik,* H. Kimmerle, ed. (Heidelberg, Carl Winter Universitätsverlag, 1959), Ms. I, 8.

10. See also Col. 1:25-27; Heb. 1:1-2; Rev. 6:9. Cf. *TDNT,* Vol. IV, pp. 124-126, and *GuV,* Vol. I, pp. 265-266, 289-290.

and nothing other than the word is his 'means of work' [*Arbeitsmittel*]."[11] Thus the identification of Jesus' person with his work of proclamation and teaching can be traced to Jesus himself, although the specific formulae by which this work is described derive from the Gospels. Moreover, word is the instrument for the third of Jesus' tasks designated by the Evangelists: healing. The association between healing and speaking is made explicit in Matt. 8:16b (". . . he cast out the spirits with a word [ἐξέβαλεν . . . λόγῳ], and healed all who were sick") and Lk. 4:36 par. ("What is this word? For with authority and power he commands the unclean spirits, and they come out"). The connection between "exorcism" and "word" is seen in the many pericopes where a saying of Jesus (especially a saying concerning "faith") is associated with an act of healing. Here the word in a quite specific sense is an action; the good news becomes a good deed.

The high value of words accorded by Jesus himself is worthy of note. In Lk. 6:45 (par. Matt. 12:34b-35) Jesus says: "The good man out of the good treasure of his heart produces good, and the evil man out of his evil treasure produces evil; for out of the abundance of the heart his mouth speaks." Bultmann regards this saying as probably authentic, although it may represent the combination of two originally independent sayings; in the Matthean version, the order is reversed.[12] In any case, the association of word (or mouth) and heart, with its consequent high valuation of word, is most likely original with Jesus. This association is more forcefully stated in Matt. 15:1-20 (par. Mk. 7:1-23), a pericope concerning the dispute between Jesus and the Pharisees over what defiles a man. Jesus' disciples have been accused of transgressing "the tradition of the elders" for eating with unwashed hands. In turn, says Jesus, the scribes and Pharisees have transgressed "the commandment

---

11. *GuV*, Vol. I, p. 273. The description of Jesus' word as his *Arbeitsmittel* is from Adolf Schlatter, *Die Geschichte des Christus* (1921), p. 135.

12. *SynT*, p. 84.

of God" by speaking falsely. "For the sake of your tradition, you have made void the word of God." Then follows the core saying of the pericope, Matt. 15:10-11, which Bultmann regards as belonging to the oldest tradition:[13] "Hear and understand: not what goes into the mouth defiles a man, but what comes out of the mouth, this defiles a man." In an "interpretation" of this saying (Matt. 15:17-20), which probably derives from the Evangelists or from a Hellenistic author, it is explained that "whatever goes into the mouth passes into the stomach, and so passes on," but that "what comes out of the mouth proceeds from the heart, and this defiles a man. For out of the heart come evil thoughts, murder, adultery, fornication, theft, false witness, slander." In this catalogue of vices, three of the seven have to do with false speaking in one form or another. The word is vital because it reveals the essence or "heart" of a man: it, rather than cultic conventions, is the means by which a man defiles himself or lives in purity and truth.

Käsemann considers this pericope important for understanding the unique authority and freedom of Jesus' teaching. Whoever denies that impurity from external sources can penetrate into man's essential being, says Käsemann, is striking at the presuppositions not only of the Torah but also of the whole classical conception of cultus. ". . . he is removing the distinction (which is fundamental to the whole of ancient thought) between the *temenos*, the realm of the sacred, and the secular, and it is for this reason that he is able to consort with sinners. For Jesus, it is the heart of man which lets impurity loose upon the world. That the heart of man should become pure and free, this is the salvation of the world. . . ." By this saying Jesus also rejects a metaphysical dualism and the classical demonology based upon it. Man is threatened not by the powers of the universe but by the evil in his own heart; similarly, he is saved not by the descent of a cosmic Redeemer but by having his

13. *Ibid.*, pp. 17-18, 74.

heart claimed for God and restored to righteousness through
the ministry of Jesus.[14] In short, it is recognition of the
centrality of the word for human existence that eliminates
the distinction between the sacred and the secular, demy-
thologizes evil, and points to the real meaning of salvation.
This is why "faithful speaking" is so important for Jesus.

Words also have a high value in defining the relation
between Jesus and his followers, as well as the relation
between Jesus and God. According to Lk. 12:8f. (par. Matt.
10:32f.; Lk. 9:26; Mk. 8:38), Jesus claims that the destiny
of men will be determined by their verbal attitude toward
him and his words: "Every one who acknowledges me
[ὁμολογήσῃ ἐν ἐμοί] before men, the Son of man will acknowledge [ὁμολογήσει ἐν αὐτῷ] before the angels of God; but he
who denies me before men will be denied before the angels
of God."[15] The original version of this saying is difficult to
determine, and it has been the subject of extensive discussion. According to Norman Perrin, its original form probably
consisted of the first half of the Lukan doublet (Lk. 12:8),
with the use of the passive voice as a circumlocution for
divine activity in place of "Son of man." Thus, the earliest
form would have read: "Everyone who acknowledges me
before men, he will be acknowledged before the angels of
God." Perrin argues that the use of ὁμολογεῖν with ἐν is very
unusual in Greek, and reflects an Aramaism that may point
to an original saying of Jesus.[16] Ὁμολογεῖν describes a relation of verbal correspondence between Jesus and his followers, by which their destiny before God will be deter-

14. *ENTT*, pp. 39-40.
15. The parallels are as follows:
  Matt. 10:32-33. "So everyone who acknowledges me before men, I also will
acknowledge before my Father who is in heaven; but whoever denies me
before men, I also will deny before my Father who is in heaven."
  Lk. 9:26 (par. Mk. 8:38). "For whoever is ashamed of me and of my
words, of him will the Son of man be ashamed when he comes in his glory
and the glory of the Father and of the holy angels."
  According to Bultmann, the original subject in the saying could have been
either the person of Jesus or his words; "in any event the significance would
be the same" (*SynT*, p. 112). As to whether "Son of man" or "I" was used
in the original version of the saying, see below.
16. Perrin, *op. cit.*, pp. 185-191.

mined. If correspondence to the person and words of Jesus
determines the destiny of man, then Jesus himself and his
word must exist in homologous relation to God and his
word. So the Evangelists reason in ascribing to Jesus what
was originally the function of God in vindicating faith,
assuming that Perrin's reconstruction is correct. The
phrases, "the Son of Man will acknowledge before the angels
of God" (Lk. 12:8), and "I also will acknowledge before
my Father who is in heaven" (Matt. 10:32), both of which
are constructions of the Evangelists, suggest a relation of
homology between the word of Jesus and the word of God.
Jesus' word corresponds to and in fact "is" the word of God,
for it is a definitively faithful word; a word in relation to
which the destiny of men is decided by their either con-
curring in it (speaking it further) or denying it. A christology is implied by this passage, which in its present form
is the work of the Evangelists, but which may have its
roots in a saying of Jesus.

Bultmann cites Lk. 12:8 par. and 9:26 par. in discussing
the relation between Jesus' person and his word. In this
saying, Jesus makes no mention of his personal qualities, and
elsewhere he specifically denies that he should be believed
on account of miracles or signs (cf. Mk. 8:11-12). Only the
spoken word establishes a relation with him and legitimates
him. The interchangeable usage of "me" (Matt. 10:32;
Lk. 12:8) and "my words" (Mk. 8:38; Lk. 9:26) in the
several versions of this saying shows, according to Bultmann,
"that Jesus' person is absorbed into his word, but also that
his word is event, event of power and of the will of God, like
the prophetic word in Israel."[17] Hence this saying is
evidence not only for the correspondence between the word
of Jesus and the word of God but also for the identity of
Jesus' person and his word: he *is* what he says, and his word
is event, personal event.

17. *GuV*, Vol. I, p. 274. Bultmann also cites Matt. 7:24-27 (par. Lk. 6:47-
49): "Every one then who hears these words of mine and does them will be
like a wise man who built his house upon the rock. . . ."

The word with which Jesus' person is identical and which designates his correspondence to God is *faithful* word. By my formula, Jesus as "the word of faith," I have adopted a Pauline expression (τὸ ῥῆμα τῆς πίστεως, Rom. 10:8) and have applied it to Jesus, thus attempting to make explicit the connection between Jesus and christology. For Paul, "the word of faith" refers to Christian kerygma, the confession (ὁμολογία) from the heart that Jesus is Lord and that God raised him from the dead. The task of christology is to interpret this confession by reference to the historical Jesus as the ground, criterion, and witness of Christian faith. If Jesus is the *ground* of "the word of faith," then he himself must *be* the word of faith, and that means he is the word of God. "Faith" means speaking a true, liberating, and wholesome word by a power not at one's disposal.[18] "Faith" describes the homologous relation between the word of God and the word of man. I introduced the concept of homology in analyzing the "transcendence" of word, i.e., the unity-in-distinction between the primordial word that gathers into presence and human speech.[19] The root meaning of homology is "same word" (ὁμός, same + λόγος, word). A homology stands between an analogy ("similar word": ἀνά, up + λόγος) and a sheer identity, and the concept is probably best translated as "correspondence" or "concurrence" (from which the connotations of "acknowledgement" and "confession" are derived). In Lk. 12:8 par., the verbal relation between Jesus and his disciples and Jesus and God is described as "homologous"; and in Rom. 10:8-9, Paul associates ὁμολογία with "the word of faith which we preach."[20] Faith as homology means speaking the "same word" or the "corresponding word"—for Christian believers, the word that corresponds to the word

18. Ebeling, *WF*, pp. 325-327; *God and Word,* trans. by James W. Leitch (Philadelphia, Fortress Press, 1967), pp. 26-29, 45.

19. See above, pp. 101-102.

20. The association of ὁμολογία and πίστις is also frequently found in the Johannine writings and in Hebrews. See Jn. 9:22; 12:42; I Jn. 2:23; 4:2; II Jn. 7; Rev. 3:5; Heb. 3:1; 4:14; 11:13; 13:15.

that came to speech in Jesus; for Jesus the word that corresponds to and in fact "is" the word of God, since the word of God is not a suprahistorical word that invades from another sphere of reality and is miraculously inserted into or between human words, but is the "same" word as human words when the latter are redeemed from sinfulness and brought to authentic correspondence, i.e., when they become words of faith. Christian faith as homologous speaking makes present the word which is itself presence (ὁμολογία), namely, the definitively faithful word of Jesus of Nazareth. Such speaking is not a human accomplishment but the gift of the word of God itself. When I say that Jesus is *the* word of faith, I mean that in him the homologous relation between the word of God and the word of man finds its completion.

The similarities and differences between the concept of *homologia* and the *homoousion* of the Chalcedonian definition need to be pointed out. The use of *homologia* to define the co-presence of God and man in Christ means that the christology proposed here stands in continuity with the classical tradition, yet with decisive differences. According to the Chalcedonian definition, Jesus Christ is "truly God and truly man," "*homoousion* with the Father as to his Godhead" and "*homoousion* with us as to his manhood." Here the critical word in the trinitarian controversy of the fourth century, *homoousion*, is recalled, this time to be used not of the consubstantiality of Father and Son in the Godhead, but of Godhead and manhood in Christ, because of the Monophysite challenge to which the Council of Chalcedon was the response.[21] Yet Chalcedon must predicate *homoousion* twice, once of the Godhead and once of the manhood. These two "natures" are then said to "combine" (συντρεχούσης) into one *prosopon* and one *hypostasis*, "without confusion, without change, without division, without separation." Thus *homoousion* describes not the unity of Christ but the duality of his natures (with both of which he is consubstantial).

21. Aloys Grillmeier, *Christ in Christian Tradition*, trans. by J. S. Bowden (London, A. R. Mowbray, 1965), pp. 481, 484-485.

Unity is to be sought on a different "level," that of "person" or of *hypostasis*, and the unity is achieved by a Stoic concept of the "conjoining" ($\sigma\nu\nu\tau\rho\epsilon\chi o\acute{v}\sigma\eta s$) of properties. By substituting *homologia* for *homoousion* I propose to avoid the abstract distinction between "nature" and "person," and to find a more adequate way of describing the unity of Christ. The homology in Christ is comprised by the concurrence of the word of God (the power that gathers into presence and constitutes personhood, although it is not itself personal agency) and definitively faithful human speech. Homology describes both the unity and the distinction of God and man in Christ, a unity-in-distinction that is to be understood as an event of language and is fundamentally constitutive of human personhood. Apart from the homology of divine and human word (the third horizon of presence), human personhood (the other two horizons of presence) would collapse. That this is true of all mankind comes clearly to focus in Jesus.

On the one hand, "faith" defines the homologous word that Jesus himself is. On the other hand, faith itself is a verbal reality and must be defined as word. Thus the relation between word and faith is an essential one from both sides: authentic word is faithful, and faith is a word-event.[22] The Hebrew stem *'mn* for terms meaning "faith" is closely associated with the stem *'mr*, meaning "word." This leads to the parallel between *ōmen* ("fidelity," "truth") and *ōmer* ("word"), and between *āman* ("to make firm") and *āmar* ("to say"). The parallel becomes explicit in the verbal adjective *'āmēn*, which means to speak firmly, truly,

22. Bultmann was not led in this direction, despite his excellent exegetical study of $\pi\acute{\iota}\sigma\tau\iota s$ in the Kittel *Wörterbuch*, because he wanted to stress theologically, in accord with Barth against liberalism, only that faith is not a human quality, phenomenon, or subjective psychological experience. Rather faith belongs purely to the salvation-event and shares in its worldly "imperceptibility." (See *Existence and Faith*, trans. and ed. by Schubert M. Ogden [New York, Meridian Books, 1960], pp. 77, 79, 87, 141-142; *Jesus Christ and Mythology* [New York, Charles Scribner's Sons, 1958], pp. 40-41, 65, 70-72, 84-85; *ThNT*, Vol. II, p. 239.) From this point of view it is difficult to appreciate the *word*-character of faith.

faithfully, certainly.[23] The association of *'āmēn* with word
is strengthened by Jesus' use of the term in a formula that
introduces many of his sayings, ἀμὴν λέγω ὑμῖν, "faithfully I say
to you" (see Sec. 2.c). The *hiph'il* form *he'emīn* ("to
believe"), ordinarily translated in the LXX by πιστεύειν, can
be defined most simply, according to Weiser, as "saying
Amen to something with all the consequences for the subject
and the object." It can be used in a profane sense to express
a relationship between persons or between persons and
things, and in a religious sense to describe the relationship
between man and God. "It pronounces God to be *ne'emān*
[faithful] or, if we paraphrase, it says Amen to God."[24] Also
noteworthy is the association by usage in the Old Testament
of the term *'emeth*, which is related to the stem *'mn* and
means "truth" or "fidelity," with the term *dābār*, meaning
"word": the words (*debārīm*) of Yahweh are true (*'emeth*)
(II Sam. 7:28; cf. Ps. 119:160).[25]

It should be clear from everything said thus far that if
I identify Jesus' person with his word, and more specifically with his word of faith, I do not intend a psychologizing
interpretation of Jesus. "Faith" is not a psychological
phenomenon interior to the believer and prior to his words.
"Faith" and "unfaith" rather refer precisely to the objectification of a person in his historical words and actions.
Moreover, I am not motivated by a biographical interest or
by a curiosity about Jesus' "own" faith. I am concerned to
describe the peculiar quality and content of Jesus' words
and actions, not to move behind them to some sort of
"personal faith" that lies at their basis and whose psychological development could be traced in biographical fashion.
Hence if I have chosen "faith" as a way of characterizing
generally the peculiar quality and content of Jesus' speaking

23. Artur Weiser, "Faith," in *Bible Key Words*, Vol. III/1, trans. from Gerhard
Kittel, ed., *Theologisches Wörterbuch zum Neuen Testament*, Vol. VI, pp.
174-230 (New York, Harper & Row, 1960), pp. 8-10.
24. *Ibid.*, pp. 10-11.
25. *TDNT*, Vol. IV, p. 93. The connection between word and faith is pursued further in Secs. 2-3, with specific reference to Jesus.

and conduct, this term is not to be construed in a psychologizing direction.[26]

The threefold sense in which I understand Jesus to be "the word of faith," and the way in which his faithful word functions as the medium of presence to self, world, and God, will be summarized in Sec. 1.b., and then more fully developed in the remainder of the chapter.[27]

b. Jesus' Word and the Qualities of Presence

In the preceding chapter I argued that word is the medium of presence in a threefold sense: presence to oneself (temporal presence), presence to the world (spatial presence), and presence to God (whose word is the power of the future that gathers into presence and enters into a homologous relation with human speech). Man's speaking as the means of presence to himself and the world is founded in a power, a gracious word, not his own. This word is named by theology "word of God." At the point where human speech comes authentically to expression, a reality, a power,

26. Ebeling has dealt with this misunderstanding in his reply to Bultmann, *ThP*, pp. 124-130.

27. My christological formula, "Jesus as the word of faith," and the way I hope to elaborate this formula systematically, are to my knowledge without specific precedent. Nevertheless, my basic approach is indebted to Gerhard Ebeling, who has brought christological reflection into the context of the relation between word and faith. (See *WF*, Chapters 7, 10; *ThP*, Chapters 3, 4; and *The Nature of Faith*, trans. by Ronald Gregor Smith [Philadelphia, Fortress Press, 1961], Chapter 4.) In recent writings and lectures, Ebeling has attempted to develop a word-christology more systematically. To understand the person of Jesus (or to answer the question, "Who is Jesus?") in the widest possible horizon of interpretation, our claim concerning Jesus, according to Ebeling, must be introduced into three fundamental horizons of human existence: the relation to God, the relation to co-humanity, and the relation to the world. Corresponding to these three relational horizons are the following three christological statements: Jesus is the word of God, Jesus is the brother of men, Jesus is the Lord of the world. Corresponding, in turn, to these three ways of identifying Jesus, one can develop systematically a threefold definition of the person of Jesus (authority, surrender and death, exaltation and resurrection), of discipleship (faith, love, hope), of sin (unfaith, hate, anxiety), and of salvation (justification of the godless, new life, kingdom of God). In each case, the first definition, following from the claim that Jesus is the word of God, is the most basic, shaping the other two. This systematic structure is sketched in "Was heisst: Ich glaube an Jesus Christus?", *Was heisst: Ich glaube an Jesus Christus?* (Stuttgart, Calwer Verlag, 1968), pp. 72-77, and is developed more fully in Lectures on Christology, University of Tübingen, Summer Semester 1967. The similarities and differences between Ebeling's project and my own will become apparent in the next sub-section.

a word is encountered that "transcends" man, yet has no independent subsistence as a metahistorical entity apart from him. I characterized this transcendence as "finite" because it can be located, not by looking away from man, either "above" him or "before" him, but precisely towards him as historical agent endowed with the gift of speech. The task now is to argue that Jesus' word, as the word of faith, was the means by which these three horizons of presence were definitively accomplished. His word gathered into presence temporally and spatially in a way that defined the structures of man's historical existence; and it existed in a relation of homology or co-presence to the word of God as the power of presence, in such a way that as *the* word of faith Jesus *was* the word of God. In Jesus, the three constitutive horizons of human existence were fully realized: presence to self, world, and God. Jesus *was* presence in a multidimensional sense.

The concept "word of faith" is also multidimensional. It refers, first, to the *quality* of Jesus' speech: his word was, in a unique fashion, "faithful word." In the second place, "word of faith" means that Jesus spoke *about* faith as a distinctive mode of human existence. Indeed, faith was the characteristic subject of his teaching. Finally, "word of faith" refers to Jesus' *enactment* of faith in his deeds and conduct: he lived the life of faith par excellence. An adequate treatment of Jesus as the word of faith must consider these three dimensions as distinguishable but not separable themes. As the word of faith, Jesus exhibited and proclaimed a new language, a new mode of existence, and a new *praxis*.

Thus the phenomena before us yield three horizons of presence (presence to oneself, presence to the world, and presence to God), and three dimensions of the concept "word of faith" (a new language, a new mode of existence, and a new *praxis*.) To provide the analysis with a systematic framework—a framework that corresponds both to general anthropological structures (the horizons of pres-

ence) and to the concrete historical realization of manhood
in the faithful word of Jesus—I shall attempt to integrate
these two sets of relations into a common schema. I shall
consider the three horizons of presence under each of the
three dimensions of Jesus' word, thus arriving at nine
qualities of presence by which his being as the word of
faith may be characterized. (1) Jesus' word as *faithful
word* was (a) an *authoritative* word, discernible especially
in the unique freedom of his teaching, by which he liberated
men from the constraints of the law, cult, religious piety,
social convention, political oppression, and showed himself
to be fully constituted as a person at one with himself. His
word was (b) a *truthful* word: the parables, as the paradigm
of his teaching as a whole, were events of disclosure, opening
reality, bringing the truth to bear upon a deceitful world.
His word was (c) *homologous,* existing in a relation of
correspondence to the word of God—as he himself acknowledged by prefacing some of his sayings with the quite
unique formula, "faithfully I say to you" ($\dot{a}\mu\grave{\eta}\nu$ $\lambda\acute{\epsilon}\gamma\omega$ $\dot{\upsilon}\mu\hat{\iota}\nu$).
(2) Jesus' *word about faith* as the definitive mode of human
existence described faith (a) as *power,* improbable power
like that of a grain of mustard seed, which gathers life into
presence temporally, integrating personal existence, freeing
it from anxiety and powerlessness; (b) as *wholeness,* the
healing of physical affliction and social cleavage, gathering
life into presence spatially, making it whole, "saving" it in
the midst of estrangement and disintegration; and (c) as
openness for the kingdom of God—the coming "kingdom
of presence," which means life in the presence of God who
is presence, and which is man's final destiny but of which
we have now a foretaste and share by faith. (3) Jesus'
enactment of faith was marked by the qualities of (a)
freedom in the world, his presence to himself as "radical
man"; (b) *responsibility* for the world, his co-humanity or
being-for-others as the "brother of men"; and (c) *obedience*
to the will of God, his presence to God as the true "son of
God." Jesus' freedom, responsibility, and obedience were

climaxed by the *death on the cross*, which accordingly is to be understood as a word-event, *the* word-event of faith. The schema may be represented diagrammatically as follows:

	Faithful Word (A New Language)	Word about Faith (A New Mode of Existence)	Enactment of Faith (A New *Praxis*)
Presence to Oneself (Temporal Presence)	authority	power	freedom
Presence to the World (Spatial Presence)	truthfulness	wholeness	responsibility
Presence to God (Power of Presence)	homology with the word of God	openness for the kingdom of God	obedience to the will of God

Having proposed this schema, I must now insist that it not be construed too rigidly. In particular, the distinctions between authority and truthfulness, and power and wholeness, are tenuous ones. The authority of Jesus' teaching manifested not merely his self-presence but was also the characteristic quality of his relationship with others. His parables of disclosure were directed to personal as well as social dimensions of man's existence. Power and wholeness describe two aspects of the same basic quality of faith as a new mode of existence: it means participation in the power of the future that gathers into presence, the power that makes life "wholesome," healing the personal and social fractures of existence. In the most fundamental sense it is "salvation." The distinction between freedom and responsibility is somewhat sharper, although here too it is evident that only the free man can be responsible and only the responsible man is free. In each of these distinctions we encounter the same dialectical relation between temporal and spatial presence that was considered in the preceding chapter. Man has access to himself only by means of a circuit through the otherness of the world; and relations with the world presuppose a temporally integrated, speaking subject. Of no one was this dialectic truer than Jesus. As Karl Barth points out, the life of Jesus was unequivocally a life for others. The Gospels show no interest in Jesus' private or personal life; his was a totally "public existence."[28] This fact does not mean that Jesus' life was simply dissipated into his relationships with others. It rather means that his presence to himself and his presence to the world were so at one that they were literally inseparable. His identity as a unique, unsubstitutable human being *was* his being for others; and his presence to others was the radical, indeed the only, expression of his self-presence. Thus we may think of the true authority of Jesus' teaching in terms of his disclosure of reality; of his personal power in terms of the saving power of faith; and of his freedom in terms of his responsibility for others, taking their oppression upon himself, suffering in their place, setting them free from the bondage of sin and death, law and cult, social and political convention. Finally, the first two horizons of presence are founded in the third: presence to God as the power of presence. Faithful word is authoritative and truthful because it is homologous with the word of God. Faith as the power that makes life whole means openness for God's kingdom or rule, the new "world" constituted by his powerful word. And acts of freedom and responsibility have their basis and coherence in obedience to the will of God.

The thesis of this chapter is that, as the word of faith, Jesus *was* "presence" in a unique and definitive sense. Far from perpetuating the conventional apocalyptic orientation toward the distant future, with its consequent devaluation of present and past, it is my contention that Jesus decisively

28. *CD*, Vol. III/2, Sec. 45.1; Vol. IV/2, pp. 180-192.

shattered it.[29] Far from standing within the framework of a horizontal dualism, Jesus' proclamation of the *near* kingdom of God bound together present and future in the closest possible fashion. The future—which is God's kingdom or rule, the new "world" constituted by the power of his word—is *coming* in the present, which means that future

29. See the statement to this effect by Günther Bornkamm, quoted above, p. 135. Ernst Käsemann writes: ". . . while Jesus did take his start from the apocalyptically determined message of the Baptist, yet his own preaching was not constitutively stamped by apocalyptic but proclaimed the immediate nearness of God." ("The Beginnings of Christian Theology," *JThC*, Vol. 6 [1969], pp. 39-40.) In this article, which is generally regarded to have initiated the current interest in future-oriented theologies, Käsemann argues that Christian apocalyptic can be traced not to Jesus but to the primitive Jewish-Christian communities in Palestine. In this sense, because "the preaching of Jesus cannot really be described as theology," "apocalyptic was the mother of all Christian theology" (*Ibid.*, p. 40). The theologians of the future who wish to base their program on an appeal *to Jesus* cannot remain consistent with Käsemann. Pannenberg recognizes this fact (*JGaM*, pp. 61-63), but apparently not Carl Braaten (cf. *The Future of God* [New York, Harper & Row, 1969], pp. 21-22). The rejoinder to Käsemann by Gerhard Ebeling ("The Ground of Christian Theology," *JThC*, Vol. 6, pp. 47-68) does not question the existence of a primitive Christian apocalyptic, but rather the judgment that the preaching of Jesus does not in fact represent the "beginning" or the "ground" of Christian theology.

The non-apocalyptic character of the preaching of Jesus is made even clearer by Käsemann in his subsequent essay, "On the Topic of Primitive Christian Apocalyptic," *JThC*, Vol. 6, pp. 102-105, 115-118. The historian in particular must observe the "uniqueness" of Jesus vis-à-vis the milieu of Jewish apocalyptic (p. 115). "It is only when we reflect that Jesus began under the message of the Baptist that we realize the importance of this fact: Jesus regarded it as his task, and as the special grace conferred on him, to testify to the gracious God as present and breaking into the world. He did so . . . by taking his own message and his personal appearance on the scene to be the beginning of the action of God, just as according to Matt. 11:12 the proclaiming of the near *basileia* constitutes the nearness of this *basileia* itself. Thus he enters into his message as himself a sort of incarnate promise and can no longer like the Baptist be comprehended under the category of the forerunner but . . . that of the mediator who brings the eschatological age in announcing it. . . . Our only worry [according to Jesus] must be not to depart from our creaturely status and not to force others out of theirs. Otherwise, the very God who is near becomes the God who judges, and therewith in fact the God who is distant. If the Baptist proclaimed the [distant] God who is drawing near in judgment, Jesus understood—and lived—the gracious approach of God as a judgment upon those who are deluded into pushing law, religion, and theology in between God and themselves" (pp. 116-117). Käsemann adds that the apocalypticism of the post-Easter Jewish Christians was an appropriate, even necessary, way of responding to the openness and freedom for the nearness of God proclaimed by Jesus (pp. 117-118).

Further support for my thesis is provided by Hans Conzelmann, "Present and Future in the Synoptic Tradition," *JThC*, Vol. 5 (1968), pp. 26-44; Robert W. Funk, "Apocalyptic as an Historical and Theological Problem in Current New Testament Scholarship," *JThC*, Vol. 6 (1969), pp. 175-191; and Norman Perrin, *op. cit.* esp. Chapter 4.

and present are co-constitutive themes. The future is that which "comes"; the present is that which is "gathered" by the coming of the future. In Jesus' word, the coinherence of the modes of time was accomplished. He is the one in whom presence was fully realized, and thus also past heritage and future hope. In this sense Jesus was "the Lord of time."[30] But Jesus' lordship over time was not final and absolute in the way of God's lordship, whose eternity, we have seen, is a more primordial temporality. He was not the primordial event of time or the ecstatic unity of time, which God himself is. To be sure, in Jesus the past was fully retrieved: Israel's destiny was his own. And the future was fully anticipated: in his preaching God's rule came near. But at the same time, Jesus did not transcend the limits of finitude. Israel's past was not appropriated without remainder: tension remains between law and gospel, the old Adam and the new, Judaism and Christianity. Likewise, Jesus' proclamation of the future did not bring the end of time: the "kingdom of presence" is near, not immediately at hand; Jesus, like all men, lived *out of* the future but not *in* the future. Faith is the *historical, finite* experience of the coinherence of the modes of time. In faith, temporal tension remains; it is not the *visio beatifica* or the pure presence of God. God himself is love but not faith. Jesus' experience and realization of presence remained on the side of man, not of God: that is what I mean by saying that he was the definitively *faithful* one.

2. FAITHFUL WORD: A NEW LANGUAGE

a. *Authoritative Word: the Freedom of Jesus' Teaching*

If there is an assured result of recent critical investigations of the historical Jesus, it is that he exercised a remark-

---

30. Barth, *CD*, Vol. III/2, Sec. 47.1.

able authority,[31] an authority that created and exhibited freedom rather than destroying it, an authority that was exercised by words rather than by physical coercion. Such authority marked the central mystery of Jesus' person for it was the manifestation of his unique self-presence, a self-presence founded in the presence of God and expressed in the directness of Jesus' presence to others. The Evangelists predicate the term ἐξουσία of Jesus twenty-nine times, customarily translated "authority." However, "authority" has come to have an unfavorable connotation, meaning the power to require and receive submission in the name of law, government, tradition, or inherited privilege, although the word itself derives from the Latin *auctor*, meaning "originator" or "author." In this root sense, the word does not suggest the weight of tradition but freedom from it, a freedom exercised not by physical power (δύναμις) or legal coercion but by word. In this respect, it reflects the fact that *exousia* can also be translated as "freedom," in the sense of "freedom to act," or perhaps better, "original freedom."[32] Such "original freedom," which contains within itself its own power and authority, is usually found in conflict with "tradition," which replaces originality with the question of legitimation.

It is no accident, therefore, that Jesus' *exousia* is expressed in his conflict with the legal and cultic tradition of Israel. He comes forward as a teacher with disciples, occasionally argues in rabbinic fashion, and allows himself to be addressed as "rabbi." Yet he is independent of the scribes, belongs to no school, and founds none.[33] The Evangelists express this as follows: "And when Jesus finished these sayings, the crowds were astonished at his teaching, for he taught them as one who had *exousia*, and not as their scribes"

31. See Bornkamm, *op. cit.*, pp. 60-61; *ENTT*, pp. 37 ff.; Hans von Campenhausen, *Kirchliches Amt und geistliche Vollmacht in den ersten drei Jahrhunderten*, 2nd ed. (Tübingen, J. C. B. Mohr [Paul Siebeck], 1963), Chapter 1, esp. p. 4.

32. Kurt Niederwimmer, *Der Begriff der Freiheit im Neuen Testament* (Berlin, Verlag Alfred Töpelmann, 1966), pp. 4, 165-166.

33. *Ibid.*, pp. 166-168.

(Matt. 7:28-29; cf. Mk. 1:21-22; Lk. 4:31-32). Jesus introduced a new mode of speaking and teaching—original, not
derived, internally authoritative rather than dependent upon
external tradition. Jesus' conflict with the tradition is most
clearly seen in the opposition of his own teaching to that of
Moses and the Torah—especially in the "but I say to you"
(ἐγὼ δὲ λέγω ὑμῖν) of the antitheses found in the Sermon on the
Mount. This formula occurs six times in the Gospels (Matt.
5:22, 28, 32, 34, 39, 44; cf. Lk. 6:27), and according to Käsemann is one of Jesus' most authentic and characteristic expressions, reflecting his sense of inspiration or consciousness
of special mission: " . . . the words ἐγὼ δὲ λέγω embody a claim
to an authority which rivals and challenges that of Moses.
But anyone who claims an authority rivalling and challenging Moses has *ipso facto* set himself above Moses; he has
ceased to be a rabbi, for a rabbi's authority only comes to
him as derived from Moses. . . . To this there are no Jewish
parallels, nor indeed can there be. For the Jew who does
what is done here has cut himself off from the community
of Judaism—or else he brings the Messianic Torah and is
therefore the Messiah."[34] The same dialectical opposition
to the law (the substitution of a higher authority in pursuit
of the deeper meaning of the law) may be observed from
the conflict over the laws of purification (Matt. 15:1-20
par.), and from Jesus' attitude towards the sabbath commandments: "The sabbath was made for man, not man for
the sabbath" (Mk. 2:23-28; Matt. 12:1-8; Lk. 6:1-5).[35]

From the example of Jesus, at least four characteristics of
exousia may be distinguished.

(1) True *exousia* creates and exhibits freedom: freedom
of word and act; freedom from tradition, law, cult, social
constraint, and political authority; freedom in the root sense

34. *ENTT*, pp. 37-38; *Jesus Means Freedom,* trans. by Frank Clarke (Philadelphia, Fortress Press, 1969), pp. 24-25. See also Niederwimmer, *op. cit.,*
pp. 151, 153-158.
35. It is worth noting that the offensive statement in Mk. 2:27 (here quoted)
is omitted in the Matthean and Lukan parallels. This reflects an effort of the
community to soften the harshness of an original saying of Jesus, denying the
freedom for all men (not just the Son of Man) that Jesus claimed for them.
Cf. *ENTT*, pp. 38-39; *SynT*, p. 75.

of *auctoritas* as that of an "author" or "originator." Such authority, which is rare indeed, does not impose convention, coercion, or bondage but rather liberates from them; it "authors" a new freedom, an "original freedom." Jesus' authority vis-à-vis the tradition of Moses and the law is most clearly seen in the antitheses of the Sermon on the Mount and in the conflict pericopes. He is the new *auctor*, the one who rivals the authority of Moses and thus brings the messianic Torah.

(2) Closely related to the freedom of authority is its certainty. Such certainty, which is an outward manifestation of presence to oneself, can be seen with clarity from Jesus' answer to the Pharisees' question as to why he ate with tax collectors and sinners (Mk. 2:17; Matt. 9:12-13; Lk. 5:31-32): "Those who are well have no need of a physician, but those who are sick; I came not to call the righteous, but sinners."[36] Here may be discerned Jesus' remarkable self-possession and sense of identity: he is radically the man for sinners because he is the man for God—God's representative among men. His mission is to call sinners, i.e., to serve as the agent by whom God's word of mercy and forgiveness is spoken.

(3) The means by which Jesus' authority is exercised is that of *word*. Hence the freedom of authority may be described as a "freedom of word." The Evangelists characteristically apply the term *exousia* to Jesus' teaching and also to the power of his healing word. The connection between word and authority is made explicit in the pericope concerning the centurion's servant (Matt. 8:5-13 par.).[37] Despite the apparent powerlessness of the word, it in fact enjoys the remarkable power to accomplish what it says (" 'Go,' and he goes"; " 'Come,' and he comes"; " 'Do this,'

36. Regarded by Bultmann, in the Markan form, as an authentic saying of Jesus (*SynT*, p. 18).

37. In its present form, at least, most likely a product of the church; cf. *SynT*, pp. 38-39.

and he does it"; "Say the word, and my servant will be healed"). Of course, words often prove powerless and ineffective, but this only makes more striking the primary phenomenon that the word has power (as Ebeling has pointed out). Words are the characteristic means by which events happen among men, even when they are misused or serve as an excuse for inaction. The action of Jesus in particular is almost entirely verbal in character, even in the event of crucifixion. Or more precisely, Jesus' freedom of word issued in his freedom of act: the freedom with which Jesus spoke is the foundation of his being as "radical man."[38]

(4) True authority advances no claims on its behalf and cannot be verified by some form of objective legitimation. Although the Evangelists often refer to the *exousia* of Jesus, the term is found on his lips as a *self*-predication only four times (Matt. 9:6 par.; 21:24; 21:27 par.; 28:18), all of which are probably interpolations of the author.[39] Thus it seems clear that Jesus did not explicitly claim *exousia* on his own behalf, nor did he suggest that it could be legitimated by some future event, like the resurrection from the dead.[40] Indeed, the notions of "claim" and "legitimation" are intrinsically inappropriate to *exousia*. True authority does not require a supplementary, formal legitimation. Either it is self-legitimating or it cannot be legitimated at all, whether by appeal to past tradition or by future, verifying events. Its temporal mode is peculiarly present, for it is accomplished by a word that manifests the presence of the speaker and gathers his hearers into presence through the power and directness of his speech. Authority cannot be verified by an

38. I have been helped on this point by Ebeling's discussion of the relation between word and *exousia* in his Lectures on Christology, University of Tübingen, Summer Semester 1967, pp. 214, 216-217, 224. His thesis is summed up by the statement: *Vollmacht ist Wortmacht.*

39. On Matt. 9:6, see *SynT*, pp. 14-16. In Matt. 10:1 par., Jesus gives his disciples *exousia*, which implies a self-predication of *exousia* (only in Lk. 10:19, however, is this found in a direct quotation). Cf. also Jn. 10:18; 17:2.

40. Here I disagree with Pannenberg, *JGaM*, pp. 53-66.

objective show of power but only by the truth that free and authoritative speaking itself accomplishes.

In an age of questioning and resisting all forms of established authority, it may seem out of place to advocate "authority" as a fundamental quality of faithful speech. But, quite apart from the necessity of avoiding the temptation to choose only those parts of the story of Jesus that suit current causes, it can be argued that precisely the loss of genuine authority is a hallmark of the present cultural and religious situation. Our age awaits an authoritative word, one that grants both freedom and certainty, without having to prove itself or to rely on objective displays of force. In the absence of such a word, we experience the dangerous situation of oscillating between doubt or uncertainty on the one hand and authoritarianism on the other. In the absence of true authority, men have often enough proved willing to sacrifice freedom in order to gain a putative security.

b. Truthful Word: the Parables

All of Jesus' sayings, but in particular the parables, show that his word functioned as *disclosure,* opening reality, bringing the truth to bear upon a concealed and deceitful world. The parables, whose authenticity is now widely recognized, bring us to the heart of Jesus' proclamation and person.[41] They may be defined as word-events of disclosure by which the new "world" of God's kingdom comes to speech. It is not my intention to work through the extensive parabolic material here; such an undertaking would lead beyond the scope of this project. Rather I shall orient my discussion to

41. See Eberhard Jüngel, *Paulus und Jesus: Eine Untersuchung zur Präzisierung der Frage nach dem Ursprung der Christologie,* 2nd ed. (Tübingen, J. C. B. Mohr [Paul Siebeck], 1964), pp. 87, 173; Robert W. Funk, *Language, Hermeneutic, and Word of God* (New York, Harper & Row, 1966), p. 237; and Joachim Jeremias, *The Parables of Jesus,* trans. by S. H. Hooke, revised ed. (London, SCM Press Ltd., 1963), p. 11. Jeremias writes: "The parables are a fragment of the original rock of tradition. . . . They reflect with peculiar clarity the character of [Jesus'] good news, the eschatological nature of his preaching, the intensity of his summons to repentance, and his conflict with Pharisaism. Everywhere behind the Greek text we get glimpses of Jesus' mother tongue."

the recent critical literature and to the consensus of interpretation that seems to be emerging in this literature. Modern parable research began with the work of Adolf Jülicher,[42] who shattered the traditional allegorical interpretation by arguing that the parables convey one point of the broadest possible application. The "one point" interpretation has been perpetuated in altered form by C. H. Dodd, Joachim Jeremias, and Eta Linnemann.[43] For Dodd and Jeremias, as Robert Funk puts it, "Jülicher's moral *point* of broadest possible application has become the eschatological *point* of particular historical application." The parables are still understood to convey *a set of ideas,* not a set of general moral maxims, to be sure, but a group of basic ideas about God's kingdom and his eschatological action, which can be synthesized from the ideas conveyed by each parable in turn. Against this "ideational reduction," the most recent work on the parables by Eberhard Jüngel, Amos Wilder, Robert W. Funk, and Dan Otto Via,[44] has argued in one way or another that the parables exemplify a particular aesthetic and literary form, which closely approximates that of metaphor, and that as such they must be viewed as unitary language-events that evoke a disclosure of reality. The parable is to be understood neither as an allegory nor as a moral or eschatological maxim, but as a language-event of unconcealment, a language-event in which that about which the parable speaks—the kingdom of God—comes to speech.

In the first place, as organic literary units, internally related and meaningful, the parables are autonomous entities, independent of the author's psychology, environment,

42. *Die Gleichnisreden Jesu,* 2 vols. (Tübingen, J. C. B. Mohr [Paul Siebeck], 1888, 1899).

43. Dodd, *The Parables of the Kingdom,* 3rd ed. (London, Nisbet & Co., 1936); Jeremias, *op. cit.;* Linnemann, *Die Gleichnisse Jesu* (Göttingen, Vandenhoeck und Ruprecht, 1962).

44. Jüngel, *op. cit.,* pp. 87-215; Wilder, *The Language of the Gospel* (New York, Harper & Row, 1964), Chapter 5; Funk, *op. cit.,* Part Two; Via, *The Parables* (Philadelphia, Fortress Press, 1967). The summary of earlier parable research is based on Funk, pp. 147-150, and Via, pp. 2-4.

or subjective intention.[45] They do not permit psychological
or biographical interest in Jesus. It is not by accident that
Jesus availed himself of such aesthetic units as the primary
and characteristic form of his teaching. They focus attention not upon him but upon the "world" evoked in the
aesthetic unity of form and content. This mode of teaching
is entirely of a piece with the indirect character of Jesus'
exercise of authority. The parables have force and power,
not because of the personal prestige and authority of their
author, but because of their ability to call up a new world
out of the old, to force their hearers to decision and involvement. The authority and power of disclosure are objective
qualities of the parable itself. Jesus' person and identity
merge into the disclosive force of his word. Nowhere is
this "objectivity" of his person more clearly seen than in
the parables.[46]

Recent interpretation of the parables has concentrated
upon an analysis of their literary structure. Taking a clue
from C. H. Dodd, Funk defines the parable as a metaphor
(more precisely, a metaphor expanded into a story), which
discloses reality and creates meaning not by direct comparison of a less known with a better known, as with a simile,
but by "the juxtaposition of two discrete and not entirely
comparable entities," which "produces an impact upon the
imagination and induces a vision of that which cannot be
conveyed by prosaic or discursive speech."[47] The "logic"
of metaphor as distinguished from the logic of discursive
language or of predication "redirects attention, not to this or
that attribute but, by means of imaginative shock, to a cir-
cumspective whole that presents itself as focalized in this
or that thing or event. . . . That is to say, metaphor shatters

45. Via, *op. cit.*, p. 77, also pp. 74-75.
46. Funk makes the same point rather differently: "Although . . . the parable
may be considered the self-attestation of Jesus, i.e., as the inverbalization of
Jesus as the word, it nevertheless shifts attention away from God and from
Jesus himself, i.e., from the religious question, to a specific way of comporting
oneself with reality. God and Jesus remain hidden." *Language, Hermeneutic,
and Word of God,* p. 197, cf. p. 196.
47. Funk, *op. cit.*, pp. 136-137. See also Wilder, *op. cit.*, pp. 80, 92.

the conventions of predication in the interests of a new vision, one which grasps the 'thing' in relation to a new 'field,' and thus in relation to a fresh experience of reality."[48]

What is juxtaposed in the parables of Jesus, thus evoking disclosure by means of "imaginative shock," is the familiar and the unfamiliar, everydayness and transcendence, deceit and truth, the old world and the new. On the one hand, the parable is oriented to the familiar, deceitful, everyday world.[49] On the other hand, it cracks the shell of deceit by calling up this familiar world in unfamiliar fashion, by hyperbolic or surrealistic intensification of the real to the point where it becomes strangely unreal and thus is seen in a new light, by framing everything ordinary in the light of the ultimate, by the surprising "turn" at the end of the story. In short, "the listener is led through the parable into a strange world where everything is familiar yet radically different."[50] What is disclosed in this process is not merely the "logic" of everydayness and deceit but also the "logic" of a new and different world. The new world is not to be understood as a supernatural substitute for the old, existing alongside it or over and beyond it. Rather, it entails a transformation of the old, a new way of speaking and comporting oneself in the world. "The parable evokes a radically new relation to reality *in its everydayness*. The parable does not turn the auditor away from the mundane, but toward it. He discovers that his destiny is at stake precisely in his ordinary creaturely existence. By means of metaphor, the parable 'cracks' the shroud of everydayness lying over mundane reality in order to grant a radically new vision of mundane reality."[51] The new logic is the logic of grace; the logic of the word of God, which calls forth a new world of freedom, truth, and love in the midst of the old, a world in which human existence is healed by being gathered into presence.

48. Funk, *op. cit.*, pp. 138-139.
49. *Ibid.*, pp. 152-155; Wilder, *op. cit.*, pp. 81-82.
50. Funk, *op. cit.*, pp. 155-156, 159-161, 189.
51. *Ibid.*, pp. 194-195. Cf. pp. 235-236.

God himself does not appear in the parable, and it is unwarranted to attempt to identify certain figures (such as a king, a master, a sower, or a father) with God allegorically. But God's word is what evokes the new world of the parable, a word that comes to speech in the language of the parable itself. It is the situation of the parable as a whole that depicts the event of the word of God—an event of disclosure, unconcealment, gathering—not isolated elements in the parable.[52]

Parabolic language is peculiarly suited to this juxtaposition of the old world and the new, indeed is indispensable to it. As Funk points out, the new logic can only be heard in the language of the old (which is the only language we have); but simultaneously the language of the old logic must undergo, in Merleau-Ponty's term, a "coherent deformation" in order to become the vehicle of the new. Such is the accomplishment of parabolic metaphor, which "brings the familiar into an unfamiliar context and distorts it, in order to call attention to it anew, i.e., to bring it into a new frame of reference, a new referential totality."[53] The parable is the only way the new world can be brought to speech in the old, a fact that seems to be borne out by a remark of Jesus. In explaining why he speaks in parables, Jesus says: "To you has been given the secret of the kingdom of God, but for those outside everything is in parables; so that they may indeed see but not perceive, and may indeed hear but not understand . . ." (Mk. 4:11-12 par.). In its present form this saying has undoubtedly been reworked by the community: a distinction is drawn between the disciples and the people ("those outside"); and the purpose of the parables seems to be only that of concealing the kingdom from the latter, whereas their true function is that of disclosure (as Mk. 4:33 more accurately reflects). Nevertheless an authentic core may be concealed here. Jesus may be saying that it is easy for all (including disciples as well as "people")

52. *Ibid.*, pp. 196-198; and Via, *op. cit.*, pp. 104-106.
53. Funk, *op. cit.*, p. 195.

to "hear" the parables without "understanding" them, for they are couched in the language of the everyday and bring the new world into view only circumspectly by "cracking" the language of the old. Thus the kingdom of God remains a "secret" or a "mystery" precisely as it comes to speech in the parables. Ebeling once suggested, in referring to Mk. 4:11-12, that "the parable . . . is the form of the language of Jesus that corresponds to the incarnation."[54] This is the case because the language of the parable is able to bring the kingdom into the world, the transcendent into history, the word of God into human speech, in such a way that the former qualifies the latter, yet without the loss of the distinction between the two and without the loss of the hiddenness and transcendence of God. The matter may be put even more boldly than by Ebeling: the language of Jesus as parable *is* the event of incarnation par excellence; in the definitively faithful word of Jesus, which gathers reality into presence by bringing an unconcealing word to bear upon it, the word of God (and thus God himself) comes to speech.

Eberhard Jüngel, in his study of the parables, is concerned, above all, with the connection between the language of the parables and the reality they bring to speech, the kingdom of God. The essence of the parable, he says, is that it "gathers": it gathers the individual elements of a narrative into a focal point *(Punkte)*, which is the point *(Pointe)* or aim of the parable; it gathers the man whom it addresses into unity with himself; and it leads the gathered one to the "point" addressing him in the parable, namely, the rule of God, which is the "point" of human existence *extra nos*.[55] In other words, the parables gather men into a language-event that is the kingdom; "the kingdom comes to speech

54. Gerhard Ebeling, *Evangelische Evangelienauslegung: Eine Untersuchung zu Luthers Hermeneutik,* 1st ed., 1942; 2nd ed. (Darmstadt, Wissenschaftliche Buchgesellschaft, 1962), p. 108. Cf. Funk, *op. cit.,* pp. 129, 154.

55. Jüngel, *op. cit.,* pp. 136-137, 173. This argument is based in particular on an analysis of the Parables of the Net and of the Weeds (Matt. 13:47-48 and 13:24-30), where the theme of "gathering" is explicit (see pp. 145-148). These are parables about parables.

in the parable *as* parable."[56] The reason the kingdom comes
to speech as parable is that parable is the word-event by
which man is gathered into presence and is brought into the
presence of that which gathers. The kingdom of God is the
new "world" constituted by this event of gathering; hence
the parable is the means by which the kingdom comes to
pass. It is a defect of his otherwise excellent study that
Jüngel does not make sufficiently explicit the twofold fact
that it is *word* which gathers (as I have argued from my
etymological and philosophical study of λόγος), and that the
word of the parable gathers *into presence* (a presence that
defines man's being in relation to himself, the world, and
God). If "word" here refers to the "faithful word" of Jesus,
and "presence" to the reality of the kingdom constituted by
God's word, then we can say that the language of Jesus
as parable not only corresponds to but is the event of
incarnation for it is the place where God himself comes
into our midst.

c. *Homologous Word: Correspondence to the Word of God*

If, in virtue of its qualities of authority and disclosure, the
language of Jesus *is* the event of incarnation, then the third
aspect of Jesus' "faithful word," its correspondence to the
word of God, is already included. Authoritative and truthful speech is the objective, historical manifestation of the
homologous relation between the word of God and the word
of man. Hence, we now have to do not so much with a
third, objectively distinguishable horizon of presence as with
that horizon which founds the first two and is implicit in
them. "Presence to God" is an historically perceptible phenomenon only in terms of "presence to oneself" and "presence to the world." Relations of transcendence occur only
in the dialectical structure of language. The transcendence
in question is what I earlier described as "finite": human
speech is founded in a power, a gracious word, that is not

56. *Ibid.*, p. 135; cf. pp. 138, 168.

man's own product and thus transcends him as unexacted gift, yet has no independent subsistence as a metahistorical entity apart from the linguistic structures of his existence.

This mode of transcendence is confirmed by the fact that Jesus had surprisingly little directly to say about God, and that his relationship with God was never made the explicit warrant of his freedom of word and disclosure of world.[57] For example, Jesus never claimed to be speaking on behalf of God: he did not use the prophetic formula, "Thus says the Lord," or "the Lord said to me." Nevertheless, God and the relationship with God were at the center of the mystery of Jesus' word. To say that his word was definitively *faithful* means above all that it corresponded to the word of God. To speak faithfully *means* to speak in homology with the word of God.[58] Yet this fact emerges to the surface only infrequently in the Gospels. The Evangelists have nothing to say about Jesus' *own* faith. Perhaps the only place where the homologous structure of Jesus' language becomes quite explicit is in his use of the formula, "Faithfully I say to you" (ἀμὴν λέγω ὑμῖν), to introduce some of his most important sayings. Its uniqueness to the New Testament, the frequency of its occurrence, and the fact that it is found only on the lips of Jesus testify to its authenticity.[59] Ἀμήν is the Greek transcription of the Hebrew verbal adjective 'āmēn, which derives from the verbal stem 'mn for terms meaning "faith," which in turn is closely associated with the stem 'mr, meaning "word." 'Āmēn in Hebrew expresses explicitly the connection between "faith" and "word": it means to speak firmly, truly, faithfully, certainly. To say "amen" to something (such

---

57. The only exception in the Synoptic Gospels would appear to be the "Johannine" statement found in Matt. 11:27 and Lk. 10:22 ("All things have been delivered to me by my Father; and no one knows the Son except the Father, and no one knows the Father except the Son and any one to whom the Son chooses to reveal him"), which is surely a construction of the church.

58. See above, pp. 101-102, 143-147.

59. Ἀμὴν λέγω ὑμῖν occurs thirty-one times in Matthew (especially in the Sermon on the Mount), thirteen times in Mark, and six times in Luke; ἀμὴν ἀμὴν λέγω ὑμῖν occurs twenty-five times in John. In addition, Luke uses the similar formulae, ἀληθῶς λέγω ὑμῖν ("Truly I tell you"), and ναί, λέγω ὑμῖν ("Yes, I tell you"). Ναί is a Greek rendering of the Hebrew 'āmēn.

as a statement, command, or doxology) is to certify its reality and truth.[60] Thus when Jesus brings together the terms ἀμήν and λέγω, this is by way of indicating that his words and sayings are *eo ipso* true and faithful.

My expression "faithful word" derives from the designation of Jesus' speaking as faithful speaking by the formula, ἀμὴν λέγω ὑμῖν. This designation *implies* a remarkable claim: that in his speaking the word of God comes to speech, that his own word corresponds to the word of God. From this formula, as well as the saying in Matt. 12:28 ("if it is by the Spirit of God that I cast out demons, . . ."), Käsemann concludes that Jesus regarded himself as being inspired, the instrument of the Spirit of God.[61] Furthermore, it is noteworthy that Jesus predicated ἀμήν of *himself* (or of his own sayings), whereas the customary practice for both Judaism and Christianity was to add "amen" only to what another man says. This self-predication implies not only the correspondence between Jesus and God but also the independence of Jesus' words from corroboration by his hearers. His word verifies theirs rather than vice versa; as the word of faith he brings them to faith and thus reconciles them with God. In brief: Jesus' use of ἀμήν provides the basis for a "christology *in nuce*."[62]

3. WORD ABOUT FAITH: A NEW MODE OF EXISTENCE

a. *Faith as Power*

Not only is faith descriptive of the *quality* of Jesus' word; it is also the distinctive and characteristic *content* of his teaching. By contrast with faith, love (for example) is not central to the *distinctive* aspect of Jesus' mode of language, existence, message, and action. With the exception of Mk. 10:21, the first three Evangelists never predicate ἀγάπη of

---

60. See above, pp. 147-148.
61. *ENTT*, pp. 41-42.
62. H. Schlier, article on ἀμήν in *TDNT*, Vol. I, p. 338. Cf. *WF*, pp. 236-238.

Jesus.[63] In the Synoptic Gospels, Jesus himself speaks love only four times in a significant fashion, twice radicaliz ing the command of the Torah to love God and neighbor (Matt. 5:43-46 par.; Matt, 22:37-39 par. [cf. Matt. 19:19]; Lk. 7:42-47; 11:42). All that can be said about love has already been said by the Torah. On the other hand, love is an eschatological virtue, fully attainable only with the coming of the kingdom (hence Jesus' radicalization of love to in- clude love of enemies). For the time being, it is possible to love only in the mode of faith. By contrast, abundant mate- rial about faith is found on the lips of Jesus. These data give good grounds for constructing a christology oriented not to the concept of love but to that of faith.

In analyzing what Jesus said about faith and the life of faith (without necessarily restricting ourselves to occurrences of the vocable πίστις and related terms), three more or less distinguishable qualities may be designated: power, whole- ness, and openness. The distinction between power and wholeness is a narrow one, for it specifies two aspects of the same basic quality of faith: its power of making life whole in both personal and social aspects, gathering it into pres- ence, healing it, saving it. Faith in the fundamental sense means "salvation." Although these two aspects could be brought together and treated under the single theme, "faith as the power that makes life whole," there are some advan- tages in taking them up separately. They correspond to the distinction between presence to oneself and presence to the world, as these two horizons of presence interact dialecti- cally, as well as to a natural division in the material about faith found in sayings attributed to Jesus. Of course what is here distinguished for purposes of analysis must not be separated in actual fact. The third aspect of Jesus' teaching about faith is what I have termed "openness"—openness for the kingdom of God, and thus participation in the power of

---

63. The more distinctive concept associated with Jesus is σπλαγχνίζεσθαι ("to have compassion"), a term used by Jesus in the parables and predicated of him by the Evangelists (see Sec. 4 a II).

the future, for the "kingdom" refers to the rule of God or the power of God by which a new world is constituted. Faith is the proper mode of openness for and participation in the future kingdom. Thus Jesus' preaching of the kingdom of God is to be understood as one aspect of his word about faith.

Ebeling has pointed out, in his epoch-making article, "Jesus and Faith" (1958), that by far the greatest majority of occurrences in the Synoptic Gospels of words from the root for "faith" ($\pi\iota\sigma\tau$-) are found in sayings attributed to Jesus.[64] Both the quantitative and qualitative intensification of the concept of faith found in the New Testament vis-à-vis the possibilities inherent in the Old Testament and late Judaism can probably be traced to the fact that Jesus was remembered to have spoken about faith in quite decisive fashion. The material about faith found on the lips of Jesus falls into two groups: instances occurring in sayings of Jesus, and those in spoken parts of narratives, primarily healing stories.[65]

In regard to the first group, the most characteristic and important sayings are those concerning the *improbable power* of faith.[66] I have in mind Jesus' comparison of faith, either implicitly or explicitly, with a "seed" in the parable of the sower (Matt. 13:1-9 par.), the parable of the mustard seed (Matt. 13:31-32 par.), and the saying about faith as a

64. *WF*, p. 224; see pp. 223-226. Of the eighty occurrences of words formed from $\pi\iota\sigma\tau$- in the Synoptics (omitting the spurious ending of Mark), Ebeling counts sixty-three in direct speech by Jesus. Of the remaining seventeen passages, eleven occur in narrative contexts (above all, the healing stories) in which the concept of faith also appears in sayings of Jesus, permitting us to assume that this is a usage deriving from the instances in the sayings of Jesus. This leaves only six passages in which the concept of faith is found without any corresponding employment of it in sayings of Jesus (Lk. 1:20, 45, 24:11, 41; Matt. 27:42; Mk. 15:32), all of which, according to Ebeling, remain "within the framework of the pre-Christian possibilities." Thus we may conclude that "faith," as it occurs in the Synoptic Gospels, has been decisively shaped by what Jesus said about it.

65. *Ibid.*, p. 226.

66. Ebeling points out, that within the first group of passages there are a few which represent constructions of the church (Mk. 1:15; 9:42; 11:31; 13:21; Matt. 18:6; 21:25, 32; 24:23, 26; Lk. 8:12, 13; 18:8, 20:5), and others where the concept ὀλιγόπιστος (men of "little faith") is found. I shall discuss the latter concept in connection with the analysis of faith as wholeness. *Ibid.*, pp. 226-227.

grain of mustard seed (Matt. 17:20 par.). All critical authorities are agreed that these are authentic sayings of Jesus, well
attested in the Gospel materials, belonging to the earliest
strata of tradition. Furthermore, these three sayings help
to interpret each other in virtue of their common subject
matter. It seems quite appropriate that the word "seed"
(σπέρμα) should serve as an image for power and vitality, an
image that binds together plant life and human generation
and growth. The term was occasionally used in the Hellenistic world with this imagery in mind. Seneca, for example, compared the word, as life-giving principle, with the
seed, and the same was common in Stoic philosophy (λόγος
σπερματικός). Hence it is all the more surprising that the
imagery of sowing seed is almost never used by the Old
Testament to describe God's action, with the exception of
Hos. 10:12.[67] We must conclude that the metaphor of the
seed originated with Jesus. It was he (not the Semitic tradition to which he belonged) who seized upon an everyday
image like seed and used it to evoke a new understanding
of life.[68]

In the parable of the sower (Matt. 13:1-9; Mk. 4:1-9; Lk.
8:4-8), the harvest, to be sure, is already implied in the
sowing. But it is not automatically insured. Just as the field
without the seed is barren, unable to yield a harvest, so also
the seed without the fertile field is unproductive, subject to
misuse and decay.[69] But when it strikes good soil, what a
harvest! Here the revelatory juxtaposition of the familiar
and the unfamiliar, so characteristic of Jesus' parables, is
experienced. A tenfold yield counts as a good harvest in
"real" life, but here we find a yield of thirtyfold, sixtyfold,

---

67. Ernst Lohmeyer, *Das Evangelium des Matthäus,* 2nd ed. (Göttingen,
Vandenhoeck & Ruprecht, 1958), p. 194.
68. All but one of the Synoptic occurrences of the words for "seed" (κόκκος,
σπόρος, σπέρμα) with this metaphorical function are found in the materials
now under consideration, i.e., in Matt. 13:1-9, 18-23, 31-32; 17:20; and
parallels. In other occurrences in the Synoptic Gospels, "seed" is used in
connection with the birds that neither sow nor reap (e.g., Matt. 6:26), with
the parable of the talents (Matt. 25:24, 26), or with human offspring (e.g.,
Matt. 22:24, 25).
69. Lohmeyer, *op. cit.,* p. 198.

even a hundredfold.[70] The improbable power of the seed
first comes into view: what sort of "seed" might this be?
The same motif is at work in the parable of the mustard
seed (Matt. 13:31-32; Mk. 4:30-32; Lk. 13:18-19), where
the point seems to be the contrast between the tiny seed and
the great bush that grows from it. The bush that shelters
birds is an eschatological image, calling to mind the world-
tree of Nebuchadnezzar's dream in Dan. 4:5 ff., which was
to shelter all nations.[71]

The third of these sayings concerns faith as a grain of
mustard seed (Matt. 17:20 par.), which in Matthew is
appended to the story of the healing of the boy with epilepsy
(17:14-19). In explaining to the disciples why they could
not cast out the demon, Jesus says: "Because of your little
faith. For truly, I say to you, if you have faith as a grain of
mustard seed, you will say to this mountain, 'Move hence
to yonder place,' and it will move; and nothing will be
impossible for you."[72] The juxtaposition of the tiny seed
and the vast mountain (the removal of which is an eschatological sign; cf. Is. 49:11; 40:4 ff.), brings out the main
point of the saying very clearly: the improbable power of
faith.[73] It is significant, as Ebeling points out, that "the
comparison with the mustard seed falls out in Mark's version
of the saying [11:23-24] and its parallels in Matthew [21:21,
22], and is supplanted by the demand not to doubt, apparently because the comparison of faith with a mustard seed
was already felt unsuitable. . . ."[74] But it is just this com-

70. Jeremias, *op. cit.*, p. 150.
71. Lohmeyer, *op. cit.*, pp. 217-218.
72. In Lk. 17:6, where the saying stands as an independent unit, faith has the
power to move a sycamine tree. In Mk. 11:23 and Matt. 21:21, the saying is
inserted into the conversation about the withered fig tree; here faith is not
compared with a grain of mustard seed but is credited with the power to
move mountains. A secondary form of the saying immediately follows in Mk.
11:24 and Matt. 21:22, where unconditional fulfillment is promised to the
prayer made in faith. This complicated situation indicates that the saying
about faith as a grain of mustard seed was an independent logion, inserted
into various contexts by the Evangelists. Bultmann (*SynT*, pp. 75, 93-94) and
Ebeling (*WF*, pp. 227-229) regard Matt. 17:20 as the original form.
73. *WF*, p. 228; Lohmeyer, *op. cit.*, p. 273.
74. *WF*, pp. 228-229.

parison that is the mark of the saying's uniqueness and authenticity. The seed of faith is a hidden, strange, seemingly insignificant and mundane possession; yet it conceals the power of the future by which all that stands in the way is overcome: not only mountains or sycamine trees, but also demons, sickness, and death—everything that fragments and destroys the wholeness of human existence.[75]

It is my proposal that this saying is the hermeneutical key to the parable of the sower, and that the parable of the mustard seed is the "link" between the two. The *saying* in which faith is explicitly compared with mustard seed shows that mustard seed is to be understood as a metaphor for faith; the *parable* of the mustard seed shows that the "seed" described in the parable of the sower (which behaves very much like mustard seed) is to be understood as the seed of faith—the seed that empowers life and makes it whole.[76] When the parable of the sower is read with this "key" in mind, we realize that something further must be said about faith as seed: the seed is sown, and that means it is a power implanted in man *extra se,* not a natural possession for which he may claim credit. Nevertheless, the seed must take root in man and be nourished by him in order to come to fruition. Faith is both a gift, the gift of the power of God, and a human act or a human word for which man must assume responsibility. This double meaning is the unique function of the image of the seed as a metaphor for faith: it refers both to the word of God as the power of the future and to the faithful word of man; and it implies that the two words come to fruition only together. As I have suggested in another context, the word of God utilizes man's word as the place of its historical existence; and conversely the word of faith is not a human possession but a divine gift—a gift, nevertheless, which is the definition and fulfillment of what it means to be human. But this makes explicit what remains

---

75. Lohmeyer, *op. cit.,* p. 273.
76. Wilder also regards the parable of the sower as a "metaphor of faith" (*The Language of the Gospel,* p. 93).

only implicit and unexpressed in the parable of the sower and the saying about faith as a grain of mustard seed. In these sayings, God is never brought directly into view. Jesus does not identify God allegorically with the sower, or his word with the seed.[77] Jesus does not say who it is that sows. Similarly, in the saying about faith as a grain of mustard seed, faith is described in a completely "non-religious" way. There is no reference to God as the object of faith, nor are one's prior conceptions about God made a precondition for having faith. Faith is not a matter of religious belief *in* something. Nevertheless, it is clear from the way in which faith comes about (it is sown as a seed, implanted *extra nos*), and from what is ascribed to faith (its immense power in contrast to its apparent insignificance), that faith above all has to do with God. As Ebeling puts it: "The power of faith is marked outright as the power of God. . . . The whole point is to declare that faith is letting God work, letting God go into action, and that therefore it is legitimate to ascribe to faith what is a matter for God."[78]

b. Faith as Wholeness

Faith possesses an improbable power, a power that derives ultimately from God himself. But what is accomplished by such power? The answer is already suggested by the comparison of faith with a seed: faith brings life to fruition, completion, security, wholeness, salvation. Fruitfulness and completion—far beyond what ordinarily could have been expected—are described by the immense harvest at the end of the parable of the sower (Matt. 13:8). Security is suggested by the picture of the mustard tree with its sheltering branches (Matt. 13:32). Healing and wholeness are portrayed by the power of faith to cure a boy of epilepsy (Matt. 17:14-20). Faith, then, is the eschatological power

77. This identification is made by the so-called interpretation of the parable of the sower (Matt. 13:18-23 par.), which is a product of the early church and does not derive from Jesus himself, a fact that has been widely recognized since Jülicher. (See Jeremias, *op. cit.*, pp. 77-79.)
78. *WF*, pp. 232-233.

that makes life whole; it is the power of salvation. Salvation (from *salvare*) means to salve, to heal, to make whole, to gather—to gather man's life into presence personally and socially, temporally and spatially.

That faith is the power which makes life whole is under-scored by the fact that men without faith are anxious, afraid, doubtful—in short, disintegrated and powerless. Jesus refers to men of "little faith" (ὀλιγόπιστος or ὀλιγοπιστία), a term which occurs several times in Matthew and Luke, always on the lips of Jesus, and which is quite probably Jesus' own usage, even though it is a concept taken over from late Judaism.[79] In Matt. 6:30-31 and Lk. 12:28-29, "little faith" is associated with "anxiety" or "care": "O men of little faith . . . do not be anxious" (ὀλιγόπιστοι, μὴ οὖν μεριμνήσητε). In Matt. 8:26, it is associated with "fear"; in Matt. 14:31, with "doubt"; and in Matt. 17:20, it is contrasted with the power of faith. According to the Evangelists' "interpretation" of the parable of the sower (Matt. 13:18-23 par.), "the cares of the world" (ἡ μέριμνα τοῦ αἰῶνος) are said to choke out the seed of faith (Matt. 13:22). Here the same term, μέριμνα, is used as in Matt. 6:31 to describe the "anxiety" of the men of little faith, and hence it may reflect Jesus' own use of the term. Accord-ing to Lohmeyer, μέριμνα in these contexts does not mean the petty concerns that press upon man in his everyday life but the care (*die Sorge*) which signifies the being of the world and man's existence in it.[80] This "care" is what Heidegger has analyzed as an "existential" of man's being-in-the-world. Care has to do with man's temporality.[81] The man for whom care is inauthentic, irresolute, productive of fear and doubt, is the man who is unsettled and divided by time, whether it be in relation to the past (e.g., boasting, self-assurance, puta-tive self-salvation), or to the future (e.g., anxiety, fear, worry), or to the present (e.g., distraction by that which is ready-to-

79. *Ibid.*, p. 227.
80. Lohmeyer, *op. cit.*, p. 209.
81. *BT*, Secs. 39-44, 61-66.

hand but not timely, such as worldly riches).[82] Inauthentic
care is the loss of presence. The man who is faithful, on the
other hand, is the man whose care is transformed into a
responsible decision for the future, a decision that gathers
together past, present, and future. The past is no longer
the legacy of unfulfilled hopes and unredeemed guilt. The
future is no longer the threat of an unknown fate. Rather,
in faith, past and future are brought together in the present
moment of existence. The past is freed of its irredeemability
by being taken up into a fresh projection of possibilities. And
the future is freed of its fateful character by being disclosed
as God's future, which is near at hand. The faithful man,
as Kierkegaard put it, is contemporaneous with himself. The
life of faith is the life of presence.

The whole matter is expressed more concretely and vividly
by the healing stories, which are also concerned with faith,
and where the "gathering" accomplished by faith is seen in a
social-horizontal as well as a personal-temporal dimension.
This theme directs attention to the second of the main groups
of material in which the word "faith" is found on the lips of
Jesus, namely, the spoken parts of healing narratives. The
concept of faith is associated with nine such narratives (not
counting parallels separately), or about half of the healing
incidents in the Synoptic materials. In all but one of these
(the story of the paralytic, Matt. 9:1-8 par.), the word
"faith" is found on the lips of Jesus.[83] From the predomi-
nance of this material, the absence of parallels in late Judaism, the lack of the concept of faith in other narratives in
the Synoptic Gospels, and the "peculiar structure" of the
concept of faith associated with healing, Ebeling concludes
that Jesus himself "affirmed a connection between faith and
the event of healing," even though we cannot argue for the
ipsissima verba of Jesus in specific passages.[84]

82. *ThP*, pp. 88, 90.
83. See *WF*, p. 230, n. 2, for a brief analysis of each of these pericopes.
84. *Ibid.*, pp. 230-231.

The most striking of the formulae by which faith is associated with healing in these stories is repeated seven times in the Synoptic Gospels, "your faith has made you well" (ἡ πίστις σου σέσωκέν σε), a repetition that would seem to mark its originality with Jesus.[85] Two similar formulae are found less frequently. The first occurs in Matt. 9:29 (the healing of two blind men) and in a modified version in Matt. 8:13: "according to your faith be it done to you" (κατὰ τὴν πίστιν ὑμῶν γενηθήτω ὑμῖν). The second occurs in the Markan and Lukan versions of the story of the woman with the hemorrhage, shortly after the words, "your faith has made you well." Luke reads (8:50): "Do not fear; only believe, and she shall be well" (Μὴ φοβοῦ· μόνον πίστευσον, καὶ σωθήσεται). Mark drops off the last phrase (5:36). Finally, we may refer to Jesus' remarkable conflict with the Syrophoenician woman (Matt. 15:21-28; Mk. 7:24-30). After the woman refuses to be turned away by Jesus' insult, he says (only in Matt. 15:28), "O woman, great is your faith! Be it done for you as you desire" (μεγάλη σου ἡ πίστις· γενηθήτω σοι ὡς θέλεις).

At least three basic conclusions may be drawn from these data. First, those who are brought to faith in these incidents have no ground for faith other than the *word* of Jesus. Objectively, their situation is one of despair and hopelessness, and nothing is changed other than that now they find a ground for faith in the word of Jesus. It is word that heals, not by magically changing the human plight, but simply by addressing a hopeless man, awakening his faith, bringing him directly into the presence of God. This association of word and healing is stated thematically by the Evangelists towards the beginning of Jesus' ministry and clearly reflects an association deeply rooted in the community's memory of Jesus. For example, in the synagogue at Capernaum, where according to the tradition Jesus per-

85. It is found in the story of the woman with the hemorrhage (Matt. 9:22; Mk. 5:34; Lk. 8:48); in the Markan and Lukan versions of the healing of Bartimaeus (Mk. 10:52; Lk. 18:42); and twice in Lukan material: the woman with the ointment (Lk. 7:50), and the healing of the ten lepers (Lk. 17:19).

formed his first healing act, the people ask: "What is this word? For with authority and power he commands the unclean spirits, and they come out" (Lk. 4:36). Or Matt. 8:16: " . . . he cast out the spirits with a word, and healed all who were sick."

In the second place, all these formulae show that it is *faith* which heals, not Jesus, and indeed that faith is not simply a possession at the disposal of the one afflicted. Faith enjoys an objectivity vis-à-vis both Jesus and the believer. Jesus' role is that of *awakening* faith or of *ascribing* faith. In Ebeling's words, he "ascribed this faith to those who had no idea what was really happening to them, told them as it were to their face: You just do not know what has really happened—ἡ πίστις σου σέσωκέν σε!"[86] Jesus is not some sort of magician or wonder worker, and strictly speaking the healing stories are not "miracles." Nowhere is this clearer than in the story of the woman with the hemorrhage (Matt. 9:18-26; Mk. 5:21-43; Lk. 8:40-56). According to the "reports" that had been circulated (Mk. 5:27), Jesus possessed a miraculous "touch" that would heal instantly. So the woman thought to herself, "If I only touch his garment, I shall be made well." According to all three Evangelists, the woman did indeed touch Jesus' garment. But in the Matthean version, Jesus instantly turns to the woman and says, "your faith has made you well"; and only then is she in fact healed (Matt. 9:21-22). Jesus seems to imply that it is not physical contact that heals but faith. Mark by contrast dwells on the physical contact in apocryphal detail (5:27-33), suggesting the secondary character of his narrative. The exclusiveness of faith as the "cause" of healing is underscored in Luke's version of the story, where Jesus says: "Do not fear; only believe [μόνον πίστευσον], and she shall be well" (Lk. 8:50). Faith alone (μόνον πίστευσον) heals. Because healing is really a paradigm for salvation in these stories, we could also write: faith alone saves—not faith in Jesus (i.e., "Chris-

86. *WF*, p. 235.

tian" faith), or even faith in God, but faith in the absolute sense, as a word-event of power that gathers man into presence.[87]

The objectivity of faith vis-à-vis Jesus is brought out most sharply in the story of the Syrophoenician woman (Matt. 15:21-28; Mk. 7:24-30). Here it is really a question of faith prevailing *against* Jesus. He scorns the woman's plea for mercy and help, apparently on the grounds that she is a Canaanite, not a Jew. Even in the face of his insult she does not yield, and Jesus responds, "O woman, great is your faith! Be it done for you as you desire" (Matt. 15:28). As Bultmann points out, this is a controversy dialogue in which "Jesus proves not to be the victor, though in no sense is this a denigration."[88] Indeed, one is tempted to surmise that Jesus allowed himself not to be the victor in this instance in order to let it be seen that faith is an "objective" quality or power, independent of the attitude of either the believer or Jesus; he deliberately pitted himself against the woman in order to "test" her faith, to let it prove itself. Here we find dramatic proof that Jesus never linked the concept of faith with the believer's attitude towards himself, and that his *own* faith came into view only rarely.

Finally, the equation of faith and salvation implied in the formula, ἡ πίστις σου σέσωκέν σε, may be noted. Σέσωκα is the perfect form of the verb σῴζειν, which means to save or to preserve, both from physical dangers and afflictions and from sin and eternal death. It is related to the conventional religious term for salvation, σωτηρία. Hence the healing that results from faith is really a paradigm of human salvation as such. This is the deeper significance of Jesus' acts of healing. Salvation is accomplished by liberating man from the destructive, disintegrative powers, and by gathering him once again into a healthy, functioning entity, at one both with himself and with the world. The powers that afflict

87. *Ibid.*, p. 245.
88. *SynT*, p. 38.

and disintegrate are both physical and spiritual, internal and
external, personal and social. Consequently, healing must
take place in all these dimensions at once. On the one hand,
faith has to do with the believer's own personal existence.
Ebeling points to the unusual and unprecedented association of the personal pronoun with the concept of faith in
Jesus' sayings: "*your* faith has made *you* well"; "according
to *your* faith be it done to *you*"; "O woman, great is *your*
faith."[89] Faith is something for which the individual must
assume responsibility, and it relates peculiarly to the well-
being of his own existence. We may note also the association of faith, healing, and peace—a peace that restores man
to harmony with himself—in Lk. 7:50 and 8:48: "your faith
has made you well; go in peace" (ἡ πίστις σου σέσωκέν σε. πορεύου
εἰς εἰρήνην). On the other hand, healing is a social act. It
takes place in Jesus' encounters with men. If we inquire
about Jesus' "social action," his involvement in the process
of liberating and transforming the world, we are directed
above all to his acts of healing (which are designated, together with teaching and preaching, as one of three fundamental forms of his ministry, e.g., in Matt. 4:23-25). Healing may be taken as paradigmatic not only of the personal
but also of the social-horizontal structure of salvation as a
whole. Healing is a social reality, requiring the constitution
and preservation of a human community.[90] In Jesus' acts of
healing and the faith associated with them, his co-humanity
is given paradigmatic expression—a co-humanity willing
to shatter the conventional dehumanizing structures for the
sake of man's well-being, and issuing therefore in his death
on the cross.

89. *WF*, pp. 238-239.
90. In the story of the woman with the ointment (Lk. 7:36-50), that which
faith heals is not a physical illness, as in most other instances, but a social ill,
prostitution. Moreover, in the parable of the talents (Matt. 25:14-30 par.),
by means of the contrast between πιστός and ὀκνηρός ("slothful") (Matt.
25:21, 26), faith is shown to involve responsible action in the world rather
than fearful retreat from it.

c. Faith as Openness for the Kingdom of God

Faith is the power that makes life whole, healing human existence by gathering it into presence. In the preaching of Jesus, the "kingdom of God" refers to the new "world" constituted by the life in presence. It is that "kingdom of presence" for which man is destined by the grace of God, a future kingdom that has drawn near and even now comes to speech in the faithful word of Jesus. Faith *means* openness for and participation in the kingdom of God; hence faith means presence not only to oneself and to the world but also to God, who as man's future comes near in the coming to speech of his kingdom. Jesus' preaching of the kingdom of God may be viewed as one form of his speaking about faith, even though the connection between "faith" and "kingdom" is rarely made explicit. This connection is, however, suggested by the parable of the mustard seed (Matt. 13:31-32; Mk. 4:30-32; Lk. 13:18-19)—significantly, the only so-called "parable of the kingdom" to appear in Mark and Luke[91] as well as in Matthew. If I have been correct in arguing that the "mustard seed" is a metaphor for faith, characterizing its improbable power, then when Jesus says that "the kingdom of God is like a grain of mustard seed . . . " (Matt. 13:31), he means that God's kingdom is the new world constituted by the power of faith, a power that is not at man's disposal but is the gift of God, and thus is the manifestation of God's rule. God rules when the power of his future word comes to speech as the word of faith; in this event a new world is founded, healing man by shattering the conventions of the old world.

I use the term "kingdom of God" with considerable reluctance because of my conviction that theology must abandon the use of royalist imagery whenever possible; but I have reached the conclusion that a more adequate translation of βασιλεία τοῦ θεοῦ is not available. Perhaps the most appealing

---

91. Luke combines the parable of the mustard seed with that of the leaven (13:20-21), which is also described as a parable of the kingdom.

alternative would be "city of God," taken in the root sense of
civitas, with obvious reference to Augustine's *civitas Dei* as
well as to the not inconsiderable use of "city" (πόλις) imagery
in the New Testament, especially in Hebrews and Revelation, to designate the new world constituted by God's rule
(the new Jerusalem, the heavenly city). But the English
word "city" simply will not bear this meaning naturally; and
βασιλεία, not πόλις, was the word used in the sayings of Jesus.
Another possibility is to render βασιλεία τοῦ θεοῦ as "rule of
God," for in the preaching of Jesus the term βασιλεία is
associated with δύναμις, "power" (cf. Mk. 9:1; Lk. 11:20).
The power of the *basileia* is the power of God, the present
manifestation of his future rule.[92] There is much to com-
mend this translation. Yet it does not convey the notion of
"world" or "region" that seems intrinsic to the *basileia* concept: the *basileia* is not simply a "rule"; it is a "world" constituted by a rule. The English word "kingdom" in fact
enjoys considerable flexibility of usage. It can connote a
"realm," "region," or "world" where something is dominant
or "rules"—whether natural, political, or religious and philosophical (e.g., "wheat kingdom," "animal kingdom," "kingdom
of estrangement," "kingdom of freedom," "kingdom of identity"). For my part, I shall think of the "kingdom of God"
as the "kingdom of presence," the "region" or "world" where
presence is constituted by the power of God's future word,
which gathers into presence by its coming.

When will the kingdom come? Is it now at hand or is yet
to come? From the extensive scholarly discussion of this
question[93] as well as my own investigations,[94] the conclusion

---

92. Rudolf Otto, *The Kingdom of God and the Son of Man*, trans. by Floyd V.
Filson and Bertram Lee-Woolf (London, Lutterworth Press, revised ed. 1943),
pp. 43-44; Eberhard Jüngel, *op. cit.*, pp. 187-188; and Wolfhart Pannenberg,
Theology and the Kingdom of God (Philadelphia, Westminster Press, 1969),
pp. 55-56.

93. See Bornkamm, *Jesus of Nazareth*, pp. 91-92; Norman Perrin, *op. cit.*;
Hans Conzelmann, "Present and Future in the Synoptic Tradition," *JThC*,
Vol. 5 (1968), pp. 26-44; and Robert W. Funk, "Apocalyptic as an Historical
and Theological Problem in Current New Testament Scholarship," *JThC*,
Vol. 6 (1969), pp. 175-191. See also the works by Dodd and Jeremias cited
above, n. 43.

must be that the kingdom is neither "present" nor "future" in an unambiguous sense, and that in so far as its time reference is clarified at all it must be spoken of as having "come near" to the present. The concept of "nearness" is made explicit in several passages, whose meaning must now be examined. Jesus says: "the kingdom of God has come near to you" (ἤγγικεν ἐφ᾽ ὑμᾶς ἡ βασιλεία τοῦ θεοῦ) (Lk. 10:9; cf. Lk. 10:11; Mk. 1:15; Matt. 3:2; 4:17; 10:7). The use of the perfect rather than the future tense of the verb ἐγγίζειν suggests that the kingdom of God has *already* come near (presumably with the beginning of Jesus' ministry), and that the state of "nearness" continues into and beyond the present. Thus the "nearness" of the *basileia* is not to be construed in a strictly chronological sense; to say that it is "near" does not mean that at some not too distant date in the future it will arrive. If the nearness of God and his kingdom is construed in a strictly chronological sense, then God would seem to become remote once the parousia is delayed. Rather, "nearness" is a qualitative dimension of the present: it describes the quality or mode of God's present relationship to man rather than the "time" of his arrival. God is the *coming* one, the one who comes by means of word. Similarly, his kingdom (the new world constituted by the coming to speech of his word) is a *coming* kingdom. In this sense it is "near" to the present. The concept of coming contains elements of both non-identity and identity. On the one hand, the kingdom is not to be identified undialectically with the present, for then it would lose its critical, unconcealing, gathering function vis-à-vis the present. The *basileia* is not

---

94. A word study of the occurrences of βασιλεία in Matthew and Luke yields the following results: in roughly forty-five per cent of the eighty-one occurrences where the concept "kingdom of God" or "kingdom of heaven" occurs, the stress seems to be placed on the present coming or nearness of the kingdom; in forty-one per cent the time reference is indefinite; and in only fourteen per cent the emphasis seems to be purely futuristic. In Luke the stress on the nearness of the kingdom is more clearly marked than in Matthew. Also in Matthew the number of "indefinite" references is greater, reflecting the fact that in most of the parables of the kingdom the time of the kingdom is not clearly specified. Needless to say, such results can only give a rough picture because of the difficulty in making distinctions in many instances.

an objectively discernible historical phenomenon, which can
be located in space and time, or whose arrival can be calculated. This is the meaning of Jesus' saying in Lk. 17:20-21:
"The kingdom of God is not coming with signs to be observed; nor will they say, 'Lo, here it is!' or 'There!' for
behold, the kingdom of God is in the midst of you [ἐντὸς
ὑμῶν]."[95] Clearly, ἐντὸς ὑμῶν does not mean that the *basileia*
is an inner spiritual principle ("within you" is a misleading
translation); rather, the *basileia* is in our midst—i.e., in the
midst of those who bring it to speech by faith—without
being observable by external signs. Thus, we must take
seriously the futurity, the not-yetness, of its coming; it transcends the present not merely vertically but also horizontally.
It is now present as that for which man must remain open
towards the future by which his destiny will be fulfilled.
God is *now* present as the *coming* one; he is not yet "all in
all" (πάντα ἐν πᾶσιν) (I Cor. 15:28). This is the element of
truth in Pannenberg's insistence upon the chronological or
horizontal aspect of the kingdom's futurity.[96] On the other
hand, the kingdom's futurity is not to be understood as
strictly chronological, for then too its "coming" would be
emasculated. We could not speak of it as having now come

95. It is worth noting that only Luke adds the words "to you" (ἐφ' ὑμᾶς) in
the saying, "the kingdom of God has come near" (Lk. 10:9). Luke seems to
be especially interested in the relation of the kingdom to the community of
faith: the kingdom is "near"—not in an abstract or chronological sense, but
to those who believe. Bultmann, who regards this passage as an authentic
saying of Jesus (*SynT*, p. 25), interprets it by reference to the saying about
the sudden coming of the Son of Man, which immediately follows in vss. 23-24.
This method presupposes that Jesus actually spoke of the Son of Man as a
future, apocalyptic figure, and that such references are to be taken as an
interpretive key for sayings about the kingdom of God. Thus Bultmann interprets Lk. 17:21 as follows: "when the Kingdom comes, no-one will ask and
search for it any more, but it will be there on a sudden in the midst of the
foolish ones who will still want to calculate its arrival." *SynT*, pp. 121-122; cf.
Jesus and the Word, trans. by Louise Pettibone Smith (New York, Charles
Scribner's Sons, 1934), pp. 40-41. It seems dubious to interpret the parables
of the kingdom by reference to the Son of Man sayings rather than vice versa,
since the precise sense in which Jesus spoke of the Son of Man is so open to
dispute. Jüngel, on the other hand, interprets this saying in a direction similar
to the one I am proposing. See the next paragraph below.

96. *JGaM*, pp. 85, 192-193, 199, 226-231.

near in the perfect tense, nor could we say that it is imperceptibly in our midst. The *basileia* of God is not a chronologically distant, future aeon, confronting the present in dualistic antithesis, as portrayed by apocalypticism. Jesus' conception of the "nearness" of the kingdom of God already shatters the apocalyptic imagery in which to some extent it is couched.

My interpretation is borne out by Jüngel's important work on the parables of the kingdom. He argues that the *nearness* of the rule of God is its essence. " 'Nearness' and 'rule of God' are not *two* concepts joined together in a synthetic judgment; rather the two together constitute *the* theological concept of the proclamation of Jesus." "The nearness of the rule of God is so near that it requires the language form of the parable in order to come to speech in such fashion that man is able to enter into it."[97] Jesus' reference to the rule of God has its roots in the Old Testament concept of God's kingship, which is effective in the present although now concealed. On the other hand, the concept by which Jesus gave expression to the idea of God's rule or kingship—*basileia*—is associated not with the Old Testament kingship traditions but with the apocalyptic notion of two aeons, according to which the new aeon, the *'olam ha-ba,* stands over against the old aeon as the distant future. According to Jüngel, this merging of traditions served two purposes. First, the *distant* future of the *'olam*-terminology was associated with the *near* future of the rule of God, so that "every apocalyptic or theological distance between the present and that future is de-distanced *[ent-fernt]*: the future is *directly* present as the near future; it knows no intervening temporal realm." On the other hand, by using the *'olam*-terminology, Jesus announced the *basileia* as the end of the old aeon. Yet this end is not something to be expected in the distant future; it is already taking place. "For the *basileia,* whose yoke can be taken up at any time, is by its very essence near to history.

97. Jüngel, *Paulus und Jesus,* pp. 175-176, 168-169.

Its eschatological essence consists in its nearness to history—
a nearness that joins the future to the present."[98] On this
basis, Jüngel interprets Lk. 17:20-21 as follows: the arrival
of the rule of God cannot be calculated in terms of some
future date, nor can its place in the future be fixed in the
sense of an interval from the present; rather, "Jesus' proclamation of the rule of God calls man out of every apocalyptic
distance from this rule into the nearness of the neighbor [*die
Nähe des Nächsten*], where the power of the future rule of
God proves itself as present. The *basileia* is 'in our midst' in
the sense that the near future of the rule of God appears in
the present as the nearness of the neighbor." The story of
the Good Samaritan, which is to be interpreted as a parable
of the kingdom, epitomizes this nearness.[99]

Now, if the essence of the kingdom of God is its *nearness*,
then *faith* is the proper mode of openness for and present
participation in the kingdom. The *basileia* is near but not
undialectically present or fully realized. For this reason it
can come to speech only in parables, which are the language
of faith par excellence. Faith is the *historical, finite* experience of the coinherence of the modes of time. In faith
temporal tension remains; faith is not the *visio beatifica* or
the pure presence of God. God himself is love but not faith.
Our experience of the nearness of God and our openness
for the kingdom of presence take the primary form of faith,
not love—a faith, to be sure, which issues in love and also
in freedom and in hope, but which remains, during our historical course, their presupposition and ground. Faith determines the "mode" in which love, freedom, and hope are
exercised for the time being. The concept of faith better
preserves the eschatological tension by which we now live
in the "kingdom of presence" than the concept of love. If
this interpretation is correct, then all the parables of the
kingdom are really parables about faith. For faith is the

98. *Ibid.*, pp. 177-180; quotations from p. 180.
99. *Ibid.*, pp. 193-196, 171-173; quotation from p. 195.

present manifestation of God's future power in word, by which life is gathered into presence and made whole. And that too is the meaning of the kingdom of God.

The concept of "openness" is related to the discussion in modern anthropology of man's openness to the world. Max Scheler, Adolf Portmann, Arnold Gehlen and others have argued that, in contrast to animals, which are bound by instinct and environment, man is able to go beyond every present situation and to change his environment or *Umwelt*. His destiny is not fulfilled by any given framework of life and thus he is always driven to expand his horizons and to remain open for the future.[100] Faith shares this structure of world-openness. Yet the world for which faith is open is not ultimately the world of human culture (the world created by man's transcendence of natural environment) but the new world constituted by the power of God's rule—the kingdom of God. Because this world is "near"—not immediately available like that of human culture, nor remotely distant like a political utopia—the proper mode of openness for it, and thus participation in it, is that of faith. Faith both exemplifies the structure of world-openness and fulfills it, for it discloses that man's openness cannot finally be satisfied by any human cultural achievement. Man must remain open for that which transcends himself and all the immanent worlds of culture and politics. The only truly satisfying world, the homeland of man's presence, is that of God's kingdom; and in relation to *this* world openness assumes the form of faith.

The near future of the kingdom of presence is nothing other than the future of *God*, who *is* presence. As Jüngel puts it, the concept of the *basileia* is a circumscription for

---

100. Pannenberg has pointed out the fruitfulness of this concept for theology. See *JGaM,* pp. 199-200, 226-227; *Was ist der Mensch?* (Göttingen, Vandenhoeck & Ruprecht, 1962), pp. 5-13; and "The Question of God," *Interpretation,* Vol. 31 (July 1967), pp. 300-301. Pannenberg cites Max Scheler, *Man's Place in Nature;* Adolf Portmann, *Zoologie und das neue Bild vom Menschen;* Arnold Gehlen, *Der Mensch;* and Helmut Plessner, *Die Stufen des Organischen und der Mensch.* One could also refer to the work of Heidegger, Bloch, Sartre, and Teilhard de Chardin.

the future of God himself; or better, "rule of God" (*Got-tesherrschaft*) is a divine attribute. "It refers to the future of God determining man's present through the word of Jesus."[101] And if "nearness" is the essence of the *basileia,* then "nearness" is also a divine attribute. God is now present as the one who is near; he is the near God. The nearness of God is the meaning of Jesus' language about God as Father.[102] Jesus was not the first to use the name "Father" for God (it is found, for example, in Stoic piety and in the Old Testament). But he used it to describe the relationship between God and the individual as well as the community or nation, referring not to physical descent but to God's near presence, his being-with-us here and now. And Jesus used the child's familiar name for his earthly father, "Abba," in addressing God in prayer (Mk. 14:36), a usage that shattered Jewish piety and was taken over by the Hellenistic church (cf. Rom. 8:15; Gal. 4:6). Thus if faith is the proper mode of openness for and present participation in the *basileia* of God, it is also the proper mode of openness for the being of God. As *the* word of faith, Jesus was the one in whom this openness was fully achieved.

4. ENACTMENT OF FAITH: A NEW PRAXIS

a. Freedom, Responsibility, Obedience

The inseparability of word and practice has been a central thesis of this discussion. In addressing a third dimension of the concept "word of faith," that of *enactment,* I hope to make explicit what already was implicit in the analysis of the *quality* and *content* of Jesus' speaking. Jesus lived the life of faith primarily by means of his verbal action. Even his ministry of healing was closely associated with what he had to say about the nature of faith and the coming kingdom of

101. Jüngel, *op. cit.,* pp. 188-189, 196-197. Cf. Pannenberg: God's being is his rule. *Theology and the Kingdom of God,* p. 55.
102. Bornkamm, *op. cit.,* pp. 124-129.

God. The only important point where his action appears
not to be verbal was the death on the cross. I shall argue,
however, that the crucifixion is to be understood as the climax of Jesus' entire being as the word of faith, and hence
that it is *the* word-event of faith par excellence.

A word that is not itself an action, or that does not issue
in an act, is not a true word but an empty, powerless, illusory
vocable. The point is made in Jesus' well-known saying concerning hearers and doers of the word (Matt. 7:24-27 and
Lk. 6:47-49): "Every one then who hears these words of
mine and does them will be like a wise man who built his
house upon the rock; . . . every one who hears these words
of mine and does not do them will be like a foolish man who
built his house upon the sand. . . . "[103] A word that does not
issue in conduct produces not merely a neutral situation but
a disastrous or destructive one. Thus it is appropriate to
direct attention specifically to the conduct engendered by
the word of faith. What are the structural dimensions of
human existence when it assumes the form of the *life* of
faith? Here again an orientation is provided by the earlier
discussion of three horizons of presence (presence to self,
world, and God). Corresponding to these horizons, three
forms of Jesus' manhood and three forms of his action may
be distinguished. As truly present to himself, he was "radical
man," whose action took the form of *freedom in the world*.
As present to the world, he was "man for other men" or
"brother of men," whose action took the form of *responsibility for the world*. Finally, as present to God, he was "man
for God" or "son of God," whose action took the form of
obedience to the will of God. Thus we may speak of Jesus
as radical man, brother of men, and son of God; and we
may describe his action as assuming the three basic forms
of freedom, responsibility, and obedience. These forms of
action are not exercised apart from or in addition to lan-

103. Bultmann regards this as an authentic similitude of Jesus, although with
rabbinic parallels (*SynT*, pp. 173, 202). However, in the parallel cited by
Bultmann (*Pirke Aboth*, III.27) it is a question of the relation between wisdom
and works, not words and works.

guage; rather they are exercised primarily by words and by actions closely associated with words. The task now is to make explicit the modes of conduct engendered by Jesus' words. Moreover, these forms of action are not in fact separable, even though for purposes of analysis they may be distinguished. The horizons of Jesus' presence are so internally integrated that it is not possible to speak of his freedom apart from his responsibility, which in turn has its basis in and gives "horizontal" expression to his obedience to God. The compenetration of freedom, responsibility, and obedience reaches a climax in Jesus' death on the cross, which accordingly is to be understood as the act by which his being as the word of faith is fully accomplished. In the first part of this section, I shall take up the three forms of action separately; then I shall direct attention to the cross as the ultimate and integrating action of Jesus' life of faith.

I. *Freedom in the World: Radical Man.* With the involvement of Christians in the revolutionary struggles of our time, "freedom" and "liberation" have become central theological motifs. A "theology of revolution" requires a "theology of freedom." If Christians take seriously God's redemptive presence in the world and the nearness of his kingdom, they must commit themselves on the side of the oppressed in the contemporary struggles for freedom and justice. On the one hand, they must make common cause with a conception of and a struggle for freedom that has been given expression in forms not specifically religious or Christian, e.g., in the black revolution, in Marxism, in the so-called "new politics," and in secular humanism. Here it is a matter of engaging in common action with a human brotherhood that transcends the visible bounds of the Christian faith. On the other hand, as Jürgen Moltmann has cogently argued, Christians have a specific role to play in this common front. Their task is that of liberating the revolution from its tendency towards legalism and moralism, of bringing about a revolution within the revolution, which frees it from the law of revolution. Revolutionaries often exhibit a puritanical, moralistic bent, which results from taking themselves and their cause too seriously, and which issues in an often irreconcilable alienation from their opponents (both real and imagined). Against this tendency, the Christian presence in revolution can introduce another dimension—that of play, joy, reconciliation, humility—which results from faith in a greater liberation than man himself can accomplish. Such freedom is not to be understood as freedom *from* the world or *from* the revolution but as freedom *in* it—freedom to make common cause with the struggle for freedom, yet to remain free in this struggle, liberated from its compulsiveness, seriousness, moralism, and alienation—in short, from its legalism. Such is the specifically Christian conception of freedom, and the Christian contribution to the revolution of freedom.[104]

Such, too, is the form of freedom that came decisively to expression in Jesus' life of faith. No one has made this clearer than Karl Barth, who in his discussion of Jesus as the "royal man" refers to "the pronouncedly revolutionary character of his relationship to the orders of life and value current in the world around him. . . . He enjoyed and displayed, in relation to all the orders positively or negatively contested around him, a remarkable freedom which again we can only describe as royal."[105] Jesus was no revolutionary in the conventional sense, yet his freedom was more than revolutionary. On the one hand, Barth argues, he did not directly attack or seek to replace any of the conventional orders of society—the temple, the family, religious and cultic practices, economic and commercial relations, the political structure. On the other hand, he remained free in his relation to all these orders, calling their presuppositions and their ultimate validity radically into question in the light of a new freedom—the freedom of the kingdom of God.[106]

104. Jürgen Moltmann, "The Revolution of Freedom," and "God in Revolution," *RRF*, Chapters 4, 7.
105. *CD*, Vol. IV/2, pp. 171-172.
106. *Ibid.*, pp. 172-179.

Rather than describe Jesus' freedom as "royal," I prefer
to designate it "radical," because of my conviction that
royalist imagery can no longer illuminate the meaning of
Christian faith and is peculiarly unsuitable in this context.
I take "radical" in its etymological sense, deriving from *radix*,
root, meaning that which pertains to or proceeds from the
ultimate source, foundation, reality, or truth of things.
"Radical man" means authentic, true, finished man. "Radical
freedom" designates a freedom that has its source in the gift
of divine presence, expresses itself in acts of liberation and
reconciliation in the world, and finds its peculiar locus in the
"root" quality of one's presence to oneself. Because of this
locus, it is appropriate to treat freedom under the first of the
horizons of presence: freedom *means*, in the first instance,
presence to oneself or integral selfhood. But the reality of
freedom is not exhausted by the first of these relational
structures. It includes also the relation to the world and
to God. I have characterized these second and third relations by the terms "responsibility" and "obedience," but
"freedom" could be used to encompass all three. Thus, the
structures of freedom would include radical selfhood, responsible brotherhood, and obedient sonship, all of which
together define the life in freedom or the kingdom of freedom. That this is the case reflects the dialectical character
of the distinctions with which we are here involved.

Although Barth is right in saying that the kingdom of God
may not be identified with any of the social orders, and that
its freedom transcends that of all liberation movements,
nevertheless precisely the *nearness* of the kingdom does not
permit a stance of neutrality with respect to the political,
social, and religious issues contested around us. Rather it
demands a form of *partisanship*, a critical partisanship,
within and *for* movements of liberation rather than against
them, *critical* in the sense of working to free such movements from the compulsiveness, legalism, alienation, and
utopian designs that frequently plague them, placing them
in the perspective of the coming kingdom of freedom, of

which they are an authentic and necessary foretaste.[107] Such critical partisanship was exemplified by Jesus himself. Although he was not directly involved in a political program and was not a social revolutionary in the modern sense, Jesus identified himself with the poor, the oppressed, the diseased, the sinners, the disinherited of the earth, and advocated their cause against the rich, the pious, the religious and political "establishment"—an advocacy which, more than anything else, accounted for his arrest and crucifixion at the hands of the authorities. This self-identification of Jesus is reflected in the Gospels by such sayings and narratives as Jesus' reply to the followers of John the Baptist (Matt. 11:2-6 par.), the Lukan version of the Beatitudes ("Blessed are you poor. . . . Woe to you that are rich," Lk. 6:20-26), parables about rich young men (Lk. 12:13-21; 16:19-31; Matt. 19:16-30 par.), and above all the words from Is. 61:1-2 placed on the lips of Jesus by Luke in the story of his rejection at Nazareth (Lk. 4:18-30)—words that have become a text for black theology[108] and the theology of revolution:

> The Spirit of the Lord is upon me,
> because he has anointed me to preach good news to the poor.
> He has sent me to proclaim release to the captives
> and recovering of sight to the blind,
> to set at liberty those who are oppressed,
> to proclaim the acceptable year of the Lord.

While Jesus was not a Zealot and did not directly attack the political authority of Rome, he may well have sympathized with the Zealot cause, as evidenced by the inclusion of one of their party, Simon, among his disciples (Mk. 3:18 par.), the absence in Jesus' teaching of any condemnation of the Zealots (by contrast with his criticism of other Jewish parties, like the Pharisees and Sadducees), his delimitation

107. The elaboration of this claim would require a *dialectics* of freedom that I hope someday to be able to work out.
108. James H. Cone, *Black Theology and Black Power* (New York, Seabury Press, 1969), pp. 35 ff. Cone states that "Jesus' work is essentially one of liberation," and he argues that the Western Christian tradition, in particular white Protestant America, has ignored the political and social implications of this fact. Nevertheless, Cone does not construe the work of Jesus in an exclusively political sense either.

of the authority of Caesar in reference to the payment of
tribute money (Mk. 12:13-17 par.; Lk. 23:2), and sayings
about Herod the "fox," the sword, the carrying of weapons,
and the like (Lk. 13:32; Matt. 10:34; Lk. 22:36). It is also
clear that Jesus challenged the sacerdotal aristocracy in
Jerusalem by his act of cleansing the temple (Mk. 11:15-19
par.), that the Jewish chief priests sought his arrest and
handed him over to the Romans, trying to convince Pilate
that he was politically dangerous, and that he may have
been executed on a charge of sedition.[109] But Jesus' confron-
tation with the authorities did not take the form of a call to
political revolt and it was more fundamental than a castiga-
tion of the temple trading system. It had to do, as we have
seen, with the way that he called all of the established orders
—religious, cultic, legal, political—into question by contrast-
ing his own authority to that of his opponents. This confron-
tation began well before Jesus' entrance into Jerusalem and
it found paradigmatic expression in his conflict with the law
and all that it represented. Although always involving a call
to action and sometimes issuing in direct action itself (like

109. S. G. F. Brandon's recent study, *Jesus and the Zealots* (New York,
Charles Scribner's Sons, 1967), is instructive in this regard. Although the
entire thrust of his argument is to establish a connection between Jesus and
the Zealots, Brandon is forced to conclude "that Jesus was not a Zealot, and
that his movement was not an integral part of the Zealot resistance against
Rome" (p. 355). An important reason is the designation of *one* of the disciples, Simon, as a Zealot, thus suggesting that the other disciples and their
leader were not Zealots. Another factor is the recognition that Jesus attacked
the "Jewish sacerdotal aristocracy" rather than the Roman government, and
that his attack on the former was "symbolic" rather than direct in character.
Brandon believes that Jesus accepted the messianic role implied by his claim
that the kingdom of God is at hand, that he and his opponents understood the
kingdom as a theocracy of Israel, and that therefore his announcement of its
imminent arrival implied the reform of the priesthood and the overthrow of
the Roman tyranny. Brandon arrives at these dubious exegetical results by
excluding (as uncertain) all of the traditions containing Jesus' teaching and
substituting his own rather extensive speculations concerning Jesus' intentions.
Nevertheless, the book is valuable because it focuses attention on the political
context of Jesus' ministry, which cannot be ignored, and because its conclusions, given the bias of the argument, are cautious. See esp. Chapters 1, 2, 7.
Only a few interpreters have contended that Jesus was an outrightly political
Messiah, e.g., Karl Kautsky, *The Foundations of Christianity* (New York,
International Publishers, 1925); perhaps also Albert Cleage, *The Black Messiah*
(New York, Sheed and Ward, 1969). Brandon is not among them; nor are
most representatives of black theology, e.g., James Cone in the work cited
above.

picking corn on the sabbath or driving out money changers),
this conflict was basically verbal in character—the "but I
say to you" of the Sermon on the Mount, the verbal contro-
versies over the sabbath commandment and the laws of
purification, the parables directed against the scribes and
Pharisees, etc. Jesus opposed his own word to that of the
law and the priests; his authority was exercised by means
of word. Freedom of action has its roots in a freedom of
word. Free, authoritative word brings the truth to bear upon
the established orders, whether conservative or revolutionary, and liberates from their legalism and inhumanity by
founding a new freedom of action. Jesus is the liberator
because he is the radically free man.[110]

II. *Responsibility for the World: Brother of Men.* Jesus'
freedom of action is an expression of his presence to himself. Yet, as noted earlier, the Gospels rarely focus attention
on Jesus as a private individual. Glimpses are caught of his
freedom, authority, and personal power only as they are
exercised in the horizontal structure of his relationships with
other men. His freedom *in* the world issues immediately in
his responsibility *for* the world: precisely because he is free
he can also be responsible without coercion or compulsion;
conversely, his responsibility takes the form of freeing men
from the restrictive, disintegrating bonds of the established
order. As the radical man, he is unequivocally the man for
other men, the brother of men. His humanity is co-humanity.
"Responsibility," like "freedom," is not a term used specifically in the Synoptic tradition to characterize the action of
Jesus. It has certain advantages, however. It suggests the

110. On Jesus' authority and freedom of word, see Sec. 2.a. The motif of
liberation is an important one in the theology of Paul—liberation from bondage
to sin (Rom. 6:6, 16, 20; 7:25), to the flesh (Rom. 1:24 ff.; 6:19; 7:5, 25;
8:3-10, 12), to the law (Rom. 7), to the principalities and powers (Rom. 8:38),
to the elemental spirits (Gal. 4:3, 8-9), ultimately to death (Rom. 8:2). For
Paul, the work of Jesus is that of liberator: "for freedom Christ has set us free"
(Gal. 5:1); through him we "obtain the glorious liberty of the children of God"
(Rom. 8:21). The same is true for the author of the Fourth Gospel: "the truth
will make you free. . . . I am the way, and the truth, and the life" (Jn. 8:32;
14:6). On this theme, see further below, Sec. 4 b II. In general support of
the position argued here, see Ernst Käsemann, *Jesus Means Freedom*, trans. by
Frank Clarke (Philadelphia, Fortress Press, 1970), esp. Chapters 1, 3, 6.

close connection between Jesus' word and his conduct, and
between his relation to the world and to God. The basic
quality of Jesus' faithful word is its correspondence to the
word of God. It corresponds by responding. Responsive
speech issues in responsible action, action that is answerable
to somebody. Jesus' action is answerable *to* God *on behalf of*
the world. His answerability to God becomes concrete and
visible in his horizontal relations with the world, his co-
humanity. Thus obedience to God and responsibility for the
world are co-constitutive themes.

Although responsibility as such is not predicated of Jesus
in the Gospels, the Evangelists make use of a similar concept
to characterize the action of Jesus: σπλαγχνίζεσθαι, "to have
compassion."[111] Karl Barth has called attention to this usage.
Σπλαγχνίζεσθαι is related to the noun σπλάγχνα, which means
"viscera" or "internal organs" and is used figuratively of the
seat of the emotions, especially of love, compassion, and
mercy. Hence σπλαγχνίζεσθαι means literally "to be moved
from the viscera—or the 'heart'—to have compassion." In
Barth's words: "The expression is a strong one which defies
adequate translation. [Jesus] was not only affected to the
heart by the misery which surrounded him—sympathy in
our modern sense is far too feeble a word—but it went right
into his heart, into himself, so that it was now his misery.
It was more his than that of those who suffered it. He took it
from them and laid it on himself. . . . He himself suffered
in their place."[112]

The term σπλαγχνίζεσθαι is used by Jesus himself in three
of the most significant parables. It describes the action of
the Good Samaritan in Lk. 10:33 ("But a Samaritan, as he
journeyed, came to where he was; and when he saw him,
he had compassion, and went to him and bound up his

111. As noted earlier in this chapter (n. 63), not "love" (ἀγάπη) but the
stronger term, "compassion," is more commonly associated with Jesus in the
Synoptic tradition.
112. *CD*, Vol. IV/2, p. 184, and Vol. III/2, p. 211; see entire discussion of
Jesus, man for other men, in Vol. III/2, Sec. 45.1, and Vol. IV/2, pp. 180-192.
On this theme, see also George S. Hendry, *The Gospel of the Incarnation*
(Philadelphia, Westminster Press, 1958), pp. 100-107.

wounds . . ."); of the father in the parable of the Prodigal Son
(Lk. 15:20); and of the king in the parable of the Unforgiv-
ing Servant (Matt. 18:27). These are figures with whom
Jesus was closely associated in the Synoptic tradition;[113] thus
it is not by accident that the Evangelists should predicate
the term of Jesus himself. It is used three times in association with acts of healing, where Jesus is "moved by compassion" to perform the deed of healing in question (Mk. 1:41;
Lk. 7:13; Matt. 20:34). The occurrence in Matthew is interesting (the healing of Bartimaeus), because the Markan and
Lukan parallels (Mk. 10:52; Lk. 18:42) use in place of the
term σπλαγχνισθείς the saying of Jesus, ἡ πίστις σου σέσωκέν σε,
"your faith has made you well." Here a parallel exists between what Jesus *said* about faith as the power that gathers
life into wholeness and his *enactment* of faith in deeds of
compassion and responsibility. The term σπλαγχνίζεσθαι also
occurs five times in Matthew and Mark as part of a formula:
when Jesus saw the crowds (ὄχλοι), he was moved with compassion for them (ἐσπλαγχνίσθη περὶ αὐτῶν) (Matt. 9:36 and Mk.
6:43; Matt. 14:14; Matt. 15:32 and Mk. 8:2). Barth points
out that ὄχλοι refers to "man in the mass," "the public,"
"everyman."[114] We could also translate ὄχλοι by Heidegger's
term, "the they" *(das Man)*, which is the characteristic state
of man's being-in-the-world, the state of inauthenticity, of
"everydayness."[115] It is "the they" to whom Jesus directed
his ministry, binding himself to them in the depths of his
compassion; yet for the most part "they" did not believe
him, and it is they who in the end cried, "Crucify him, crucify him." Thus Jesus had compassion not merely on individuals who found themselves in distressing states but also
on the plight of humanity as such—its "theyness," its worldly
indifference, its loss of identity and of "presence." Hence it

113. In the parables themselves, these figures refer more to the action of God
than of Jesus. In the Lukan Benedictus σπλάγχνα is predicated of God himself
(Lk. 1:78)—διὰ σπλάγχνα ἐλέους θεοῦ ἡμῶν ("through the 'heartfelt' mercy of
our God").
114. *CD,* Vol. IV/2, pp. 185-187.
115. *BT,* pp. 163-168.

is especially appropriate to speak of Jesus' responsibility, not
merely for other individuals, but *for the world* in its worldliness. "World" refers in general to the socio-political nexus
constituted by the relations between men, and the natural
environment that embodies these relations. But the term
"world" has a deeper theological sense: it refers to these
relations as they have fallen into indifference and everydayness, subjugated and controlled by the "orders" of the
established world. This subjugation is imposed, not by alien
cosmic powers, but by "the they." It is this world of "the
they" that is shattered and opened by the word of faith that
came to speech in Jesus. As Gogarten has contended, we are
not to think of two worlds in the sense of a classic dualism,
but of two modes of being world: a "closed" or "established"
world and an "open" or "living" world. The "turn" from the
one world to the other is accomplished by the son of God
having assumed *responsibility* for the world: in his compassion he took its "worldliness" upon himself, suffering in its
place, on its behalf.[116]

The expressions "in our place," "on our behalf," which
designate the deepest meaning of Jesus' compassion, also
anticipate the oldest and broadest soteriological category
for interpreting the death of Jesus, a category taken over
and refashioned by Paul: "But God shows his love for us in
that while we were yet sinners Christ died for us [ὑπὲρ ἡμῶν]"
(Rom. 5:8). Here is a specific instance of the fact that the
crucifixion cannot be interpreted apart from its backward
reference to the words and deeds of the earthly Jesus, which
it climaxed. The significance of Jesus' death is already prefigured in the Evangelists' characterization of his action as
"compassionate," and in Jesus' use of the term σπλαγχνίζεσθαι
to epitomize the action of the Good Samaritan and other
parabolic figures. Finally, Jesus' responsibility for the world
is the horizontal structure by which his transcendent rela-

116. Friedrich Gogarten, *Jesus Christus, Wende der Welt: Grundfragen zur
Christologie* (Tübingen, J. C. B. Mohr [Paul Siebeck], 1966), Chapters 10-13;
"Theologie und Geschichte," *ZThK*, Vol. 50 (1953), pp. 349-370.

tionship to God becomes concrete and visible: responsibility for the world and obedience to God are ultimately one and the same thing. In answering the question, "Who is God?", Dietrich Bonhoeffer wrote:

> Encounter with Jesus Christ. The experience that a transformation of all human life is given in the fact that "Jesus is there only for others." His "being there for others" is the experience of transcendence. It is only this "being there for others," maintained till death, that is the ground of his omnipotence, omniscience, and omnipresence. Faith is participation in this being of Jesus (incarnation, cross, and resurrection). Our relation to God is not a "religious" relationship to the highest, most powerful, and best Being imaginable . . . but our relation to God is a new life in "existence for others," through participation in the being of Jesus. The transcendental is not infinite and unattainable tasks, but the neighbour who is within reach in any given situation. God in human form . . . "the man for others," and therefore the Crucified, the man who lives out of the transcendent.[117]

III. *Obedience to the Will of God: Son of God.* Just as correspondence to the word of God is the secret of Jesus' faithful speech, so obedience to the will of God is the foundation of his freedom and responsibility. The dynamic relations by which Jesus' life was lived—his presence to himself, to the world, and to God—are not really separable. In him they cohere in a unified life-act in a fashion we can only dimly imagine, not describe. He has his identity as the one who is fully present to God, fully responsible for the world, and fully at one with himself: he *is* this man; such a one is the Christ, the son of God, the word of God. On the one hand the relation with God is the fundamental, definitive relation of his life; on the other hand this relation cannot be grasped abstractly but is visible only in the social and personal structures of his existence.[118]

117. Dietrich Bonhoeffer, *Letters and Papers from Prison*, rev. ed., Eberhard Bethge, ed.; trans. by R. H. Fuller, Frank Clarke, *et al.* (New York, The Macmillan Co., 1967), p. 202.

118. On the dialectic between "the man for other men" and "the man for God," see *CD*, Vol. III/2, Secs. 44.1, 45.1; Claude Welch, *The Reality of the Church* (New York, Charles Scribner's Sons, 1958), pp. 89-112; and George Hendry, *op. cit.*, pp. 100-102.

Jesus' obedience to God may be characterized by the term
"sonship." As the one fully obedient and responsive to the
will of God, he was *the* son of God, the true and faithful son.
Here the discussion of Jesus' sonship by Wolfhart Pannenberg and Emanuel Hirsch may be mentioned. The concept
"son of God" does not, according to them, refer to a pre-
existent divine *persona*, which enters into hypostatic union
with the human nature of Jesus. Rather it refers to the
humanity of Jesus as it is completed in perfect obedience
and self-dedication *(Selbsthingabe)* to the Father. The
"divinity" of Jesus is not a divine hypostasis but his filial
humanity. In his obedience and self-dedication, Jesus is
related to God *the Father*, not to the Second Person of the
Trinity (the "Son of God"). It is precisely in his relationship
to the Father that he *becomes* the son of God—the one in
whom the fullness of divinity dwells, the one to whom God
is fully present. Also germane to this point is Karl Rahner's
analysis of the *potentia oboedientialis* as the quintessence of
man's natural existential or finite spirituality, by means of
which he possesses the possibility for transcendental relationship with God (a potency actualized only by God's free
self-communication in word).[119] We may think of obedient
sonship as possessing both passive and active qualities. On
the one hand, it contains the element of surrender or self-
negation, of dedication or devotion *(Hingabe)*, which is so
important for Pannenberg. On the other hand, it involves
the assumption of responsibility for the world, living the life
of obedience on behalf of other men and in their place. The
definitive relation with God must be construed in positive as
well as negative terms.

According to Paul, Jesus' relation of sonship with the
Father is the consequence of a history; a history of humiliation and obedience unto death (ὑπήκοος μέχρι θανάτου), and of
resurrection from the dead (Phil. 2:8-9; Rom. 1:4; 5:19).

119. *JGaM*, pp. 181-182, 323, 334-337, 339-340, 342-343; Emanuel Hirsch,
Jesus Christus der Herr, 2nd ed. (Göttingen, Vandenhoeck & Ruprecht, 1929),
pp. 73-91; Karl Rahner, *ThI*, Vol. I, pp. 171, 183-184; Vol. IV, pp. 108-110;
Vol. V, p. 206.

At the same time, Paul stresses the originality of this sonship
—in the twofold sense of its perfection and its character as
grace—by occasional use of the mythological concept of
pre-existence.[120] In Romans 8 and Gal. 4:4, Paul uses the
language of pre-existence in referring to God's "sending his
own son" in order to redeem mankind from sin, flesh, and
the law. However, from these passages as well as from
Rom. 1:4, it is clear that it is not the concept of pre-existence
as such that is important for Paul, but rather what is
accomplished by sonship: obedience, fulfillment of the just
requirement of the law, conformity to the will of God,
entrance into an "inheritance"—an inheritance of the world,
for which men must assume responsibility as mature sons.
The latter theme, developed in Gal. 4:1-9 and Rom. 8:16-17,
is central to Friedrich Gogarten's discussion of Jesus' sonship. In Gal. 4:4, Paul writes: "But when the time had fully
come, God sent forth his son, born of woman, born under
the law, to redeem those who were under the law, so that we
might receive adoption as sons." This passage, says Gogarten,
reveals the extent to which Paul's concept of "sonship" has
been freed of mythological and "religious" connotations.
When Paul says "born of woman," this means, according to
biblical usage, that this son is a man, not a god disguised
in the flesh. "Born under the law" refers to the immaturity
of the established world, which the son takes upon himself
but to which he does not belong. "That we might receive
adoption as sons" describes the purpose of redemption in
non-cultic imagery. Redemption involves entering into the
state of mature sonship, which has two aspects: knowledge
of God as the one God and Father, rather than enslavement
to the elemental spirits of the universe (Gal. 4:8-9); and

120. Hirsch, *Jesus Christus der Herr,* pp. 83-86. F. C. Baur already
pointed out in his Pauline studies that the Apostle's intention was not to
describe Jesus as a pre-existent divine being but rather to insist that his
authentic humanity—his existence κατὰ πνεῦμα, or his true sonship to God—
was not to be regarded as a human accomplishment but as a divine gift, the
divine act of reconciliation. *Paulus, der Apostel Jesu Christi,* 2nd ed. (Leipzig,
Fues's Verlag, 1866-1867), Vol. II, pp. 271, 273-274; and *Vorlesungen über
neutestamentliche Theologie* (Leipzig, Fues's Verlag, 1864), pp. 188-189.
On the Johannine concept of the pre-existence of the word, see above, p. 80.

knowledge of the world as inheritance, as the heritage for
which man must assume responsibility (Rom. 8:16-17; Gal.
4:1-7). The world is no longer to be venerated in mythological fashion as something divine. Rather, since it is the
creation of God, man is to assume responsibility for it in
historical fashion. To be a son of God means to be *obedient*
to *God* and to assume *responsibility* for the *world*, which is
God's creation and man's inheritance. Jesus *maintains* his
sonship both to God and to the world as inheritance, whereas
we have *forfeited* ours. Forfeited sonship or disobedience
(cf. Eph. 2:2; 5:6: "sons of disobedience") becomes fear,
slavery, sin, and curse, the perversion of man's right relation
with the world. Men can forfeit their sonship either by
attempting to usurp the world (rather than accepting it as
inheritance), or by abandoning responsibility for it. Jesus'
maintenance and fulfillment of sonship brings him finally to
the cross, where in the final act of obedience he takes upon
himself the sin and curse of the world.[121]

b. *The Cross as Word-Event*

I. *Crux sola nostra theologia?* It is perhaps to be expected
that a christology oriented to the experience of the death
or absence of God should focus its attention upon the death
of Jesus on the cross, which, after all, is the original context
for *theological* talk about the death of God.[122] In fact,
christology after the death of God has tended to be either
"Jesusology" or *christologia crucis*. According to Jürgen
Moltmann, the cross is the *krisis* that divides Jesus and the
community, the past and the future, the old world and the
new. It is the prism through which our knowledge of
the earthly ministry and message of Jesus is refracted and by
which alone it must be interpreted. Thus "Jesus the Crucified" becomes the central, all-embracing theme of chris-

121. Friedrich Gogarten, "Theologie und Geschichte," *ZThK*, Vol. 50 (1953),
pp. 349-362, 366-367; *Jesus Christus, Wende der Welt*, pp. 52-53, 65-67,
75-80, 110-111, 122-123.
122. See Eberhard Jüngel, "Vom Tod des lebendigen Gottes," *ZThK*, Vol. 65
(1968), pp. 95-99.

tology.[123] This theme has been forcefully propounded of
late by Ernst Käsemann in polemicizing against what he
regards as a new Protestant "enthusiasm," which champions
a theology of resurrection and of saving deeds, and which
has thus lost sight of the critical heart of Protestantism.
Against this he proposes to advance the Reformation
particula exclusiva: we must say not only *sola Christus* and
sola fide, but also *crux sola nostra theologia.* The basis for
such a theology is put forward by Paul, and nowhere more
clearly than in the first two chapters of I Corinthians. Here
Paul argues that the cross cannot be understood as one
theologumenon among others, which can be levelled into a
chain of saving events, but rather as the center and horizon
of theology as a whole, in a sense the only theme of
Christian theology (and also, of course, the only theme of
christology). "I decided to know nothing among you except
Jesus Christ and him crucified" (I Cor. 2:2), writes Paul;
"we preach Christ crucified, a stumbling-block to Jews and
folly to Gentiles" (I Cor. 1:23).[124]

In the stark form advanced by Käsemann and Moltmann,
I am unable to accept this thesis. It would be correct to
say that "the cross alone is our theology" only if the cross
were understood in the closest connection both to what
precedes it and to what follows it, i.e., to the earthly ministry
of Jesus on the one hand and to the resurrection and present
agency of Christ on the other. The second connection is
clearly enough recognized by Paul himself (cf. Rom. 4:25;
I Cor. 15:3-4), although the first admittedly remains problematic on strictly Pauline grounds. Nevertheless, we must
insist that the cross can be rightly interpreted only in the
context of the total event of Jesus as the word of faith, i.e.,
in the context of all that he said and did before his death.

123. Jürgen Moltmann, Lectures on Christology, University of Tübingen,
Winter Semester, 1968-69.
124. Ernst Käsemann, "Die Heilsbedeutung des Todes Jesu nach Paulus,"
Zur Bedeutung des Todes Jesu: Exegetische Beiträge, Fritz Viering, ed.
(Gütersloh, Gütersloher Verlagshaus Gerd Mohn, 1967), pp. 14, 23-26; *Jesus
Means Freedom,* Chapter 3.

The saving significance of this *particular* death can be understood only from the significance of the particular life that preceded it, of which it is the final act. The cross is *the* word-event of faith par excellence. For this reason, the so-called return to the historical Jesus is of the essence of the interpretation of the death of Jesus. The alternative is to regard the cross as an abstract, ahistorical, isolated act of God, the exclusive focus of the salvation-event. Behind this position lurks either a metaphysical dualism or a pantheistic acosmism, both of which for different reasons regard the relation between God and the world in such fashion that God can act in the world only by negating it and being negated by it. God and the world intersect—on the cross. Everything else is a matter of relative indifference. When this position is pursued to the limit, the cross becomes an abstract principle of negativity (as in Hegel's philosophy), divorced from the concrete life that comes to final focus there. Far from freeing christology from a metaphysic, as Martin Kähler thought, this sort of *theologia crucis* is likely to fall into one, for death is an historical, as distinguished from a purely philosophical, theme only when it is viewed as the death of a specific human being who reaches his fulfillment there.

Specific aspects of the proclamation and conduct of Jesus are implied and reflected in the interpretation of his death by the early kerygma. Corresponding to the death of Jesus for sinners (Rom. 5:6 ff.) is the fact that the earthly Jesus was a friend of tax collectors and sinners (Matt. 11:19), a solidarity he maintained unto death. His overcoming of the demonic powers by his death (Gal. 1:4, etc.) is paralleled by his earthly struggle against these powers. That Jesus' death "brings near" those who are alien, far off, and godless (Eph. 2:12-13), is comparable with the fact that Jesus himself did not respect the limits of piety. That his death is understood as the "end of the law" (Rom. 10:4) reminds us of his rejection of cultic and ceremonial laws. Finally, as we have already observed, the central conception of the death of Jesus as "substitution" is anticipated by the way he exercised compassion "on behalf of" sinners, the downtrodden, "the people" in general, whom he brought into the presence of God by his word and deed.[125]

Furthermore, it can be shown that Jesus' death did not rest on a tragic accident or misunderstanding but was consonant with the content and claim of his word and deed. Passages such as Mk. 3:6; 11:18; 12:12; and parallels, show that Jesus spoke a word which evoked an opposition unto death. This is one of the senses in which his death can be described as a "word-event." Especially instructive is the conclusion to the parable of the wicked tenants: "The scribes and the chief priests tried to lay hands on him at that very hour, but they feared the people; for they perceived that he had told this parable against them" (Lk. 20:19; Mk. 12:12). Passages such as these provide historically more authentic grounds for understanding the reasons behind Jesus' death than the report of the trial (Mk. 14:53-72 par.), which was shaped by early Christian confession of Jesus as the Messiah. Jesus was not condemned and put to death because of an alleged messianic claim, but because his preaching and conduct brought him into irreconcilable conflict with established religious piety and the law, causing the Jewish authorities to seek his destruction by persuading the Romans that he was politically dangerous. Hence it is no accident that he died "outside the camp" (Heb. 13:12-13) and "was reckoned with transgressors" (Lk. 22:37).[126]

125. Wolfgang Schrage, "Das Verständnis des Todes Jesu Christi im Neuen Testament," *Das Kreuz Jesu Christi als Grund des Heils,* Fritz Viering, ed. (Gütersloh, Gütersloher Verlagshaus Gerd Mohn, 1967), pp. 53-54. On the last point in particular, Schrage cites Ernst Fuchs, *Zur Frage nach dem historischen Jesus,* 2nd ed. (Tübingen, J. C. B. Mohr [Paul Siebeck], 1965), p. 156; Willi Marxsen, "Erwägungen zum Problem des verkündigten Kreuzes," *Neutestamentliche Studien,* Vol. 8 (1961/62), pp. 209-212; and H. D. Knigge, "Erlösung durch Jesu Tod," *Una Sancta,* Vol. 18 (1963), p. 164.
126. Schrage, "Das Verständnis des Todes Jesu Christi," *op. cit.,* pp. 55-57. Hans Conzelmann believes it likely that the title on the cross, "The King of the Jews," was introduced by the Evangelists, since the central motif of their entire portrayal of the crucifixion is Jesus' implicit kingship. See "Historie und Theologie in den synoptischen Passionsberichten," *Zur Bedeutung des Todes Jesus: Exegetische Beiträge,* Fritz Viering, ed. (Gütersloh, Gütersloher Verlagshaus Gerd Mohn, 1967), p. 48.

There is a second reason for resisting the reduction of christology to a *christologia crucis*. We simply do not possess much historically verifiable information about the details of the crucifixion of Jesus. The historical kernel is only that Jesus was crucified, from which it may be concluded that he was imprisoned and put to trial, indeed by the Romans, for crucifixion is a Roman, not a Jewish, form of execution. Almost everything else in the course of events that make up the passion narratives is subject to dispute and reflects intensive theological interpretation by the Evangelists. Conzelmann points out that for large parts of the story no Christian eyewitnesses were on hand, e.g., the closed trials before the Sanhedrin and before Pilate. Even for those scenes where there *could* have been eyewitnesses, no eyewitness reports are given: the Last Supper, the imprisonment of Jesus, the denial of Peter, every detail of the crucifixion scene. "The entire course of the passion story, as the Evangelists portray it, can very likely not be regarded as historical." The fragments of pre-Markan materials that are still visible (e.g., 14:1-2, 10-11) offer no theological interpretation of the passion. This interpretation is provided only by the post-Easter confession that Jesus was crucified and risen as the Messiah (I Cor. 15:3 ff.; Rom. 14:9), a confession that lies at the basis of the present form of the passion narrative.[127] For this reason, Martin Kähler's well-known statement that the Gospels are "passion narratives with extended introductions"[128] is incorrect historically and highly improbable theologically. It is simply not the case that the Gospels reach their climax as "history" in the passion narratives, that here we find the highest degree of concreteness and specificity, that here Jesus' identity is most sharply

127. Conzelmann, "Historie und Theologie in den synoptischen Passions-berichten," *op. cit.*, pp. 37-40.
128. Martin Kähler, *The So-Called Historical Jesus and the Historic, Biblical Christ*, trans. by Carl Braaten (Philadelphia: Fortress Press), p. 80. See Conzelmann, *op. cit.*, p. 39; and Schrage, *op. cit.*, p. 65. Willi Marxsen reformulates Kähler's statement to say that the Gospels are "Easter stories with a detailed introduction"—which seems to me equally unsupportable. *AJN*, p. 166 (Eng. trans., p. 163).

focused. To the contrary, the whole story of Jesus' death remains—with one exception—highly stylized: it is the death of the suffering, righteous, and innocent Messiah, who will be vindicated by the hand of God.[129] Furthermore, the cross tends to dominate the narrative as a whole only in Mark, where it serves as the clue to the "messianic secret." But even for Mark the passion of Jesus cannot be made intelligible apart from the concrete life that preceded it.

In short, a christology must have a broader base, both historically and theologically, than the story of Jesus' death. And conversely, the significance of the cross can be grasped only from the broader context of tradition to which it belongs. With this in mind, I shall consider the death of Jesus in two contexts or interpretive spheres: as the completion of his historical word and deed, and in relation to his resurrection and present agency.

II. *Jesus' Death on the Cross as Word-Event.* The death of Jesus is the completion and integration of the modes of conduct by which he enacted the word of faith. In the crucifixion, freedom, responsibility, and obedience come to fullest expression. I shall consider these three themes separately by looking at several aspects of Paul's theology of the cross. Then I shall ask what it means to say that the cross is a word-event.

(1) Liberation is one of the central themes in Paul's interpretation of the cross. Although he was aware of the motif of redemption from slavery, he did not use the term "redemption" thematically.[130] Rather he speaks of "liberation" or "freedom" (ἐλευθερία), of being "set free" (ἐλευθεροῦν): "the creation itself will be set free from its bondage to decay and obtain the glorious liberty of the children of God" (Rom. 8:21). Such liberation means freedom from sin and

---

129. For the opposite judgment, see Hans W. Frei, "Theological Reflections on the Gospel Accounts of Jesus' Death and Resurrection," *The Christian Scholar*, Vol. 49 (1966), pp. 263-306, esp. pp. 292 ff.

130. Käsemann, "Die Heilsbedeutung des Todes Jesu nach Paulus," *op. cit.*, p. 22. See also Schrage, "Das Verständnis des Todes Jesu Christi," *op. cit.*, p. 85. Paul does use the verb ἐξαγοράζειν ("to redeem," "to purchase one's freedom") twice in Gal. 3:13; 4:5. See also 1 Cor. 6:20; 7:23.

death, from flesh and the law, from the enslaving powers of
the world (see Rom. 6:18; 8:2; I Cor. 7:21-23; II Cor. 3:17;
Gal. 2:4; 5:1; 5:13). This freedom may be viewed as the
perpetuation of Jesus' "radical freedom" in the world, which
becomes the property of all men through the freedom of his
death, by which the enslaving powers are permanently
conquered and the established orders are broken. For
Jesus' death resulted, as we have seen, from the revolutionary
freedom with which he questioned and opposed these
orders. The cross is his act of freedom par excellence. It is
also the mediating link between the freedom of the "radical
man" and the "glorious liberty of the children of God."

(2) The fulfillment of Jesus' responsibility for the world
in his death is envisioned by the oldest and broadest of
soteriological categories, the *pro nobis* formula, which has
its roots in the Jewish expiation theology. It is preserved
in I Cor. 15:3 ("Christ died *for our sins* in accordance with
the scriptures"), Rom. 5:8 ("God shows his love for us in
that while we were yet sinners Christ died for us [$\dot{v}\pi\grave{\epsilon}\rho$
$\dot{\eta}\mu\hat{\omega}\nu$]"), and other places. Although Paul was familiar with
the tradition of blood sacrifice (Rom. 3:24-25; I Cor. 5:7;
10:16 ff.; 11:25), the ideas of sacrifice and substitutionary
punishment no longer had any essential significance for him,
according to Käsemann. Rather Jesus' death was a matter
of his dedication to God and of the self-dedication of his
love (Gal. 1:4; 2:20; II Cor. 5:14-15). ". . . love for Paul
means the demonstration of existence for others, concretely
and especially emphatic, particularly in death. The Apostle
gives a disinctive and for his theology important nuance to
the formula when he speaks of death for the ungodly and
for sinners in Rom. 5:6 ff., for the Christian brother in
Rom. 14:15, and for all men in II Cor. 5:14. The 'for us'
remains always the central motif. It encompasses the two
meanings, 'for our benefit' and 'in our place,' and the recipro-
cating interpretations characterize its intensity and range."[131]

131. Käsemann, *op. cit.*, pp. 18, 21; see also Schrage, *op. cit.*, pp. 77-80.

This interpretation of the death of Jesus is prefigured in the Evangelists' characterization of his action as "compassionate" and in Jesus' own use of the term σπλαγχνίζεσθαι in certain of his parables. Hence we may say that the cross is his act of responsibility par excellence, and also the mediating link between the compassion of the "man for other men" and the "greatest" of Christian virtues—love (I Cor. 13).

(3) Jesus' death is his final act of obedience, whereby he acknowledges the rule of God and establishes the right relationship between God and man—the relationship of Creator and creature, of Father and son, of word of God and word of faith. Significantly, Käsemann regards obedience as the central motif in Paul's theology of the cross. Paul designates the dying Jesus as the obedient one (Rom. 5:12-19; cf. Phil. 2:8), because by his death he restores men to the righteousness of true obedience—an obedience that acknowledges God to be Creator and man to be creature, a creature who renounces all pious and rebellious attempts at self-salvation. Obedience is the sign of regained creature-hood, of regained humanity.[132] In Rom. 5:18-19, where the antithesis between Adam and Christ is brought to a climax, the association of "obedience," "righteousness," and "life" becomes especially clear: "Then as one man's trespass led to condemnation for all men, so one man's act of righteousness [δικαιώματος] leads to righteousness of life [δικαίωσιν ζωῆς] for all men. For as by one man's disobedience many were made sinners, so by one man's obedience [ὑπακοῆς] many will be made righteous." Obedience means justification in the sight of God, which is the basis of new life; life beyond the death brought by sin and disobedience. Jesus' life as the faithful one is brought to completion by his obedience unto death.

But may the cross in fact be considered Jesus' final act of obedience, the fullest expression of his faith? Undoubtedly, both the literary and historical climax of the passion narrative is found in Jesus' cry of God-forsakenness from the cross:

132. Käsemann, *op. cit.*, p. 20; see also Schrage, *op. cit.*, p. 81.

"My God, my God, why hast thou forsaken me?" (Matt.
27:46; Mk. 15:34; cf. Ps. 22:1). If any detail of the crucifixion story is historically authentic, this is probably it. Ellen
Flesseman-van Leer has made a study of the Old Testament
citations in the passion story.[133] The basic purpose of intro-
ducing these citations, she concludes, was to remove the
contingent and scandalous elements from the passion of
Jesus, to show that Jesus' humiliating death was not astonish-
ing because the righteous of the Old Testament had always
suffered, and to insure that God would in the end vindicate
him. This is especially the case with the Psalms cited in
the crucifixion scene (Pss. 22, 31, 69). All of these Psalms
are jeremiads, and their laments are so stereotyped that
the innocent, suffering, righteous one almost attains a suprapersonal form.[134] But the citation from Ps. 22:1 is another
matter. With its expression of deep anguish and God-
forsakenness, it scarcely serves the stereotyped image of the
suprapersonal innocent sufferer. To the contrary, it is the
deepest expression of Jesus' humanity and finitude; it
appears to be a cry of despair rather than of faith. For this
reason, it is difficult to imagine that this last word of Jesus
was freely composed by the Evangelists. Indeed, the texts
show that it was received only with difficulty by the tradition.[135] Furthermore, the word is quoted first in Aramaic,
which for the Synoptic tradition represents an effort to
preserve the authority and authenticity of Jesus' sayings.[136]
Miss Flesseman-van Leer concludes that the cry of God-
forsakenness is probably the authentic historical kernel on

133. "Die Interpretation der Passionsgeschichte vom Alten Testament aus,"
Zur Bedeutung des Todes Jesu: Exegetische Beiträge, Fritz Viering, ed.
(Gütersloh, Gütersloher Verlagshaus Gerd Mohn, 1967), pp. 79-95.

134. *Ibid.*, pp. 82, 91-92, 96.

135. The D text for Mk. 15:34 and Matt. 27:46 reads *zaphthani* rather than
sabachthani in the Aramaic, which in Mark (not Matthew) is translated into
Greek by ὠνειδίσας ("shamed") rather than ἐγκατέλιπές ("forsaken"). John
does not have this word at all, and Lk. 23:46 replaces it with Ps. 31:5
("Father, into thy hands I commit my spirit!").

136. *TDNT*, Vol. IV, p. 107.

the basis of which the Evangelists introduced other citations from Ps. 22 to designate individual stages of the crucifixion scene.[137]

But what is to be made of this final cry of anguish and forsakenness? Not only is it most likely historically authentic, but also it sums up the entire crucifixion event. It gives expression to the agony, despair, estrangement, isolation of death. It is the quintessence of the event of death itself, in so far as death is an experience undergone by man. For this reason the cross may be considered a *word*-event; for death becomes a *human* experience when it is brought to expression and accomplished by words. It is perhaps not insignificant that the only factual detail of the trial and execution about which we can be reasonably certain is Jesus' final cry of God-forsakenness, his death-cry. Yet it must now be acknowledged that this cry of forsakenness is a word of despair, not of faith, and that despair or hopelessness before God is an act of *sin*. By what right, then, can I propose that the cross is *the* word-event of faith? The answer can only be understood paradoxically. Jesus' final act of obedience is his identification with sin and death, which characterize the human condition in its state of broken presence. His obedience is an "obedience unto death, even death on a cross" (Phil. 2:8). We could also write: "obedience unto sin and death," for sin and death are causally related by Paul. Death is the consequence of and punishment for sin: "the wages of sin is death" (Rom. 6:23); "the sting of death is sin" (I Cor. 15:56).[138] Here it must be understood that Paul distinguishes death proper ($\theta\acute{a}\nu\alpha\tau o\varsigma$) from mere mortality ($\theta\nu\eta\tau\acute{o}\varsigma$), which has not yet acquired

---

137. "Die Interpretation der Passionsgeschichte," *op. cit.*, pp. 92-93. Matt. 27:35 par. = Ps. 22:18; Matt. 27:39 par. = Ps. 22:7-8; Matt. 27:43 = Ps. 22:22-24.

138. Bultmann, *TDNT*, Vol. III, p. 15. Other Pauline texts cited by Bultmann in which sin and death are connected include Rom. 1:32; 6:16, 21; 7:5; 8:6, 13. Cf. also James 1:15; Gal. 6:7-8; II Cor. 7:10; Jn. 8:21, 24; I Jn. 5: 16-17; and various texts from the Apostolic Fathers. For the Old Testament, see Prov. 14:27; 21:6, etc.

the character of θάνατος. He says that death (θάνατος) came
into the world through Adam (I Cor. 15:22), through
Adam's sin (Rom. 5:12, 17-18). Θνητός he associates with
σάρξ or σῶμα (II Cor. 4:11; Rom. 6:12; 8:11). It refers to
man's transient, impermanent, perishable nature, which of
itself is not evil or sinful but which can become an occasion
for sin when man regards himself solely from the perspective
of σάρξ, living by its criteria, seeking to gain his life from it,
or denying and defying it in a bid for immortality.[139] When
that happens, θνητός becomes θάνατος, mortality becomes death
—a form of bondage, an enslaving power (cf. Rom. 8:2), a
wounding power: "the *sting* of death is sin." Some men die
without going through a phase of despair and defiance.
Jesus was apparently not among them. We do not need to
suppose that he did not experience other psychological
phases in the process of dying, such as acceptance and
affirmation. But if the cry of God-forsakenness is authentic
we know that he in fact experienced the despair of death,
and that in his case mortality became an occasion for sin.
Further confirmation for this interpretation may be found
in Rom. 8:3: "For God has done what the law, weakened
by the flesh, could not do: sending his own Son in the likeness of sinful flesh and for sin [ἐν ὁμοιώματι σαρκὸς ἁμαρτίας καὶ
περὶ ἁμαρτίας], he condemned sin in the flesh." Whether the
expressions "likeness of sinful flesh" and "for sin" are to be
taken to mean that in Paul's view Jesus *in fact* sinned, as
the mark of his identification with sinful humanity, has been
extensively debated.[140] The more radical interpretation is
arguable in light of the cry of God-forsakenness. He who
was without sin *became sin* for our sake.

Although despairing, Jesus' word from the cross is nevertheless a truthful word in the sense that it speaks the truth
about death. Because it is a truthful word, it is also a

139. *Ibid.*, Vol. III, pp. 15-16, 21-22.
140. Does Phil. 2:7 mean to imply that Jesus was not *in fact* man by the
expression, "born in the likeness of men"?

"faithful" word. Here despair and faith become inextricably intertwined, as they in fact so often are in human experience. Sometimes a despairing, hopeless cry can become an occasion for unconcealment rather than concealment. This is further evidence that faith is not something at our disposal. The point now is that Jesus was so fully identified with the human condition that he too experienced this intermixture of despair and faith, that in this one instance at least he was able to speak a truthful word only despairingly. The truth about death (both as mortality and as θάνατος) is that it *means* to be forsaken by God.[141] It is the most intensive experience of God's absence, the final evidence of man's own powerlessness and finitude. Jesus offers no palliatives for death in his cry from the cross. The power by which Jesus recognizes death for what it is and speaks a truthful word about it remains the power of God. For death is recognized to *be* death (and not some form of hidden deity) only when God is acknowledged to *be* God by the *power* of God. Death may be defined only vis-à-vis God, and God, vis-à-vis death. Thus, paradoxically, in his cry of God-forsakenness, Jesus' identity with God is maintained. It is God himself who speaks in the cry from the cross. Hegel has reminded us of this fact by adopting the words from the Lutheran passion hymn, "God himself is dead." Even heretics, he notes, can agree to the death of Jesus as a sensible human being. But Christians must confess that *God* has died, that God *himself* is dead, that therefore the negation of death has been taken up into the being of God

141. Cf. Gerhard von Rad, *Old Testament Theology*, Vol. I, trans. by D. M. G. Stalker (Edinburgh, Oliver and Boyd, 1962), pp. 388-389: ". . . death begins to become a reality at the point where Jahweh forsakes a man, where he is silent, i.e., at whatever point the life-relationship with Jahweh wears thin. . . . The decisive declaration about the state of the departed, which keeps recurring, is again theological: 'Thou rememberest them no more, and they are cut off from thy hand' (Ps. 88:6[5]). . . . The dead stood outside the cult and its sphere of life. Properly, this was what constituted their being dead. In death there is no proclamation and no praise (Ps. 88:12[11]; Is. 38:18); the dead stood outwith the action of Jahweh in history (Ps. 88:11[10]), and for Israel death's real bitterness lay in this exclusion."

himself.[142] *God* has died, we may suggest, in the sense that
he makes Jesus' cry of God-forsakenness to be his *own* word,
and that therefore not only Jesus but God himself participates in sin and death as human experiences. The only
answer to death is that God takes it upon himself, transforming its absence into the presence of his living being.
The cross reveals the radicalism of God's word-presence:
here he is present in the very depths of humanity, in the
shame of crucifixion,[143] in the anguish of death, in the
sinfulness of a despairing word. In the self-negation of his
obedience unto sin and death, Jesus' being as the word of
God is brought to completion.

III. *Resurrection of the Crucified.* Hegel notes that,
according to Christian faith, the course of affairs did not
come to a standstill with the death of God. Rather a
reversal ensues: "God maintains himself in this process, and
the latter is only the death of death. God rises again to life."
Hence this "deepest anguish" is at the same time the "highest
love."[144] Here we are brought to the second of the spheres
in which the death of Jesus is to be interpreted, his resurrection and present agency, and also to the brink of my
second main systematic thesis, "Jesus as Present." For
Jesus' resurrection and contemporary presence *mean* the
death of death, the negation of absence, the taking up of
death into the being of God, or of absence into the presence
of God. As Jüngel points out, the resurrection does not
mean that the son of God who suffered death now leaves
death behind and returns to life. For whoever leaves death
behind in order to return to life still has death before him.

142. Hegel, *Vorlesungen über die Philosophie der Religion*, Georg Lasson,
ed. (Hamburg, Verlag von Felix Meiner, 1966), Vol. II/2, pp. 157-158 (1821
MS.), 165 (1824 notes), 167 (1840 *Werke*), 172 (1827 notes). See Eberhard
Jüngel, "Vom Tod des lebendigen Gottes," *ZThK*, Vol. 65 (1968), pp. 98-99.

143. Crucifixion was a form of death reserved for criminals and sinners; hence
the significance of the phrase "even death on a cross" in Phil. 2:8. The Crucified One died "outside the camp" (Heb. 13:12-13) and "was reckoned with
transgressors" (Lk. 22:37).

144. Hegel, *Philosophie der Religion*, Vol. II/2, pp. 167 (1840 *Werke*); 158,
163 (1821 MS.); 166 (1824 notes).

Rather, the death of Jesus, in which God himself shares, means that death itself is altered. And this altering of death is the real meaning of the resurrection. At least this is Paul's understanding of the matter: "For we know that Christ being raised from the dead will never die again; death no longer has dominion over him. The death he died he died to sin, once for all, but the life he lives he lives to God" (Rom. 6:9-10). "Death is swallowed up in victory" (I Cor. 15:54); "what is mortal [is] swallowed up by life" (II Cor. 5:4). God puts death to death by taking it up into his own being, his own life. Thus death is deprived of its essential character as negativity, estrangement, *absence,* and is converted into *presence,* the presence of the living God. The death of death means the "essencing" (or "presencing") of absence. In Jüngel's words: "The essence deprived of death becomes essential in the being of the living God as allowance of an eternal place [cf. Jn. 14:3] for those who, existing ἐν Χριστῷ, are chosen and determined to be in God's eternal being."[145] The living presence of Jesus as risen from the dead means that the absence of death has been taken up into the presence of God once and for all. Jesus' present work of reconciliation involves making efficacious for us this presence, which came to definitive expression in his life and death.

I shall pursue this theme further in the next chapter. My concern now is to show the inseparable connection between crucifixion and resurrection. If Jesus' resurrection means the death of death, then it is precisely the Crucified who is risen. Käsemann and others have rightly warned against the dangers of a resurrection "enthusiasm" on the part of a new *theologia gloriae.* The reconciling agency of the risen Christ must not be allowed to imply an uncritical anthropology, a triumphalistic ecclesiology, or an apocalyptic

---

145. Jüngel, "Vom Tod des lebendigen Gottes," *ZThK,* Vol. 65 (1968), pp. 111, 113-114. Although Jüngel does not deal explicitly with the dialectic of absence and presence, it is implicit in his discussion of the essence of death as estrangement and the "essencing" of this estrangement by taking it up into the being of God.

eschatology. Such a temptation was clearly present in the
early community, as evidenced by some of the primitive
Christ-hymns that praise the lordship of the risen one but
overlook his suffering and death (I Tim. 3:16; Col. 1:15 ff.;
Phil. 2:6 ff.); by the early post-Easter apocalyptic that
regarded Easter as the immediate beginning of the general
resurrection of the dead (cf. Mk. 14:25); and by the Gnostic
Christianity that Paul encountered in Corinth.[146]

Paul attempted to guard against this danger by drawing
the themes of crucifixion and resurrection together into the
closest unity (cf. Rom. 4:25; 8:34; I Cor. 15:3-4; II Cor.
5:15; 13:4). He did this, not by subordinating the resurrection to the crucifixion or by making it a chapter in the
theology of the cross (as Käsemann sometimes argues), but
rather by insisting (as Käsemann also says) that the cross
remains the "signature of the risen one."[147] In Paul's view,
according to Käsemann, "Only the Crucified is risen, and
the dominion of the Risen One today extends only so far
as the Crucified is served."[148] This is undoubtedly correct
as far as it goes, although I should want to expand it to say:
only the earthly Jesus—the one identified by his words,
deeds, and death as *the* word of faith—is risen, and the
dominion of the Risen One today extends only so far as
these words and deeds and this death are brought to expression anew in the life of faith. Or as I have also expressed
it thematically: the one who *was* presence is *now* present.
His past presence determines the mode of his contemporary
presence, identifying the one who is now present, preventing
a resurrection theology from becoming a mere ideology of
presence. But his past presence is defined not merely by
his death but by his life *and* death, or better, by the death

146. Käsemann, "Die Heilsbedeutung des Todes Jesu nach Paulus," *op. cit.*,
pp. 23-24, 30-32; Schrage, "Das Verständnis des Todes Jesu Christi im Neuen
Testament," *op. cit.*, pp. 61-63, 68. See also Käsemann, *Jesus Means Freedom*,
Chapter 3.
147. Käsemann, "Die Heilsbedeutung des Todes Jesu nach Paulus," *op. cit.*,
pp. 31, 34; cf. pp. 24-26.
148. *Ibid.*, p. 32; cf. pp. 33-34.

of the one who lived the life of faith and spoke the word of faith. Such a one is now present. That this death and life remain the signature of the Risen One reminds us that his presence today does not signal the end of time and history. Now is the time of the work of reconciliation; it is not the time of the end, the final consummation. The future has come near; it is not yet fully at hand. Presence remains an eschatological reality.

PART THREE

JESUS AS PRESENT

5

RESURRECTION AND THE
PRACTICE OF PRESENCE

1. THE TIME OF THE RESURRECTION

a. Resurrection as Present Event

In Sec. 4, Chapter 2 I considered the connection between the two main themes of this essay, "Jesus as presence" and "Jesus as present," as these themes relate to the classical distinction between the person and the work of Christ. The doctrine of the person of Christ, I argued, directs its attention to the historical Jesus, the one who was presence in virtue of God's self-presentation in word. The doctrine of the work of Christ is properly concerned with the one who is present, the one who is risen from the dead and "comes to stand" in the world as the agent of reconciliation. "Resurrection" means the contemporary practice of presence, which is reconciliation, atonement, salvation. Thus the doctrine of the work of Christ and the doctrine of the resurrection are ultimately one and the same, a connection I shall attempt to bring out by defining the resurrection as *praxis*. It refers to an act of God by which Jesus "comes to stand" in the world as agent, mediating his presence to us and thus taking up death into life. The "place" where his agency is exercised is the community of the faithful as it engages in mission to the world. This mission is practiced by bringing to expression anew the faithful word and deed of Jesus. If we may hold to the *homological* structure of Christian speech and action, then we may say that Christian mission, when it is true and faithful, brings to speech the *same* word and the *same* deed that came to speech in Jesus, and that in this sense Jesus himself is present in the practice of mission, indeed as its chief agent or as "the head over all things" (Eph. 1:22). This homologous structure does not involve the mere repetition of what Jesus said and did; to the contrary, it requires ever-new forms of speech and action, many of which in our time will prove to be quite non-religious in character.[1]

In the present chapter, I shall attempt to lay out this thesis in some detail by directing attention to three sets of related questions: "When" does the resurrection take place? "What" does it entail? "How" (or in what modality) does it happen? The "when" question requires a discussion of the time of the resurrection (Sec. 1). The "what" question concerns the reality of the resurrection as *praxis* (Sec. 2). And the "how" question involves an analysis of the modes of Jesus' personal presence (Sec. 3). I shall conclude with some reflections on the eschatological character of presence (Sec. 4).

It may seem odd at first to raise a question about the "time" of the resurrection. Nevertheless, since in a sense the resurrection has to do with time, this is a crucial question, and the way we answer it will determine the way we also address its reality and modality. In popular piety and traditional theology, the resurrection has commonly been thought of (in Gerhard Koch's words) "as a miraculous episode that had its place in the brief interval between Good Friday and Pentecost, thereby serving merely as the introduction, visible in the historical sphere, to a lordship of Jesus in the heavenly

1. The relation between resurrection and presence is suggested by Bultmann. According to Paul, he says, the cross and the resurrection are not to be understood as mere facts of the past but only as they are "made present" or "contemporized" (*vergegenwärtigen*) for individuals in baptism and preaching. This permits a participation both in the crucifixion of Christ and in his resurrection, "which refers not to a single fact of the past but to the beginning of a new humanity." (*GuV*, Vol. I, pp. 288-289.) See also Gerhard Koch, who argues that the "resurrection" concerns "the question of the direct presence of that history which God allowed to happen as revelation in the person of Jesus of Nazareth." (*AJC*, p. 151.)

heights, withdrawn from the earth."[2] A distinction has
customarily been drawn between "resurrection" (the
"awakening" from death, the miraculous transition from
death to life), "ascension" (the removal from earth to
heaven), and "session" (Christ's present dominion at the
right hand of the Father). The resurrection is thus locatable
as a past episode in the chain of saving events. I propose
to dispense with this salvation-history schema and its neat
chronological distinctions—distinctions that rupture the
unity of temporal-historical experience, reduce the resurrection to the level of a miraculous fact, and elevate the present
dominion of Christ to an other-worldly realm.

I shall seek to understand the resurrection in the most
comprehensive sense possible, as an event embracing all
three modes of time but with a peculiar focus upon the
present: the *future promise* of new life is based on the *past
occurrence* of the raising of Jesus, the experiential basis of
which is the *present faith* of the community, its encounter
with him as the living agent of God who sends into mission.
This temporal dialectic marks the logic of Paul's argument
in I Cor. 15:8-28. His starting point or premiss is the
"appearance" of Jesus, which founds his apostolate (vss.
8-10), together with the preaching of the resurrection and
the faith of the Corinthian community (vss. 11, 12, 14, 17).
The appearance, the preaching, and the faith together constitute the experiential basis for affirming that "in fact Christ
has been raised from the dead" (vs. 20a). But what happened to Jesus is only the "first fruits" of what also is
promised for us, namely, that "in Christ all shall be made
alive," that the Son shall reign in the name of the Father,
that God shall be "all in all" (vss. 20b-28). The argument
moves from the present through the past to the future and
embraces the modes of time in a dynamic unity. The tense
of the verb used by Paul in vs. 20a is perfect: "Christ *has
been raised* [ἐγήγερται] from the dead." The same tense is

2. *AJC*, p. 154.

found in the ancient confession quoted by Paul in I Cor.
15:4 and elsewhere in the New Testament. Thus, according
to Christian faith, the resurrection is an event that occurs
in the perfect mode: it began in the past (the "raising up"
of Jesus), continues into the present (the agency of Jesus
who calls to faith and sends into mission), and bears consequences for or is open towards the future (new life in the
presence of God, by which death itself is overcome). In the
discussion to follow, I shall attempt to show the unfortunate
results of viewing the resurrection as *merely* a past occurrence (Pannenberg and his school), a present experience
(Bultmann, Koch, existentialist theology), or a future hope
(Moltmann, Käsemann). In my view, the present *is* the
epistemological and ontological fulcrum of the resurrection
event as a whole, as may be demonstrated by the New
Testament appearance traditions, but it would be a mistake
to try to reduce the resurrection *just* to the experience of
and participation in the present lordship of Jesus. For
that lordship has a past basis and contains a promise for
the future as well.

Nowhere in the New Testament does the resurrection of
Jesus from the dead come directly into view as a past
occurrence. There were no witnesses to it, and on principle
there could not have been any. It is always a matter of
encounters with Jesus after his death, from which the
inference could be drawn that something happened between
the crucifixion and these encounters. But no witnesses were
available to corroborate this inference, and no attempt was
made to describe what had happened.[3] The inference was
important as a formal matter, but no content could be given
it. The substance of the resurrection focuses on the present:
its primal datum is a coming-to-faith and being-sent-to-
mission on the basis of encounters with Jesus as the living,

3. Willi Marxsen, *AJN*, p. 70 (Eng. trans., pp. 66-67); and "Die Auferstehung
Jesu als historisches und als theologisches Problem," *Die Bedeutung der Aufer-
stehungsbotschaft für den Glauben an Jesus Christus*, Fritz Viering, ed.
(Gütersloh, Gütersloher Verlagshaus Gerd Mohn, 1966), pp. 17-18.

present agent of God, who is at work in the ministry of reconciliation. This datum was interpreted in various ways by the biblical writers and continues to be interpreted by theological reflection. The Evangelists, for example, interpreted it by constructing a "course of events," an Easter *narrative*, which explained the encounter with Jesus in story form (moving, in varying sequences, from the crucifixion to the empty tomb to the several appearances of Jesus to the disciples). Interpretation could also be provided by *concepts*: for the biblical writers, such concepts as "resurrection," "exaltation," "appearance," "newness of life"; for Schleiermacher, "living action," "spiritual presence," "redeeming agency"; for Marxsen, "furthering Jesus' cause," "sending into mission," to cite just a few examples.[4] In each of these instances, the reference is to an event that happens in the present experience of the interpreter, although the interpretation itself may point to the past or the future.

The association of the resurrection with the presence of Jesus, independent of a literal raising from the dead, has its modern theological roots in Schleiermacher. His entire discussion of the work of Christ (*Der christliche Glaube,* Secs. 100-105), and of "the manner in which fellowship with the perfection and blessedness of the Redeemer expresses itself in the individual soul" (Secs. 106-112), is in fact concerned with the presence of Christ, or with what he calls "the living action of Christ" (*die lebendige Einwirkung Christi*). *Einwirkung* has customarily been translated as "influence," which suggests that Christ's presence is simply a matter of historical "memory" or "influence," much like that of other important figures of the past. But this is not Schleiermacher's intention. For him, Christ's redeeming work is clearly the result of his own present personal agency. "The essence of redemption," he writes, is "that the God-consciousness already present in human nature . . . is stimulated and made dominant by the entrance and the living

4. *AJN*, pp. 129-131, 159-160 (Eng. trans., pp. 126-129, 155-156).

action of Christ," with the result that "the individual on whom this action is exercised attains a religious personality not his before."[5] The exercise of this action is the work of Christ himself in conjunction with the divine activity. Schleiermacher speaks, for example, of the "self-communication of Christ," the "action of Christ" in "producing faith within [man's] living receptivity," the "agency [*Wirksamkeit*] of Christ in conversion."[6] This living action of Christ in redemption is, in fact, the meaning of "resurrection," although Schleiermacher makes it clear at the outset of his discussion that this action is not dependent upon a literal doctrine of the raising of the body and ascension into heaven. ". . . Neither the spiritual presence [*die geistige Gegenwart*] which he promised nor all that he said about his enduring influence [*fortwährenden Einfluss*] upon those who remained behind is mediated through either of these two facts [resurrection and ascension]. This may well depend upon his sitting at the right hand of God—by which . . . we must understand simply the peculiar and incomparable dignity of Christ, raised above all conflict—but not upon a visible resurrection or ascension, since of course Christ could have been raised to glory even without these intermediate steps; and if so, it is impossible to see in what relation both these stand to the redeeming agency [*die erlösende Wirksamkeit*] of Christ."[7] In effect, Schleiermacher is replacing the ancient metaphor of "resurrection" with concepts such as "spiritual presence," "living action," "redeeming agency," to express and interpret the same fundamental reality.

That the event of resurrection has its focus in the present —the present work of Jesus, the coming-to-faith and being-sent-to-mission of the community on the basis of an encounter with the risen Jesus—may be observed from the

5. *ChrG*, Sec. 106.1, Redeker ed., Vol. II, p. 147; Eng. trans., p. 476.
6. *Ibid.*, Secs. 108.6, 109.3, Redeker ed., Vol. II, pp. 171, 177; Eng. trans., pp. 495, 500.
7. *Ibid.*, Sec. 99.1, Redeker ed., Vol. II, p. 82; Eng. tr., p. 418.

New Testament appearance traditions. It is commonly
argued that the appearances were limited to the immediate
disciples of Jesus, i.e., to those who had known Jesus as an
historical figure and were in a position to confirm the
identity of the one seen. As such, they are claimed to be a
strictly past event although enormously important, since
subsequent faith in the resurrection is based on the testimony
of those eyewitnesses to the Risen One and is maintained
by the slender thread of continuity with those original
witnesses. As such the appearances together with the empty
tomb become part of the past "proof" of the resurrection.[8]
In my judgment, this is a fundamental misinterpretation of
the appearances. To be sure, the first witnesses had known
Jesus as an historical figure and thus were able to confirm
from direct experience the identity of the historical and the
risen Lord. But we, too, are able to confirm this identity on
the basis of the Synoptic traditions concerning the historical
Jesus. His accessibility as a past figure is not restricted
merely to his immediate disciples. Hence chronological
priority did not give the first witnesses any special advan-
tage, nor did it mean they experienced something extraor-
dinary and singular in Easter.[9] They were not eyewitnesses
to some sort of unrepeatable, miraculous epiphany. As
Kierkegaard has pointed out, true contemporaneity is
not a function of temporal proximity. The best evidence for
this fact is Paul. That Jesus "appeared" also to him, who
had never known Jesus in the flesh and indeed had been the
arch-opponent of the first Christians, is proof that the "appearances" were not limited to the immediate disciples and
indeed were intended in principle to continue. Paul's statement in I Cor. 15:8, "Last of all [ἔσχατον δὲ πάντων], as to one
untimely born, he appeared also to me," need not be taken
to imply that after Paul there would be no more appear-

8. Gerhard Delling, "Die Bedeutung der Auferstehung Jesu für den Glauben
an Jesus Christus. Ein exegetischer Beitrag," *Die Bedeutung der Auferstehungsbotschaft für den Glauben an Jesus Christus*, Fritz Viering, ed. (Gütersloh, Gütersloher Verlagshaus Gerd Mohn, 1966), p. 89.
9. On this point, see *AJC*, pp. 195-196.

ances. Used adverbially, the neuter ἔσχατον simply means "finally" or "at last." More significantly, the adjective ἔσχατος means "last" not simply in a temporal sense but also in rank and succession: it can refer to those who are "the least," "the most insignificant."[10] Indeed, it is precisely this that Paul makes explicit in the next verse (vs. 9), "For I am the least [ἐλάχιστος] of the apostles, unfit to be called an apostle, because I persecuted the church of God." The word play between ἔσχατον and ἐλάχιστος suggests that Paul is the "last" to whom Jesus appeared in the sense of being "the least," the one most unworthy of being called to apostleship. Ἔσχατον has the double function of saying that "finally" Jesus has appeared even to Paul, who nevertheless is "the least" worthy of being brought to faith and sent to mission.

But what, in fact, does the concept of appearance refer to? "Appeared" is the customary translation of ὤφθη, the aorist passive of the verb ὁρᾶν ("to see"), used by Paul in I Cor. 15:5-8, and of Peter in Lk. 24:34. It also occurs several times in Acts (9:17; 13:31; 26:16). Marxsen has pointed out that several possibilites exist for translating this tense of the verb and that consequently its precise sense is uncertain: "he was seen," "he appeared," "he let himself be seen," "he showed himself." Or the passive voice can be viewed as an expression that avoids the divine name, in which case the meaning would be: "God has made visible."[11] It seems clear from the tradition that after Good Friday, Peter was the first who came to faith on the basis of a "seeing" of Jesus (Lk. 24:34; I Cor. 15:5), a "seeing" closely associated with his call to mission (Jn. 21:15-22), by which others were also to be brought to faith. Ὤφθη became associated in the tradition first with Peter, then with the twelve, then with other early Christians (I Cor. 15:5-7). By using the same term, Paul intended to place his own experience in the same series

---

10. W. F. Arndt and F. W. Gingrich, *A Greek-English Lexicon of the New Testament and Other Early Christian Literature* (Chicago, The University of Chicago Press, 1957), pp. 313-314.

11. *AJN*, p. 101 (Eng. trans., p. 98); "Die Auferstehung Jesu," *op. cit.*, pp. 20-21.

with Peter's.[12] But of course Peter tells us nothing about his own experience of "seeing." In fact, we cannot even be sure that Peter used this term himself, since it is predicated of him by the community. We can only interrogate Paul, not Peter.

But Paul himself does not say much about the actual experience of "seeing" either. In the Pauline corpus there are three brief references to it: Gal. 1:15-17; I Cor. 9:1-2; and I Cor. 15:8. The latter passage has already been discussed. In Gal. 1:15-17, the earliest of these references, Paul writes: "But then in his good pleasure God, who had set me apart from birth and called me through his grace, chose to reveal his Son to me and through me [ἀποκαλύψαι . . . ἐν ἐμοί], in order that I might proclaim him among the Gentiles. When that happened, without consulting any human being, without going up to Jerusalem to see those who were apostles before me, I went off at once to Arabia, and afterwards returned to Damascus" (New English Bible). From this passage we must conclude that Paul did not find it *necessary* to describe his Damascus experience as a "seeing." He can use another concept, whose root meaning is "to unveil something that previously was concealed" (ἀποκαλύπτειν = ἀπό, remove from + καλύπτειν, to conceal).[13] In Chapter 3 I argued that word, not sight, is the fundamental means of unconcealment: word unconceals by gathering into presence, by making present in a manifold sense. Hence it is not by accident that Paul associates this "revelation" of the Son with God's gracious *call* (καλέσας) to *proclamation* (εὐαγγελίζωμαι) among the Gentiles. Paul's Damascus experience is in fact an encounter with the Lord that takes the form of a revelatory word-event in the double sense of a *call* from God to

12. *AJN*, pp. 90-99 (Eng. trans., pp. 86-96); Emanuel Hirsch, *Jesus Christus der Herr*, 2nd ed. (Göttingen, Vandenhoeck & Ruprecht, 1929), pp. 38-41.

13. *AJN*, pp. 104-105 (Eng. trans., pp. 101-102). The concept of "revelation" is also associated with the resurrection in Jn. 21. But here the verb is φαίνειν, and the meaning is quite different, namely, to show oneself or to appear in a visible epiphany.

a ministry of *words*. It has nothing to do with a visible epiphany or a factual seeing of Jesus.

Paul uses the verb "to see" for the first time in I Cor. 9:1-2. "Am I not free? Am I not an apostle? Have I not seen [ἑώρακα, perfect tense] Jesus our Lord? Are not you my workmanship in the Lord? If to others I am not an apostle, at least I am to you; for you are the seal of my apostleship in the Lord." Here, as in I Cor. 15:8-9, Paul directly associates his "seeing" with his apostolate (which had been contested by some in Corinth). Here again there is no attempt to describe the "seeing." The "proof" of his apostolate is not to be found in a detailed description of the Damascus experience. Rather, it is proved by its effects in the community (*"you* are the seal of my apostleship in the Lord"). By means of Paul, the Corinthians have been brought to faith; their faith, their existence as a community, is the only proof of his apostolate, proof that Paul has been touched from without, that his Gospel is from God. In Willi Marxsen's words: "*Historically*, to be sure, Paul grounded his apostolate in the Damascus experience; *theologically*, however, he grounded it in the existence of the community."[14]

From these passages we may conclude that for Paul the event of the resurrection of Jesus is closely associated with his experience of being called to apostleship, an experience that involves both a coming-to-faith in Jesus on the basis of an encounter with him as living, present Lord, and a call to carry forward the work of Jesus, serving as the instrument of his present work of reconciliation. Paul can describe this experience of encounter and call by the concept of "seeing" or "appearance," but it is not necessary for him to do so. He can also describe it as a "revelation" of Christ "to me and through me," a concept closely associated with the function of word. That he uses the concept of "appearance" is probably attributable to the fact that it had already been associ-

14. *Ibid.*, p. 107; see pp. 105-107 (italics his), (Eng. trans., pp. 102-104).

ated by the tradition with the experience that he himself has now undergone, a tradition to which he attaches himself in I Cor. 15:8, even though his own experience was not mediated by the tradition but was direct, personal, and present (Gal. 1:15-17). In any case, "appearance" or "seeing" is a concept used to *interpret* the more fundamental experience of the presence of Jesus, an experience that involves both a coming-to-faith and a being-sent-to-mission. It is this present experience that is the fulcrum of the resurrection event as a whole.[15]

My conclusion may be further substantiated by a brief reference to the Emmaus tradition found in Lk. 24:13-35, which will be of concern in the analysis of the modes of Jesus' presence in Sec. 3 of this Chapter. Here it is sufficient to note that, by associating the appearance of Jesus with the celebration of the Eucharist (Lk. 24:30-31, 35) and indeed with the cult in general, Luke underscored the fact that the appearance of Jesus was fundamentally a *present* experience, indeed an experience of the *community* as it engaged in acts of worship, i.e., in acts of "service" both to God and to man. ". . . the coming of the Lord was expected and experienced at the Lord's Supper in the early Church."[16] The Emmaus tradition in Luke also associates the presence or "nearness" of Jesus not so much with a seeing as with a hearing and a doing. Although Jesus himself "drew near and went with" the disciples, nevertheless, "their eyes were kept from recognizing him" (Lk. 24:15-16). What ensued was an intensive *conversation* with the risen Lord, who was

---

15. I cannot agree with Marxsen's attempt to distinguish chronologically between "resurrection" (as a past event) and "appearance" (as a present experience). This distinction is based on the way he interprets the "resurrection" metaphor, in a backward-moving, personal direction rather than in a forward-moving, functional direction. It leads him to the rather peculiar statement that at Damascus Paul experienced Jesus as living, but that he did not experience the "resurrection." See *AJN*, pp. 109-110, 113 (Eng. trans., pp. 106-108, 110-111). Against this position I shall want to argue that the resurrection as ἀνάστασις, Jesus' "coming to stand" in the world, is identical with the experience described as "appearance."

16. L. Brun, *Die Auferstehung Christi in der urchristlichen Überlieferung* (1925), p. 74.1 (quoted by Bultmann, *SynT*, p. 291). See also, *AJC*, Chapters 12, 13.

finally revealed to the disciples in the *action* of the breaking of the bread (vss. 30-31, 35), an action associated both
with the word of blessing and all that he had said to them
on the way to Emmaus (vss. 30, 32).[17]

b. Resurrection as Past Occurrence

From the present encounter with Jesus it can and, indeed,
must be inferred that something happened in the past which
made this encounter possible. He who died on the cross is
now experienced to be alive and active. This experience
presupposes that he must have undergone a process of
transition from death to life, a transition in which death was
not merely left behind but fundamentally altered. According to the tradition, this transition occurred at a specific
point in time, namely, the third day after his burial. It is not
necessary, of course, to infer that the transition occurred all
at once at a specific moment in past time; it could just as
easily be imagined as a continuing event, an event in the
perfect mode, whose beginning lay in the past but whose
effects extend into the present. But it is at least necessary
to infer that something was initiated or set under way
during the interval between the crucifixion of Jesus and
his first "appearances" to the disciples. In this respect,
it is proper to speak of the resurrection of Jesus as a
past occurrence.

In so speaking, however, two qualifications are essential.
The first is that language about the resurrection as a past
occurrence has precisely and peculiarly the character of an
inference. It is an inference from a present experience to a
past occasion for this experience. The resurrection of Jesus
from the dead as a past occurrence comes into view only
as an inference, never as a directly experienced fact. There
were no witnesses to it, and the New Testament traditions
never make any attempt to describe what had happened.

17. For further discussion, see below, pp. 268-269.

The inference to the past occurrence of the resurrection was important as a formal matter, but no substance or content could be given to it, since witnesses were not available and what was inferred (the transition from death to life) transcends in principle "immanent human epistemological possibilities," as Marxsen puts it.[18] For these reasons, it is incorrect to regard the narratives concerning the "course of Easter events," and in particular the empty tomb traditions, as "historical" reports, i.e., as reports referring to a historically observable and describable event. These narratives are the result of an inference from a present experience and represent an effort to interpret this experience. They have their epistemological basis in the present rather than the past. They do not have the form of historical judgments. The resurrection is an *historical* event in its *present* modality, not as an historically observable past fact.

The second qualification is that, given the inferential structure of language about the resurrection as past occurrence, theological interest must not focus or come to rest at this point, but simply view it as one aspect in the total temporal complex of the resurrection event. Indeed, it is that aspect about which there is the least to say, given the purely formal character of the inference, and for that reason it is of least significance, theologically. Theological interest must focus on the present and the future, while acknowledging formally that the resurrection of Jesus is also a past occurrence. It is appropriate to speak metaphorically of the transition from death to life (which is the "something" inferred as a past— or at least a perfect—occurrence) only in the context of the future promise of life, as Paul makes clear in I Cor. 15:35-57 and Rom. 6:2-11. In other words, what happened to Jesus in the past can be conceived, if at all, only eschatologically.

Much of the recent interest in a theology of resurrection violates these two qualifications. Theological interest has been focused on the resurrection as past occurrence rather

18. *AJN*, p. 121 (Eng. trans., p. 118).

than present event or future promise. And the Easter narratives have been regarded as historical reports whose credibility can be confirmed or questioned. Representative of this tendency is the work by Wolfhart Pannenberg, Hans Grass, Ulrich Wilckens, K. H. Rengstorf, and others,[19] who stand in the tradition of the seminal essay by Hans von Campenhausen of 1952, "The Course of the Easter Events and the Empty Tomb."[20] The most articulate theological statement is provided by Pannenberg.

In reviewing his treatment of the resurrection in his christology, Pannenberg introduces a revealing distinction between the resurrection-*reality* and the resurrection-*event*.[21] The former refers to the reality or concept of new life after death, which has no spatio-temporal locus and can be described only metaphorically or symbolically. (For Pannenberg, the late-Jewish apocalyptic metaphor of "rising from sleep" is indispensable for conceptualizing this reality.) "But the *event* of the resurrection of Jesus, in contrast to the reality which results from this event, has to do with the transition from our earthly reality to that resurrection-reality which is no longer locatable in space." The *event* or

19. *JGaM*, Chapter 3; Hans Grass, *Ostergeschehen und Osterberichte*, 3rd ed. (Göttingen, Vandenhoeck & Ruprecht, 1964); Ulrich Wilckens, "Der Ursprung der Überlieferung der Erscheinungen des Auferstandenen," *Dogma und Denkstrukturen*, W. Joest and W. Pannenberg, ed. (Göttingen; Vandenhoeck & Ruprecht, 1963), pp. 56-95; and "Die Überlieferungsgeschichte der Auferstehung Jesu," *Die Bedeutung der Auferstehungsbotschaft für den Glauben an Jesus Christus*, Fritz Viering, ed. (Gütersloh, Gütersloher Verlagshaus Gerd Mohn, 1966), pp. 41-63; K. H. Rengstorf, *Die Auferstehung Jesu: Form, Art und Sinn der urchristlichen Osterbotschaft*, 4th ed. (Witten-Ruhr, Luther-Verlag, 1960). Also standing in this tradition are: Gerhard Delling, "Die Bedeutung der Auferstehung Jesu für den Glauben an Jesus Christus. Ein exegetischer Beitrag," in Viering ed., *op. cit.*, pp. 65-90; and Berthold Klappert, *Diskussion um Kreuz und Auferstehung* (Wuppertal, Aussaat Verlag, 1967). For an interesting comparison of the Pannenberg-Wilckens line of interpretation with that of Marxsen and Ebeling on the one hand and Bultmann and Barth on the other, see Hans-Georg Geyer, "Die Auferstehung Jesu Christi. Ein Überblick über die Diskussion in der gegenwärtigen Theologie," in *Die Bedeutung der Auferstehungsbotschaft für den Glauben an Jesus Christus*, pp. 91-117.

20. *Der Ablauf der Osterereignisse und das leere Grab*, 2nd ed. (Heidelberg, Carl Winter Universitätsverlag, 1958).

21. Wolfhart Pannenberg, "Response to the Discussion," *Theology as History*, J. M. Robinson and J. B. Cobb, Jr., ed. (New York, Harper & Row, 1967), p. 266, n. 76.

actuality of the resurrection, as distinguished from its concept, is a spatially-temporally locatable occurrence of transition from death to life. It took place, according to the
New Testament Easter traditions, at a specific time and place
in first-century Palestine. Pannenberg's theological interest
clearly focuses upon an analysis and corroboration of these
traditions as historically reliable reports. For the resurrection is interpreted, in the context of his christology as a
whole, as a past act of God that verifies Jesus' earthly work
and discloses his identity as the Son of God. If Jesus' resurrection can be "proved," so also can his divine sonship and
the redemptive action of God generally.[22] In fairness to
Pannenberg, it must be noted that he subsequently has
drawn a distinction between the probable certainty obtain-
able by historical study and the certainty of faith, which
involves total trust.[23] The implication would seem to be that
historical study of the resurrection traditions cannot of itself
legitimate faith in the resurrection. Furthermore, toward
the end of his chapter on the resurrection, Pannenberg makes
the following interesting statement:

> The ultimate divine confirmation of Jesus will take place only in the
> occurrence of his return. Only then will the revelation of God in Jesus
> become manifest in its ultimate, irresistible glory. When we speak
> today of God's revelation in Jesus and of his exaltation accomplished
> in the resurrection from the dead, our statements always contain a
> proleptic element. The fulfillment, which had begun for the disciples,
> which was almost in their grasp, in the appearances of the resurrected
> Lord, has become promise once again for us.[24]

This statement means that the resurrection as a past historical event, corroborative both of Jesus' pre-Easter claim
to authority and of our present confession of the Christ,
itself requires corroboration by a future event, which is
beyond the reach of empirical inspection, namely, the general resurrection from the dead. This whole intricate, inter-
locking network of corroborations, by which one moves from

22. *JGaM*, pp. 53-73.
23. Pannenberg, *Theology as History*, pp. 273-274.
24. *JGaM*, p. 108.

the future to a focal past event (the resurrection of Jesus), from it to other past events (e.g., his ministry), and thence to the present, could be avoided if Pannenberg abandoned the attempt to view the resurrection of Jesus as an event of the historical past on which our present faith in the divinity of Jesus is based.

Since I do not regard the Easter narratives to be historical judgments, but rather theological interpretations of the original experience of coming-to-faith in Jesus on the basis of an encounter with him as living agent, Pannenberg's attempt to treat them as historical reports about a past event strikes me as inappropriate in principle. The appearances, for example, he judges to be instances of extrasensory perception in which a reality objective to the perceivers themselves was encountered by a specific group of men in first century Palestine.[25] But as Marxsen has argued, the whole discussion of "objective" versus "subjective" visions is beside the point. Of course the disciples themselves believed that their faith was caused *extra se.* However, we do not have direct access to their experience but only to interpretations of it, for the most part by persons other than those who had the experience itself. Under these circumstances it is impossible to say whether the visions were objective *in fact,* as opposed to being *believed* to be objective by those who experienced them and by their followers.[26] In the second place, to speak of the appearances as "extrasensory perception" implies that they involved an objective mental *vision* or at least some sort of quasi-*sensory* perception. But I have already argued that the concept of "seeing" ($\overset{\text{\'{}}}{\omega}\phi\theta\eta$) cannot be taken as a literal description but as an *interpretation* of an experience which, for Paul at least (who is the only witness we can interrogate), did not involve a visible epiphany or a factual seeing of Jesus but rather a coming-to-faith and a being-sent-to-mission. Finally, I have

25. *Ibid.,* pp. 94-99.
26. *AJN,* pp. 116-119 (Eng. trans., pp. 113-117); "Die Auferstehung Jesu," *op. cit.,* pp. 22-23.

contended that the appearances do not belong to the past (constituting in part the transition from death to life that Pannenberg calls "resurrection-event"), but are interpretations of the ever-present experience of being caught up in the action of the living agent.

Pannenberg does not lay as much store in the empty tomb traditions as he does in the appearances, but, nevertheless, he believes their authenticity can be established by the fact that early Jewish polemic against the resurrection, of which traces are left in the Gospels (Matt. 27:62-66; 28:11-15), did not contest the claim that Jesus' grave had been opened and found empty, but argued rather that the corpse had been stolen.[27] However, it seems much more likely that these traces, which are found only in Matthew, are not early but quite late, representing Matthew's addition to the Easter narrative in order to counter Jewish polemic against Christians in Jerusalem during his own time, after the empty tomb stories were well-known. Besides, even if Pannenberg's argument was correct, it would only establish that the tomb was found empty, not how it got that way. It could be argued that the corpse was stolen (as the Jews later claimed), or that it was resuscitated and ascended from the tomb. The first argument seems much more plausible, but it could be verified with certainty only if the stolen corpse had actually been found. To maintain the second not only would demand a *sacrificium intellectus* but also would require the reality of the resurrection to be interpreted as the revivification of a corpse, the return to life of the same fleshly body, which is contrary not only to Paul's entire argument in I Cor. 15:35 ff., but also to Pannenberg's own intention.[28] Against this whole approach, the conclusion must be that the empty tomb traditions are not to be judged as historical reports but as later interpretations of the belief that Jesus was risen and at work in the world—interpretations, furthermore, that de-emphasize, or at least do not

27. *JGaM*, pp. 100-102.
28. *Ibid.*, pp. 75-76.

argue from, the emptiness of the tomb.[29] The antinomies
that arise in Pannenberg's treatment of the Easter narratives
as factually verifiable reports demonstrate the futility of
focusing theological interest upon the resurrection as an
occurrence in the historical past.

c. Resurrection as Future Promise

With Jürgen Moltmann's treatment of the resurrection in
Theology of Hope, we seem to find the diametrically opposite emphasis from that of Pannenberg: rather than focus-
sing theological interest on the past, Moltmann proposes to
direct it quite radically to the future. Against Pannenberg,
he does not believe that the *historisch,* i.e., the historical-
critical, approach to reality can be "expanded" sufficiently to
bring the reality of the resurrection into view. For the resurrection does not involve the merely analogically new but the
eschatologically new: it is a *novum ultimum,* a *nova creatio
ex nihilo,* which fundamentally shatters all *historisch* categories. The resurrection is a *geschichtlich,* not an *historisch*

29. On this point, see Marxsen, *AJN,* pp. 159-160, 164-165 (Eng. trans., pp.
155-156, 161-162); "Die Auferstehung Jesu," *op. cit.,* pp. 19-20; H.-W. Bartsch,
Das Auferstehungszeugnis: sein historisches und sein theologisches Problem
(Hamburg-Bergstedt, Herbert Reich Evangelischer Verlag, 1965), pp. 13-15,
26. It is important to note the sequence of events in Mk. 16:6-7 and Matt.
28:5-6. *First* the women are *told* by the angel that "he has risen"; *then* they
are shown the empty grave. This sequence would seem to indicate that the
emptiness of the grave is intended as an interpretation of the confession that
"Jesus has risen," not as the foundation of it. Finally the women are referred
to the forthcoming appearances in Galilee, which would suggest that the
tomb narratives were originally intended to or even as a prolegomenon to or even as a
substitute for (Bartsch) the appearance stories. In fact, in Matthew (as in
Jn. 20:14-18) an appearance occurs at the tomb itself (28:9-10). Regarding
the Lukan account (Lk. 24:1-12), Paul Schubert has shown that Luke
"noticeably diminishes the interest in the empty tomb as providing by itself
direct or even inferential evidence for the fact of Jesus' resurrection." This
is to be seen from the rhetorical question of the "two men," "Why do you
seek the living among the dead?" (24:5); Luke's interest in proof from
prophecy (rather than from historical evidence) (24:6, 7); the lack of belief
in the women's report on the part of the apostles (24:11); and the fact that
there was no appearance at the empty tomb (in contrast to Matt. 28:9-10)
(24:24). See Paul Schubert, "The Structure and Significance of Luke 24,"
*Neutestamentliche Studien für Rudolf Bultmann: Zu seinem siebzigsten
Geburtstag am 20. August 1954* (Beiheft 21 of *Zeitschrift für die neutestamentliche Wissenschaft;* 2nd ed.; Berlin, Alfred Töpelmann, 1957), pp.
167-168, 172.

reality. In Moltmann's theology, the terminological distinction between *historisch* and *geschichtlich* marks what we
might call an "horizontal" dualism. *Historisch* refers to
unredeemed past (and present) reality, or to what he has
described as the "history of death." *Geschichtlich* refers to
reality as it is drawn toward the future, the "new creation."
In order to be grasped at all, the resurrection requires a
new concept of history as *Geschichte*. Thus no efforts are
made by Moltmann to "corroborate" the resurrection by an
historisch examination of the accounts concerning the empty
tomb and the appearances. Rather than taking place "within"
history at all, the resurrection constitutes a new history,
establishing the *geschichtlich* character of all reality by
drawing it toward the future. "The raising of Christ is then
to be called 'historic' [*geschichtlich*], not because it took
place *in* the history to which other categories of some sort
provide a key, but it is to be called historic because, by pointing the way for future events, it *makes* history in which we
can and must live. It is historic, because it discloses an
eschatological future."[30] To be sure, the raising of Jesus is
an event that occurred in the past sometime between the
burial and his Easter appearances. Yet what actually happened "is left in the darkness of the still unknown and still
hidden God." It is covered by a term—"raising from the
dead"—"for which there is no basis in experience hitherto
and elsewhere," "no analogies in the history we know." "From
the two mutually radically contradictory experiences of the
cross and the appearances of Jesus, [the Easter narratives]
argue to the event in between as an eschatological event for
which the verifying analogy is as yet only in prospect and
is still to come."[31] Thus the resurrection of the dead is a
totally future, totally eschatological promise, which nevertheless has occurred once proleptically in the past. As such,
the "resurrection" becomes a supernatural or suprahistorical

30. Moltmann, *Theology of Hope* (New York, Harper & Row, 1967), pp. 76-
84, 172-182, 302; quotation from p. 181.
31. *Ibid.*, p. 197.

(supra-*historisch*) event, representing not a vertical super-naturalism but a supernaturalism of the future. In principle it is an event that cannot yet have happened; yet, miracu-lously, it has happened once.[32]

Moltmann has undoubtedly recognized an important di-mension of the total temporal structure of the resurrection event. We have already noted the logic of Paul's argument in I Cor. 15:8-28: the future promise of a general resurrec-tion from the dead is based on the accomplished fact that "Christ has been raised," the experiential basis of which is Paul's encounter with the living Lord, together with the existence of the community, its faith and its proclamation. The argument moves from the present through the past to the future. Hence Paul's basic orientation and direction throughout Chapter 15 is eschatological: his central propo-sition is that "in Christ all shall be made alive" (15:22). The *meaning* of the resurrection is that Christ "must reign" (until even death is brought under his dominion), in order that God may be "all in all" (15:25-26, 28). Furthermore, in the context of this future promise (and *only* in this con-text), it is appropriate to speak metaphorically of the transi-tion from death to life. Paul sets himself to this task in I Cor. 15:35-57. Here his reference is not to what happened to Jesus in the past (as though this were some sort of realis-tic account of the course of events between Good Friday and Easter Sunday), but rather to the future, to an eschatologi-cal reality. In this context Paul does not rely on the apoca-lyptic metaphor of "rising from sleep." Indeed, he shatters the basic apocalyptic image of the return to life of the same decayed fleshly body. He rejects as foolish the question, "How are the dead raised? With what kind of body do they come?" (15:35). He insists that we all shall be qualitatively "changed" (ἀλλαγησόμεθα): from mortality to immortality, from weakness to power, from a physical body to a "spiritual body" (σῶμα πνευματικόν) (15:42-44, 51-54). This "change"

32. *Ibid.*, pp. 226-227; and Pannenberg, *Theology as History*, p. 262.

involves not merely a return to the same old life, leaving death—temporarily at least—behind, but rather a qualitative transformation of death itself (15:54-55), and hence also of life.[33]

Although "resurrection" *means* the final dominion of Christ, and although it can be described only eschatologically, it must be recalled, nevertheless, that Paul's argument *begins* with the present—with his present experience of "seeing" Jesus, with the present faith of the Corinthian community (*"you* are the seal of my apostleship in the Lord") (I Cor. 9:1-2; 15:8-19). "If in this life we who are in Christ have *only* hope, we are of all men most to be pitied" (I Cor. 15:19). Unlike faith, hope cannot be construed by a *particula exclusiva:* we cannot live "by hope alone." Just this is the weakness in Moltmann's position.[34] By totally eschatologizing the resurrection, by focusing theological interest exclusively there, the present reality of the resurrection is made to evaporate; it becomes a supernatural magnitude, rupturing our present experience, requiring a new concept of "history." If there is "no basis in experience" for imagining the reality of resurrection, "no analogies in the history we know," then on what grounds can we possibly base an intelligible "hope" in it? If we do not *know* what we are hoping for, and if we do not have some grounds for believing that the hope is a *true* hope, then hope itself is senseless, or, in Paul's words, "to be pitied." One of the curious consequences of this position is that the time "in between" the past raising of Jesus and the future *nova creatio* becomes strangely insignificant and quiescent. It is a time of waiting, hoping, and resisting; waiting upon the eschatological act of God, to which man himself can contribute nothing.[35] It is not clear how this theological understanding of resurrection accords with Moltmann's equal insistence upon the involvement of Christian mission in the

33. I shall return to these themes below, pp. 256-257.
34. See especially *Theology of Hope,* p. 16.
35. *Ibid.,* pp. 82-83, 203, 221, 225, 227-229, 278, 300-302.

political, social, and economic revolutions of our time.[36]

Against this position, we must contend with Paul that the coming dominion of Christ is also a present reality, one which we can even now experience and in which we are called to participate by faith. In the next section, an effort will be made to concentrate attention upon this present reality without losing sight of its genuinely eschatological character. The resurrection of Jesus means the *presence* of that which is promised as our *future*, namely, the presence of God, the reconciliation of all things with him so that he (and not death) may be "all in all." Because it is the *future* that is present, it can be present only in unfulfilled, unfinished fashion. We are reminded of this by the fact that it is the *Crucified* who is risen. If we are able successfully to maintain the temporal dialectic of the resurrection (present —past—future), then perhaps we shall succeed in avoiding a resurrection "enthusiasm."

2. RESURRECTION AS PRAXIS

a. *Resurrection as an Action of Jesus*

"Resurrection" is to be construed as both an "objective" and a "subjective" reality. It refers to an action that involves

36. What I have described here is Moltmann's position up to 1964, the time of the writing of *Theology of Hope*. In recent essays and lectures, a shift in position is discernible. Although still holding to the suprahistorical character of the resurrection and insisting upon the qualitative newness of the future, Moltmann is now beginning to speak of the resurrection as a present as well as a future event. He says, for example, that the resurrection belongs to "the history of the practice of Christian freedom." According to Paul, the resurrection is a past event happening now (in the perfect tense), opening the present and freeing the future. The resurrection as an eschatological reality is now present in terms of the dialectic of faith in unfaith (constituting a new community), of love in estrangement (demanding a new obedience in the body), and of hope in death (evoking the vision of a new world). See Lectures on Christology, University of Tübingen, Winter Semester 1968-69; "Gott und Auferstehung" and "Die Revolution der Freiheit," in *Perspektiven der Theologie* (München, Chr. Kaiser Verlag, 1968), esp. pp. 49-54, 209 (this material is not in the English translation). Now Moltmann can write that "in [Jesus], the Crucified and Risen One, the coming God himself is present" (*RRF*, p. 105; my translation; cf. *Perspektiven der Theologie*, p. 145). With Moltmann's emerging position I have no quarrel, although it is not yet developed with sufficient clarity.

Jesus as agent, and, thus, ultimately the agency of God. But it also requires human response and practice, including both a coming-to-faith (where the personal-individual aspect is prominent) and a being-sent-to-mission (where the social-communal aspect is prominent). Neither the objective nor the subjective dimension is separable from the other. Man's speech and agency (when it is true and faithful) may be considered the visible "place" where the action of the risen Jesus occurs; and the latter may be considered the ontological foundation of the former, that which becomes perceptible in it as its true basis. The resurrection is not to be reduced, on the one hand, to a purely objective, transcendent fact that happened (or still happens) to Jesus at some remote distance from us, or, on the other hand, to an existential transformation in the believer. Neither orthodoxy nor existentialism has been able to give adequate account of the full reality of the resurrection.

The category by which I am proposing to interpret the resurrection of Jesus, namely, "action," "agency," or *praxis,* derives originally, as we have seen, from Schleiermacher, who speaks of "the living action of Christ" or "the redeeming agency of Christ."[37] Schleiermacher, however, concentrated on the personal-individual aspects of Jesus' redemptive agency. The theme of Secs. 106-112 of the *Glaubenslehre* is "the manner in which fellowship with the perfection and blessedness of the Redeemer expresses itself in the individual soul"; and the key concepts are "regeneration," "conversion," "justification," and "sanctification." By contrast, I shall be more directly concerned with the social-communal aspects of Jesus' reconciling agency: only as the individual is caught up in the worldly mission of the community does he come to faith, experiencing the presence of the risen Christ.

My concept of "agency" or *praxis* is also indebted to Dorothee Soelle. An "agent" is one who *acts,* both on his own behalf and on behalf of another; an agent is a "repre-

37. See above, pp. 53-55, 224-225.

sentative" or a "deputy." Thus the validity of Soelle's title
for Jesus, "the representative,"[38] may be acknowledged, although not her thesis that Jesus represents the now *absent*
God, acting in his place. Rather the future God is *present*
precisely through the agency of his representative; the action
of Jesus is ultimately the action of God. I shall propose to
speak of the risen Christ not as "Lord" but as "agent,"
because royalist and cultic imagery is no longer a serious
possibility for theology,[39] and because the essence of the
risen Christ is precisely *praxis*—the action by which he
gathers men into presence, "saving" them in both personal
and socio-political dimensions. The title κύριος ("Lord")
originated in the Hellenistic Church and was borrowed from
oriental Hellenism, although it was Paul who established its
use as the most characteristic designation of the risen Jesus.
Nevertheless, to say the same thing that Paul intended in
appropriating this title, we must now say it differently.[40]

In taking up first the theme of the action *of Jesus,* I shall
contend that "resurrection" means Jesus' "coming to stand"
in the world as the agent of God, engaged in the work of
reconciliation or "presencing." It means the nearness of the
one in whom God himself has come near, constituting a world
by the nearness of his rule. Jesus' agency is not exercised
in some remote realm or "heaven," or in some transcendent
dimension of "salvation history." Rather it is exercised
in our midst. Resurrection means his coming, his presence, not his departure or absence. Because his being-as-
risen is essentially that of presence, he has conquered and

38. *Christ the Representative,* trans. by David Lewis (Philadelphia, Fortress
Press, 1967). For a discussion of the thesis of this book, see Sec. 1, Chapter 1.

39. *Ibid.,* p. 141; and Dorothee Soelle, *Atheistisch an Gott Glauben: Beiträge
zur Theologie* (Olten, Walter-Verlag, 1968), p. 24.

40. Ernst Käsemann supports this argument, although he does not suggest
the specific term "agent." He says that Paul did not take *kyrios* in the cultic
sense. Rather, as *kyrios* Jesus is the "exalted cosmocrator," "the one who holds
God's place [*der Platzhalter Gottes*] in a world which is not yet wholly subject
to God"—terms that are clearly related to my concept of agency. ("On the
Topic of Primitive Christian Apocalyptic," *JThC,* Vol. 6 [1969], p. 129; cf.
ZThK, Vol. 59 [1962], p. 280.) See also *ThNT,* Vol. I, pp. 124-125; and *GuV,*
Vol. I, p. 260.

transformed death, which is essentially absence. In developing this theme, first I shall examine the root meanings of
the biblical words for "resurrection." Next I shall consider
Paul's association of the concepts "resurrection," "salvation,"
"justification," "new life." Then I shall argue that, as an
action of Jesus, the resurrection is also an action of God,
"who gives life to the dead and calls into being the things
that have no being" (Rom. 4:17).[41]

The most common verbs in the New Testament meaning
"to raise the dead" or "to rise from the dead" are ἐγείρειν and
ἀνιστάναι—ἐγείρειν is used more frequently than ἀνιστάναι in the
verbal form, but ἀνάστασις is the standard noun for "resurrection."[42] It is commonly argued that the basic meaning of

41. My conception of the agency of the risen Christ raises a question about
the distinction between the work of Christ and that of the Holy Spirit. For
orthodoxy, this distinction was no problem, since Christ was believed to be
removed to heaven, where he rules at the right hand of the Father, while the
Spirit carries on the work of redemption on earth. But if we conceive the
risen Christ as the one who comes to stand *in* the world as agent, then we face
the difficulty of distinguishing between the agency of Christ and the agency
of the Spirit. This distinction, if it can be drawn at all, must be understood
as a dialectical one. *Opera trinitatis ad extra indivisa sunt.* Bultmann points
out that for Paul "in Christ" can interchange with "in the Spirit" (Rom. 8:9;
14:17; *ThNT*, Vol. I, p. 311). In so far as a distinction can be made, we may
say that the agency of Christ is objective and present (historical), whereas
that of the Spirit is subjective and eschatological. In I Cor. 12, 14, Paul understands the Holy Spirit as the subjective agency by which Christ constitutes
his dominion in the world. I suggested earlier that God as word exists triunely in three modes of subsistence and in a twofold structure of self-
communication. He is the uncreated one ("Father") who communicates
himself in faith ("Son") and in love ("Spirit"). Faith is an historical virtue
(marking the mode of present participation in the kingdom of God), whereas
love is an eschatological virtue (descriptive of the final kingdom of presence).
Man hears the word of God in faith as one who is under way in history
through discipleship to Christ; he responds to the word in love as one who
is completed by the return to God through the inner witness of the Spirit.
Here the subjective and eschatological dimensions of the Spirit's agency are
conjoined, in contrast to the objective and historical agency of Christ. Nevertheless, these distinctions remain relative, for history and eschatology, faith
and love, objective and subjective agency are but different aspects of God's
one self-communication *ad extra.* On the relation between Christ and the
Spirit, see especially Claude Welch, *The Reality of the Church* (New York,
Charles Scribner's Sons, 1958), Chapter 7; George S. Hendry, *The Holy Spirit
in Christian Theology* (Philadelphia, The Westminster Press, 1956); Dietrich
Bonhoeffer, *Sanctorum Communio* (London, Collins, 1963).

42. *TDNT*, Vol. II, p. 335.

these terms is "to awaken from sleep" (both transitive and intransitive), and that this meaning was applied metaphorically in the apocalyptic tradition to the resurrection of the dead. Thus Wolfhart Pannenberg: ". . . in the same way that one is awakened from sleep and rises, so it will happen to the dead. . . . The familiar experience of being awakened and rising from sleep serves as a parable for the completely unknown destiny expected for the dead."[43] Pannenberg also notes, however, that "the notion of the resurrection of the dead that is most obvious on the basis of the analogy of sleeping and waking would be that of a revivification of the corpse in the sense of what has died standing up and walking around."[44] Despite the fact that this is *not* the meaning of the resurrection according to Paul and the primitive Christian tradition, Pannenberg nevertheless proposes to hold to this apocalyptic metaphor because it implies, by contrast with the Greek concept of "immortality of the soul," that life after death must be "another mode of existence of the *whole* man," body and soul together. It is essential for a monistic anthropology.[45] Willi Marxsen apparently regards as correct this understanding of the resurrection metaphor, rooted in late Jewish apocalyptic. But it is just this difficulty with it—the fact that it suggests a revivification of the corpse—that causes Marxsen to supplant it with other concepts by which the experience of "seeing" Jesus after his death and being called to faith through him might be "interpreted."[46] The way Marxsen understands ἐγείρειν and ἀνιστάναι leads him to an ambivalent position toward the whole "resurrection" concept: on the one hand he has serious doubts about the adequacy of this interpretative metaphor, but, on the other hand, he continues to use the term (as in the title of his book) and does not believe the concept can

43. *JGaM*, p. 74.
44. *Ibid.*, p. 75.
45. *Ibid.*, pp. 86-87.
46. Marxsen, "Die Auferstehung Jesu," *op. cit.*, pp. 30-36; *AJN*, pp. 133-151 (Eng. trans., pp. 130-148).

ever be completely avoided.[47] It also causes him to draw a
distinction, as we have noted, between "resurrection" and
the experience of encountering Jesus as living.

But is the apocalyptic understanding of resurrection of the
dead, based on a particular reading of ἐγείρειν and ἀνιστάναι,
the only proper or correct one? A closer examination of these
two verbs reveals that the notion of "awakening from sleep"
is not necessarily central to their biblical usage. Although
the etymological root of ἐγείρειν apparently is "to waken,"[48] it
was not commonly used in this literal sense in the Septuagint. There it had two basic spheres of meaning. First, it
referred to God's action in "raising up" a figure in history
(cf. Judges 2:16, 18; 3:9, 15; I Kings 11:14, 23), a usage
carried over into the New Testament as well (Acts 13:22;
Matt. 3:9; Lk. 1:69). It could also be used in the passive
sense of "being stirred" or "raised up" to an action (Jer.
6:22; Is. 19:2); the New Testament, for example, speaks of
prophets "being raised" (Matt. 11:11; Lk. 7:16; Jn. 7:52).
The second sphere of meaning had to do with the notion
of "setting up" something, such as an idol (I Sam. 5:3),
an animal (Matt. 12:11), "the poor" (I Sam. 2:8), the sick
(Mk. 1:31; 9:27; Acts 3:7), etc. In a deponent sense it
could also be used to mark the beginning of an action, "to
commence" (Ex. 5:8; I Chron. 10:12; 22:19; II Chron. 21:9;
22:10; Matt. 9:19; Jn. 11:29).[49] In none of these usages is
the literal sense of "wakening from sleep" in evidence; the
meaning is rather that of raising up, sending, or establishing
a historical figure, of rising to an action, of setting something
under way. There is no reason to assume that, when the
New Testament authors appropriated this term to interpret
the conviction that Jesus was alive and active in the world,

47. *AJN*, p. 151 (Eng. trans., p. 148).
48. The perfect form ἐγρήγορα is closely related to the Old Indian jā-gāra,
"I awoke." See Hjalmar Frisk, *Griechisches etymologisches Wörterbuch*
(Heidelberg, Carl Winter Universitätsverlag, 1960 ff.), Vol. I, p. 438.
49. *TDNT*, Vol. II, pp. 334-335. Of course it was also used occasionally in the
Old Testament to refer to "raising the dead" (II Kings 4:31; Greek Sirach
48:5).

they necessarily had in mind the picture of wakening from sleep, applied metaphorically to an awakening from death. They could just as well have thought of ἐγείρειν as God's sending or establishing Jesus in his function as Lord or agent. This would seem to be especially true of Paul, for whom the ἐγήγερται of Jesus had nothing to do with the resuscitation of a corpse, as I Cor. 15:35 ff. makes unmistakably clear.

This conclusion is reinforced by an analysis of the second set of biblical terms used of Jesus' resurrection from the dead, ἀνιστάναι (verb) and ἀνάστασις (noun). Here the notion of wakening from sleep does not belong to the root meaning of the word, although it was occasionally used in that sense. More commonly it meant "to institute or install" someone in a function, e.g., the "installation" of a high priest (Heb. 7:11, 15). Heb. 7:15 is important because the author speaks of Jesus' being "installed" (ἀνίσταται) as a priest forever after the order of Melchizedek. In the context of Heb. 7-10, this expression refers precisely to Jesus' "resurrection." The author of Hebrews interprets the Easter experience by the concept, "installation as a priest forever." It is no accident that the term he chose to express this interpretation was the same one associated by the tradition with Jesus' being "raised from the dead." 'Ανιστάναι was also commonly used in the following senses: "to rise" to an action, such as speaking (Lk. 10:25; Acts 5:34; 13:16; 15:5); to mark the beginning of an action (Gen. 21:32; Judges 13:11; I Kings 19:21); to raise up offspring (Gen. 38:8; Judges 4:5, 10; Matt. 22:24); to raise up or to "send" a figure in history (Deut. 18:15, 18; I Sam. 2:35; I Kings 14:14; Jer. 23:4; Ez. 34:23; Acts 3:22; 7:37). In Acts 3:26, this latter concept was applied to Jesus himself: "God, having raised up [ἀναστήσας] his servant, sent [ἀπέστειλεν] him to you first. . . ."[50]

The basic term used in the Septuagint to describe God's

50. *TDNT*, Vol. I, pp. 368-369.

action of "giving life" or "making alive" in nature and history
was ζωοποιεῖν, a word Paul continued to use in association with
the resurrection of Jesus. When the notion of life after death
arose, ἐγείρειν and ἀνιστάναι were also applied to the idea of
God's "giving life" by a metaphorical extension of their
original meaning. The precise sense in which the metaphor
was to be taken is not immediately evident. I have been
arguing that the image of wakening from sleep is not central
to the biblical usage of these terms and that it is erroneous
to suppose that the New Testament authors took the terms
in the metaphorical sense of awakening from death when
used to interpret the Easter experience. More likely, the
extension of meaning was along the lines of installation in
a function, rising to an action, sending a historical figure,
or inaugurating a course of affairs.

This thesis is confirmed by a closer look at the root meaning of ἀνιστάναι and ἀνάστασις. These terms are made up of the
prefix ἀνά plus the verb ἱστάναι or the noun στάσις. 'Aνά, used
as a prefix, means "up," "again," "throughout," "in the midst
of." The verb ἱστάναι means, transitively, to "set up," "establish," "confirm," and intransitively, to "stand," "be," or "exist."
Στάσις refers to "the act of standing" or "existence" (especially "continuing, permanent existence"). This etymology
suggests as a translation of ἀνάστασις: "standing up to" a function or action, or more figuratively, "coming to stand in the
midst of." That in the midst of which the risen Jesus stands
is the world. Hence, "resurrection" (ἀνάστασις) means: "Jesus'
coming to stand in the midst of the world," his "continuing
existence in the world," his "presence." This translation of
ἀνάστασις as a term used to interpret the Easter experience
accords better with the ordinary biblical usage of both
ἐγείρειν and ἀνιστάναι than does that interpretation based on the
image of wakening from sleep, which requires (when applied to the "raising" of Jesus) the notion of a resuscitation
of the corpse. It also enables us to retrieve the "resurrection" concept and to employ it positively in contemporary

theology, rather than finding it necessary either to eliminate it (Schleiermacher) or to qualify it (Marxsen).[51]

The New Testament ordinarily uses the verb ἐγείρειν and the noun ἀνάστασις. To this may be added that the New Testament knows a distinction between ἐγείρειν and ὤφθη ("appeared") (I Cor. 15:4-5; Mk. 16:6-7; Lk. 24:34), but not between ἀνάστασις and ὤφθη.[52] From this evidence we may conclude that ἐγείρειν refers to God's *act* of bringing Jesus to stand, whereas ἀνάστασις refers to the *state* or *function* of Jesus' having come to stand, a function identical with the disciples' experience of "seeing" Jesus and of being caught up in his mission. Or to paraphrase Gerhard Koch:

51. Unfortunately, the English word "resurrection" (*re*, again + *surgere*, to rise; hence "to rise again") does not convey the root sense of ἀνάστασις as successfully as the German *Auferstehung*. But even if we take "resurrection" in the literal sense of "rising again," the mode and meaning of "rising" is not specified, and we can argue that Jesus has "risen to" (i.e., "taken up" or "come to stand in") his function as agent. The interpretation of ἀνάστασις offered here is indebted to Gerhard Koch. He writes: "The Risen One [*der Auferstandene*] in his graciousness has to do with men, for whom God has raised him. Jesus Christ draws men into his active being and thereby liberates them from their forgetfulness of God and their fallenness. Thus it is no accident that this being of Jesus is designated by a word [ἀνάστασις] which even in Scripture has its place in everyday colloquial talk. Resurrection [*Auferstehen*] means to rise up to a work [*sich zu einem Werk erheben*]. The resurrection [*Auferstehen*] of Jesus means standing up [*Auferstehen*] to a work; it means being and work in 'stand.' This work in stand happens through the 'Father' (Rom. 6:4; Gal. 1:1). . . . God's own work happens in the stand of the Risen One in history. The *doxa* of God has appeared in the world through him. His work thus interpreted is brought from the half-darkness of a history of the gods into the bright light of the historical world." (*AJC*, pp. 177-178.) In showing the relation between ἀνάστασις and στάσις, Koch refers to Johann Gerhard, *Loci theologici*, F. Frank, ed. (Leipzig, 1869), Vol. VIII, Chapter 13, p. 504.

Dietrich Bonhoeffer, in his christology lectures, *Christ the Center*, trans. by John Bowden (New York, Harper & Row, 1966), very subtly develops a theology of the resurrection informed by the root meaning of ἀνάστασις as "coming to stand." He inquires after the "place" of the risen Christ: "Everything depends on Christ being present to his church as a person in space and time. . . . The mode of existence of the person of the Risen One [*der Auferstandene*] is temporal-spatial. So we must ask the question, 'where?' 'Where does he stand?' [*Wo steht er?*] He stands *pro me*. He stands in my place, where I should stand and cannot." (*Christ the Center*, p. 61. Trans. altered slightly; cf. *Gesammelte Schriften*, Eberhard Bethge, ed. [München, Chr. Kaiser Verlag, 1960], Vol. III, p. 194.) According to Bonhoeffer, the risen Christ stands as and at "the center" (*die Mitte*)—the center of human existence, of history, and of nature; he stands as the center in his *pro me* structure as word, as sacrament, and as community. (*Christ the Center*, pp. 49-67.) These allusive proposals will be of value for our consideration of the modes of Jesus' personal presence in Sec. 3 of this chapter.

52. *AJC*, p. 179.

God *has raised up* (ἐγήγερται) Jesus in order that he might *come to stand* (ἀνάστασις) in the world, taking up his work there.[53] This formulation expresses the temporal dialectic of the resurrection for which I have contended: it is a present event (Jesus' coming to stand in his agency of reconciliation), having its origin in an event of the perfect mode (God's act of having raised up), and containing the eschatological promise of the ultimate victory of life over death.

My interpretation of ἀνάστασις implies that Jesus was not raised to an extra-worldly "heaven" where he is now removed from us, but to *this* world, where he comes to stand as agent, constituting the world as God's kingdom by his present reconciling *praxis*. For the biblical writers, "heaven" (οὐρανός) does not refer to an extra-worldly region in any case. Heaven and earth together constitute the world, the cosmos. Heaven is a region of *this* world, the "place" occupied by the "principalities and powers" (Rom. 8:38-39), which ought to subserve God as agents of his rule but have in fact been corrupted. The risen Jesus goes to "heaven" precisely to assume dominion over this world and the powers that control it. Koch writes: "[God] does not call [Jesus] to himself in his glorious Zion, his 'above'; he does not call into eternity. In the raising of Jesus Christ he calls into the reality of the world, into history! . . . The word of the God who makes history, who calls into existence the things that do not exist, calls the Crucified in the resurrection. The call of God in the resurrection is a call into the world. Resurrection [*Auferstehung*] is the summons [*Aufruf*] to the world." Hence resurrection is a "historical" event in the most fundamental sense, for it is a history-constituting event.[54]

---

53. Koch's words are: "Dazu hat Gott Jesus Christus auferweckt, dass der in die Welt hinein Auferstandene dort sein Werk treibe." *AJC*, pp. 176-177. See pp. 172 ff. The parallel is not precise because the German *auferstehen* is always intransitive, whereas ἀνιστάναι is not.

54. *AJC*, pp. 174-175; see pp. 236-282, where the "nearness" of the Risen One is developed as a major theme.

Moreover, it is Jesus *of Nazareth* who is thus called, who comes to stand in the world as the near agent. The continuity between the earthly Jesus and the risen Christ is one of the central themes in the Evangelists' Easter narratives. This continuity means that the post-Easter faith has no other content and character than the pre-Easter faith into which Jesus himself called.[55] The same faithful word and the same free, responsible, and obedient deed that came to expression in Jesus come to expression anew in the practice of Easter. Thus it is *he* who is now present, engaged in the work of reconciliation.

Thus far the analysis has been limited strictly to the resurrection concept. When the theological context in which this concept appears in the theology of Paul is examined, it is apparent at once that the reality of Jesus' resurrection from the dead is closely linked with the occurrence of the salvation event as an eschatological reality bearing upon the present. In Pauline usage, the title κύριος refers to Jesus' work of salvation as the Risen One (see Rom. 1:4-5; 4:24; 10:9; I Cor. 15:24-25; II Cor. 4:14). Salvation is linked with resurrection in such passages as Rom. 8:34 ("Christ Jesus, . . . who was raised from the dead, who is at the right hand of God,[56] who indeed intercedes for us"); II Cor. 5:15 ("And he died for all, that those who live might live no longer for themselves but for him who for their sake died and was raised"); and especially Rom. 10:9 (". . . if you confess with your lips that Jesus is Lord and believe in your heart that God raised him from the dead, you will be saved"). The

---

55. This is one of the central theses of Willi Marxsen's book, *Die Auferstehung Jesu von Nazareth,* expressed even in its title ("The Resurrection of Jesus of Nazareth"), and in Marxsen's two basic "interpretations" of the resurrection: "he still comes today"; "the cause of Jesus is carried further." See pp. 127-129, 166-175 (Eng. trans., pp. 125-127, 162-172).

56. This phrase appears in the Pauline corpus only once (assuming that Eph. 1:20 is non-Pauline). Here Paul has taken over the traditional confessional language of the church. Cf. Acts 2:32-33 ("This Jesus God raised up, and of that we all are witnesses. Being therefore exalted at the right hand of God . . ."). Its rarity in Paul indicates that for him Jesus' resurrection does not involve his removal into another realm. "At the right hand of God" is not to be taken literally as the designation of a place but metaphorically as a description of Christ's authority and dominion.

latter passage is especially significant because it shows the connection for Paul between faith (as ὁμολογία), resurrection, and salvation.[57] That Jesus is "raised from the dead" has its proper locus in the homologous speaking of faith; the consequence of such speaking is that the event of salvation comes to pass. The *reality* of Jesus' resurrection is the present salvation event; the "place" where this event happens is the homologous speech and action of men.

The event of salvation, in turn, includes two elements: justification (δικαίωσις, δικαιοσύνη) and newness of life (καινότης ζωῆς) in Christ. The motif of justification is most clearly linked with the resurrection of Jesus in Rom. 4:25: ". . . Jesus our Lord, who was put to death for our trespasses and raised for our justification [καὶ ἠγέρθη διὰ τὴν δικαίωσιν ἡμῶν]."[58] The Pauline association of resurrection and justification was an important theme for the Reformers. For example, Luther wrote: "Resurrectio eius a mortuis est nostri iustificatio per fidem solam."[59] The second of the elements, newness of life, marks Paul's most basic definition of the resurrection: resurrection itself *means* new life, the new life that Jesus himself is as he comes to stand in the world as agent, the new life that is ours as we share in his dominion, as we live "in Christ." The identification of resurrection and life is reflected in the fact that Paul sometimes uses the verb ζωοποιεῖν ("to give life") as a synonym for or in conjunction with ἐγείρειν ("to raise"), referring clearly to the resurrection from the dead.[60]

For Paul, newness of life is both a present and a future reality. In some texts, such as Gal. 2:20; Rom. 6:11; II Cor. 4:10-11, the present participation of the faithful in the new

57. See above, pp. 143-146.

58. This linkage is also implied in Rom. 5:18-21, although here the resurrection is not specifically mentioned.

59. *WA*, 39/II, 237, 2. Quoted in Ernst Bizer, "Über die Rechtfertigung nach Luther und der Confessio Augustana," *Das Kreuz Jesu Christi als Grund des Heils*, Fritz Viering, ed. (Gütersloh, Gütersloher Verlagshaus Gerd Mohn, 1967), p. 23.

60. See Rom. 4:17; 8:11; I Cor. 15:22, 36, 45. A similar usage of ζωοποιεῖν is found in Jn. 5:21; 6:63.

life of the risen Christ is stressed.[61] In other texts, however, the emphasis is on the eschatological character of new life. In Rom. 6:4-9 Paul writes: "We were buried therefore with him by baptism into death, so that as Christ was raised from the dead by the glory of the Father, we too might walk in newness of life [ἐν καινότητι ζωῆς περιπατήσωμεν]. . . . We know that our old self was crucified with him so that the sinful body might be destroyed, and we might no longer be enslaved to sin. . . . But if we have died with Christ, we believe that we shall also live with him. For we know that Christ being raised from the dead will never die again; death no longer has dominion over him." Likewise, in I Cor. 15:35-57, Paul stresses the qualitative difference between the "physical body" and the "spiritual body"—the σῶμα πνευματικόν (vs. 44), which may be taken as an image for the creation of new life after death, not for the continuation of individual bodily existence after death in some miraculously transposed form. The concept of the σῶμα πνευματικόν must be read in the light of what Paul says immediately following (vs. 45), that the last Adam became a "life-giving spirit" (πνεῦμα ζῳοποιοῦν). Here Paul uses the verb ζῳοποιεῖν, which means "to give life." Hence we may assume that the essence of "spirit" (πνεῦμα) is not individuated bodily existence but that which has been given and gives "life," especially life in which death itself is overcome. Ernst Käsemann has argued[62] that, with the exception of the image of the church as the body of Christ, Paul does not have a physical organism in mind when he uses the concept of "body" (σῶμα). Σῶμα for Paul means participation in a world or a dominion— the dominion of Adam or the dominion of Christ. "Physical body" means participation in the old order of Adam, and "spiritual body," participation in the new world constituted by the action of Christ. Σῶμα is not, fundamentally at least,

61. Here, too, may be added the deutero-Pauline texts, Col. 2:12-13; Eph. 2:1, 5-6.

62. Lectures on I Corinthians, University of Tübingen, Winter Semester 1968-69.

an individualizing but a communal phenomenon. Thus the
"anthropological" questions of vs. 35—"How are the dead
raised? With what kind of body do they come?"—are
shattered. Paul is not interested in how individual men are
raised bodily from the dead. He is rather concerned to
show that resurrection means participation in the dominion
of Christ. In vss. 38-43, 47-54, he introduces a series of
images to stress the qualitative difference between life
under the old dominion and life under the new—a difference
grounded in the fact that death itself is altered, taken up
into life, by the resurrection from the dead (Rom. 6:9-10;
I Cor. 15:51-55). It is perhaps significant that after vs. 44
Paul drops the term σῶμα itself, as though to stress that
resurrection has nothing to do with a prolongation of individuated bodily existence after death. The difference
between the old life and the new is too basic to permit
that. Thus Paul himself can make no attempt to *describe*
the "new life," other than to say that it *means* participation
in the dominion, the agency of Christ, of which even now
we have a foretaste; it means being made alive "in Christ"
(I Cor. 15:22-27). And that means ultimately being made
alive "in God," who *is* life and who *is* presence (vs. 28).
"New life" means life in the presence of God.[63]

b. *Resurrection as an Action of God*

This analysis of the resurrection as meaning essentially
justification and *new life* leads, thereby, to a closely related
point—that as an action of Jesus the resurrection is also the
action of God. For the creation of life in which sin and
death are overcome is essentially an affair of God, not of
man. Gerhard Ebeling is right in understanding the resurrection as, in the final analysis, a definition of God, indeed
from a Christian perspective the sharpest and most decisive

---

63. The resurrection is nowhere more explicitly identified with "life" than in
the words of Jesus found in Jn. 11:25: "I am the resurrection and the life
[ἐγώ εἰμι ἡ ἀνάστασις καὶ ἡ ζωή]." However, limitation of space prevents discussion of the Johannine theology of resurrection.

definition of God. According to Paul God is the one "who gives life to the dead [ζῳοποιοῦντος τοὺς νεκρούς] and calls into being the things that have no being [καλοῦντος τὰ μὴ ὄντα ὡς ὄντα]" (Rom. 4:17). Ebeling writes: "[This] is the God-predicate which, in contradiction to that which contradicts God to the uttermost, affirms God's being as God to the uttermost. Death is the uttermost test for what the word 'God' means, for whether we are deadly serious in using the word 'God.' . . . God's action always has its object in the antithesis to his being: in nothingness, in sin, in death. Creation, justification, and resurrection—these are the three mutually corresponding works of the one mode of his action. Only when they are all brought into view together may each of them be rightly understood. . . . Resurrection means being sheltered in the life of God from the nothingness of temporal existence and from the power of sin, through the completion of the life of death. But this is nothing other than the fulfillment of life, whose dawn faith is."[64]

Ebeling here confirms what I have attempted to establish in my exegesis of Paul: that "resurrection" means justification and new life. Or, to put it differently, the concept of "resurrection" embraces and brings to fruition the concepts of "creation" and "justification." Resurrection is the creative and justifying action of God par excellence, for death is the quintessence of non-being and of sin. Furthermore, according to a profound insight of Paul, this action of God is exercised by means of a *call*: God "calls [καλοῦντος] into being the things that have no being." Here Paul undoubtedly reflects the account of creation in Gen. 1, thereby associating the act of resurrection with that of creation. It is by his *word* that God creates, justifies, and raises (or gives life to) the dead. It is by means of the *word of God* that Jesus comes to stand in the world,[65] mediating that life-giving word to us anew.

---

64. Gerhard Ebeling, "Was heisst: Ich glaube an Jesus Christus?" *Was heisst: Ich glaube an Jesus Christus?* (Stuttgart, Calwer Verlag, 1968), pp. 66-67.
65. *AJC*, pp. 174-175, in a passage quoted above, p. 250.

The resurrection, as God's call into being, is in fact a
call into the presence of the future God, whose being *is*
presence. Paul makes this explicit in II Cor. 4:13b-14:
". . . We too believe, and so we speak, knowing that he who
raised the Lord Jesus will raise us also with Jesus and bring
us, together with you, into his presence [. . . ἐγερεῖ καὶ
παραστήσει . . .]." The verb Paul here uses in parallel with
ἐγείρειν is παριστάνειν, "to bring into the presence of" someone.
In terms of structure it is related in an interesting way to
ἀνιστάναι. It is made up of the same root verb, ἱστάναι ("to
place," "to stand"), with a different prefix, παρά ("beside,"
"near," "with"). Hence, whereas ἀνιστάναι means "to bring to
stand" or "to stand in the midst of," παριστάνειν means "to
present" or "to be present to."[66] Its usage in this passage
suggests that Paul intends it as a substitute or synonym for
ἀνιστάναι, a way of saying what ἀνάστασις really means. Jesus
comes to stand in the world as the one who "presents (us)
to" God. "Resurrection" as "new life" means being brought
into the presence of God, or, as Ebeling puts it, "being sheltered in the life of God."[67] For man has life—true life, in
which death itself is overcome—only in the presence of God,
who himself *is* life and presence and thus the antithesis of
death and absence.[68]

66. The verb is found several times in the Pauline corpus. In Rom. 6:13, 16,
19, it is used in the sense of "putting oneself at God's disposal." In Rom. 12:1,
Paul appeals that we should "present" our bodies as a living sacrifice to God.
In II Cor. 11:2 he writes: "I betrothed you to Christ to present you as a pure
bride to her one husband." A similar usage is found in Eph. 5:27 ("that the
church might be presented before [Christ]") and in Col. 1:22, 28 ("in order
to present you holy and blameless and irreproachable before [God]"; "that
we may present every man mature in Christ"). In other words, the verb is
used in several ways to express an intensive relationship between the believer
and God or Christ; it describes existence in the presence of God. The verb is
also related to παρουσία ("being-with"), which I shall discuss shortly.
67. Ebeling, "Was heisst: Ich glaube an Jesus Christus?", *op. cit.*, p. 67.
Ebeling also writes that Jesus' resurrection "means that he, the dead one, has
death (not just dying, but death) finally behind him, and is finally *with God*,
and for this reason is *present in this earthly life.*" *The Nature of Faith*, trans.
by Ronald Gregor Smith (London, Collins, 1961), p. 71 (italics mine).
68. See also Rev. 21:3-4: "Behold, the dwelling of God is with men. He will
dwell with them, and they shall be his people, and God himself will be with
them; he will wipe away every tear from their eyes, and death shall be no
more, neither shall there be mourning nor crying nor pain any more, for the
former things have passed away."

If resurrection means life in the presence of the one who is presence, then death itself must be essentially altered by it. Death means absence, the loss of presence, the disintegration of being into that structureless, opaque chaos we call "nothingness." Resurrection means the death of death, the negation of absence, the taking up of absence into the presence of God. Being raised from the dead, we shall never die again, and death has thus lost its dominion over us (Rom. 6:9); death is swallowed up in victory (I Cor. 15:54), mortality in life (II Cor. 5:4). This means that death itself is taken up into the being of God and is there essentially altered, deprived of its character as negation, nothingness, absence, and converted into presence, the presence of the living God. In Eberhard Jüngel's words, "death becomes a God-phenomenon"; it is "essenced" in the being of the living God.[69] The ultimate meaning of the resurrection is that *God* and not death shall have dominion over all things (Rom. 6:9; I Cor. 15:26), that "*God* will be all in all [$\mathring{\eta}$ $\dot{o}$ $\theta\epsilon\grave{o}s$ $\pi\acute{a}\nu\tau a$ $\dot{\epsilon}\nu$ $\pi\mathring{a}\sigma\iota\nu$]" (I Cor. 15:28 NEB). This is another way of saying that God's being *is* presence. He is present to his creation as the one who gathers into presence, who brings life out of death, through the power of his word. He is present to himself as the primordial word-event that is the event of time itself, the living unity of time. Death, by contrast, means strictly speaking the loss of time, timelessness. It is the disintegration of the modes of time into a "dead" past, a sterile present, and a never-coming future. It is cessation, immobility, petrifaction, rigor mortis. Thus it is the direct antithesis of the being of God. When death is taken up into God, "essenced" in his being, it is in effect "temporalized," vitalized, brought to life; for life means being-in-time, or better, being-as-time. When God "gives life" to his creatures by gathering them into presence, he gives them time—that living time which is the ecstatic unity of future-past-present. To live "timefully" is to live by faith.

69. Jüngel, "Vom Tod des lebendigen Gottes," *ZThK*, Vol. 65 (1968), p. 114; see also the passage from p. 111 quoted above, p. 215.

If Jesus is the one who presents us to God in virtue of his resurrection from the dead, then his being as risen is essentially that of presence. His being present to us today as the one who comes to stand in the world is a function of this alteration of his status vis-à-vis death. The New Testament expresses this idea with the concept of παρουσία, which means literally "presence" ("being-with," παρά, with + οὐσία, being). In ancient writers it became a *terminus technicus* for the visit of a king, and in the New Testament was used to describe the second coming, the "return visit," of the risen Messiah. Yet we need not think of this "coming" just as an event in future time. Rather it describes the state, condition, or mode of Jesus' present relationship to men. He is now with us as *the coming one,* the one over whom death no longer has dominion, the one whose *ousia* is a constant *par-ousia.* This interpretation is suggested by the Pauline formula, ἐν τῇ παρουσίᾳ τοῦ κυρίου ἡμῶν Ἰησοῦ Χριστοῦ, "in the coming of our Lord Jesus Christ," which recurs several times (I Cor. 15:23; I Thess. 2:19; 3:13; 5:23; cf. also I Jn. 2:28). Here the apocalyptic notion of a specific future date is muted. "In the *parousia* of our Lord Jesus Christ" refers to an abiding in the presence of the Risen One. "As in Adam all die, so also in Christ shall all be made alive. But each in his own order: Christ the first fruits, then in his *parousia* those who belong to Christ" (I Cor. 15:22-23).

c. *Resurrection as an Action of Community*

At the beginning of this section I argued that the resurrection is to be understood as both an objective and a subjective reality, involving not only the agency of Jesus but also the speech and action of men, which may be considered the visible "place" where the action of the risen Jesus (and thus ultimately that of God) occurs. I also suggested that the human agency involves both a coming-to-faith (where the personal-individual element is predominant) and a being-sent-to-mission (where the social-communal element is predominant). Of the two elements, the latter is more fundamental in the sense that it is only as the individual is caught up in the mission of the community to the world that he comes to faith. This mission represents the "embodiment" of the new life in Christ, whose individual manifestation is a new and faithful mode of existence. In this section I shall briefly examine these two dimensions of the action of the community—the personal and the sociopolitical. Then in Sec. 3 I shall ask in what sense we can speak of Jesus himself as present in the word and action of the community.

The first dimension—resurrection as a coming-to-faith in Jesus—is the one that has received major attention in existentialist theology. In a classic statement Bultmann wrote: "The real Easter faith is faith in the word of preaching which brings illumination. If the event of Easter Day is in any sense a historical event additional to the event of the cross, it is nothing else than the rise of faith in the risen Lord. . . . The historical event of the rise of the Easter faith means for us what it meant for the first disciples—namely, the self-attestation of the risen Lord, the act of God in which the redemptive event of the cross is completed."[70] In a later comment on this argument Bultmann adds the following clarification: "It is often said, most of the time in criticism, that according to my interpretation of the kerygma Jesus has risen in the kerygma. I accept this proposition. It is entirely correct, assuming that it is properly understood. It presupposes that the kerygma itself is an eschatological event, and it expresses the fact that Jesus is really present in the kerygma, that it is *his* word which involves the hearer in the kerygma. . . . To believe in the Christ present in the

70. Rudolf Bultmann, "New Testament and Mythology," *Kerygma and Myth*, Hans Werner Bartsch, ed. (New York, Harper & Row, 1961), p. 42. Gerhard Ebeling has pursued this same line of interpretation in stating that "the point of the appearances is precisely the arising of faith in the Risen One." The resurrection *means* that Jesus as the *witness* of faith becomes the *basis* of faith. See *The Nature of Faith*, Chapter 5; quotation from p. 68.

kerygma is the meaning of the Easter faith."[71] It is important to understand precisely what is being said here. First, the resurrection event as "the rise of faith" in Jesus is an eschatological event in the sense that it is the event of salvation (*Heilsgeschehen*) itself; second, this event involves the "self-attestation" of the risen Lord, the "real presence" of Jesus; and finally, it is a word-event, an event that takes place in the proclaiming and hearing of the word, which itself is an action of the community. That the resurrection is the salvation-event underscores the fact that it is an act of God, not merely a subjective human phenomenon, even though the "place" where the event occurs is the faith of men—definitively so, the faithful word of Jesus, but also the faith of those who confess him Lord.[72] The claim that the resurrection involves the "self-attestation" of Jesus, that he is "really present" in the kerygma, and that "*his* word" encounters the hearer in the kerygma, means that for Bultmann the resurrection entails an action of Jesus, his contemporary living presence, as I have contended throughout this chapter.

Finally, and for present purposes most important, the resurrection is a word-event, an event that takes place in the proclaiming and hearing of the word. Hence Bultmann's famous statement: "Jesus has risen in the kerygma."[73] This

71. Rudolf Bultmann, "The Primitive Christian Kerygma and the Historical Jesus," *The Historical Jesus and the Kerygmatic Christ*, Carl E. Braaten and Roy A. Harrisville, eds. (Nashville, Abingdon Press, 1964), p. 42 (italics his).

72. On the resurrection as *Heilsgeschehen*, see Bultmann, *ThNT*, Vol. I, Sec. 33. Bultmann himself would not agree that the "definitive" place of the salvation-event is the word and deed of the historical Jesus. He would rather place the stress on the present proclamation of the community, i.e., on the kerygma rather than the historical Jesus.

73. Marxsen believes this statement is correct but "terminologically inexact," because it identifies "resurrection" with Jesus' *presence* in the kerygma of his witnesses, whereas "resurrection" is a metaphor referring to an awakening from death. Hence it is better, in Marxsen's judgment, to eliminate the resurrection concept entirely and to substitute for Bultmann's statement the following: "The 'cause of Jesus' is carried further"—the "cause" in this instance being Jesus' own kerygma, his word of reconciliation, which is carried further by the community. See "Die Auferstehung Jesu," *op. cit.*, p. 29. I have already criticized this argument by attempting to retrieve the "resurrection" concept in such a way as to let it mean more precisely what Bultmann is here contending for.

aspect of the matter comes especially into view in Bultmann's analysis of Paul's theology of resurrection. According to Paul, "the salvation-event [Jesus' death and resurrection] is nowhere present except in the proclaiming, accosting, demanding, and promising word of preaching."[74] The fact that the salvation-event takes place by word means that it is transposed out of "the dimension of cosmic-natural event," where it remained in the Gnostic myth, into "the dimension of genuinely historical event [*die Dimension echt geschichtlichen Geschehens*]. The union of believers into one σῶμα with Christ now has its basis not in their sharing the same supernatural substance, but in the fact that in the word of proclamation Christ's death-and-resurrection becomes a possibility of existence in regard to which a decision must be made, and in the fact that faith seizes this possibility and appropriates it as the power that determines the existence of the man of faith."[75] This passage is crucial. It means that the resurrection is not an event by which Jesus is translated into another world, on the model of the Gnostic redeemer-mythology. Rather, it is a "genuinely historical event" by which Jesus comes to stand, constituting a new "world" in our midst; the "place" where this event happens is the word of proclamation. This word concerns the individual: it confronts him as "a possibility of existence in regard to which a decision must be made"; it is "the power that determines the existence of the man in faith." But, as Bultmann's statement also makes clear, the act of proclaiming is a *communal* function in a twofold sense. It is a community-*constituting* function, for by means of proclamation believers are united into one σῶμα with Christ (σῶμα here being understood as participation in his dominion or "world"). And it is a community-*engaging* function, for the purpose of the community is precisely to carry forward the "ministry

74. *ThNT*, Vol. I, p. 302. Eng. trans. slightly altered; cf. Bultmann, *Theologie des Neuen Testaments*, 5th ed. (Tübingen, J. C. B. Mohr [Paul Siebeck], 1965), p. 301.
75. *ThNT*, Vol. I, p. 302. Eng. trans. slightly altered; cf. *Theologie des Neuen Testaments*, p. 302.

[διακονία] of reconciliation," which Paul identifies with the "word [λόγος] of reconciliation" in II Cor. 5:18-19. It is through this "word of reconciliation" that God confronts us (II Cor. 5:20), and that Christ himself is speaking and working (II Cor. 13:3; Rom. 10:17; 15:18).[76] Hence the first of the dimensions under consideration—the resurrection as a coming-to-faith in Jesus—already entails the second—the being-sent-into-mission (or ministry, διακονία).

In developing this theme, two important differences from Bultmann may be noted. First, Jesus is present not merely in the word of preaching but wherever and whenever a free, truthful, and salvific word comes to speech—whether within the Christian community or beyond its domain, in the language of piety or in the discourse of the world. The "word of reconciliation" encompasses far more than the word of preaching. Both Bultmann and Barth tended to restrict the word of God and the word of faith to church proclamation, thus losing a sense of the historicity and worldliness of the word by which salvation is mediated. Second, the communal embodiment of word must be thematized more rigorously than by Bultmann and existentialist theology. Man is confronted with the call to decision by which his existence is determined not as an isolated monad but as he engages in the work of the world and participates in the various intersecting social and political communities that make up his worldly existence. The mission or *diakonia* of the Christian is not merely *to* the world but engagement *in* it—engagement in the struggle for a liberated and reconciled society, which provides the only viable context for the freedom of the person and inner redemption. The community in which the Christian participates is not only the church but the world as a socio-political nexus. The dialectic between church and world is a theme to be considered shortly. Precisely in the context of this dialectic, the presence of

76. *ThNT*, Vol. I, pp. 302, 306.

the risen Christ is to be understood as a social phenomenon rather than as a matter of inner experiential certainty.[77] Or more precisely, the embodiment of Christ in the language and *praxis* by which the human community is liberated and redeemed creates the context in which the individual also comes to faith.

The primacy of the communal over the personal may be observed in the case of Paul. His Easter experience did not entail a literal physical seeing of Jesus but a twofold experience of coming-to-faith and being-sent-to-mission. The second of these elements—the so-called "functional" element[78]—is stressed by Paul in his own accounting of the Damascus experience. In Gal. 1:16, Paul writes that God "chose to reveal his Son to me and through me, *in order that I might proclaim him among the Gentiles.*" In I Cor. 9:1-2, he associates his "seeing" of Jesus with his "apostleship." And in I Cor. 15:8-9, he says: "Last of all, as to one untimely born, [Christ] appeared also to me. For I am the least of the apostles, unfit to be called an apostle, because I persecuted the church of God." In none of these passages is there a direct reference to Paul's coming-to-faith in Jesus, although that of course must be assumed since prior to the experience Paul had been a persecutor of the church. Rather, the focus of attention is on the connection between the encounter with Jesus and the *call to apostleship.* It is precisely and only in the exercise of his apostolate that Paul's personal faith becomes visible. His own faith has its substance in the faith and life of the community. (cf. I Cor. 15:10-11, 14, 17).

77. This theme is forcefully propounded by Wolf-Dieter Marsch, *Gegenwart Christi in der Gesellschaft: Eine Studie zu Hegels Dialektik* (München, Chr. Kaiser Verlag, 1965). The development of such a theme lies beyond the province of this book, but I want to acknowledge my sympathy with the efforts of Marsch and others to transcend the individualistic ethic of existentialism and to relate a theology of resurrection to the dialectic of social liberation.

78. The term is Marxsen's. See "Die Auferstehung Jesu," *op. cit.*, pp. 28 ff.; *AJN*, pp. 88 ff., 104 ff., (Eng. trans., pp. 84 ff., 101 ff.).

The association of "appearance" and "mission" (or "apostolate") is also found in the Peter traditions,[79] especially in Jn. 21:15-19. When Jesus appeared to Peter, according to this tradition, he did not ask whether Peter *believed in* him but rather whether he *loved* him. Upon Peter's affirmative response ensued the threefold call to mission: "Feed my lambs," "Tend my sheep," "Feed my sheep"—a call summed up by the simple words, "Follow me." Marxsen suggests that the story of the great catch of fish in Lk. 5:1-11, where Peter and others are called to discipleship, may in fact be an Easter tradition closely related to Jn. 21. He also points out that the implication of Lk. 24:34 ("The Lord has risen indeed, and has appeared to Simon!") is that Jesus' appearance to Peter has brought *others* to faith, which means that the functional element was associated with the appearances from the beginning.[80] Just as the author of the Fourth Gospel ended his work on the motif of the missionary charge of the risen Lord, so it is with Matthew and Luke.[81] The Matthean formula (28:16-20) is especially important because it binds together directly a seeing of Jesus (vs. 16), the call to discipleship (which involves both baptism and teaching, vss. 19-20), and the assurance of Jesus' continuing presence ("Lo, I am with you always, to the close of the age"). In Lk. 24:47-48 the functional motif is less precise, but in Acts 1:3-8 it is picked up again and formulated in distinctively ecclesiastical fashion: "You shall receive power when the Holy Spirit has come upon you; and you shall be my witnesses in Jerusalem and in all Judea and Samaria and to the end of the earth" (vs. 8).

We may conclude, then, that for the Evangelists, as for Peter and Paul, the "Easter event" was above all a community-constituting event: an event constituting it in its definitive function as mission. This mission was to be exer-

79. This has been pointed out by Marxsen, *AJN*, pp. 90-99 (Eng. trans., pp. 86-96) and Hirsch, *op. cit.*, p. 39.
80. *AJN*, pp. 91, 94, 99 (Eng. trans., pp. 87, 90, 95).
81. This motif is also found in the longer ending of Mark (16:15-20).

cised by means of word (preaching, teaching), but also by action, by deeds of love ("Feed my lambs," "Tend my sheep"). These words and actions are not an autonomous product of the community, although it is by the community's agency that they are accomplished. They are rather the words and actions of Jesus himself, brought to expression anew. In this sense he himself is present, at work, in the action of the community. It is *his* cause that is carried further by the mission of the community.[82] In the terms of my analysis, the "cause of Jesus" is his *faithful word*—the word that is liberating, truthful, and homologous; the word of power that heals life and constitutes a new world (God's "kingdom"); the word that is embodied in acts of freedom, responsibility, and obedience. Where this faithful word is carried further, there Jesus himself is personally present. The bringing to speech of this word is the definitive function of that community known as "Christian"; but it is a function that transcends the bounds of this community and becomes the common task of the world.

3. MODES OF JESUS' PERSONAL PRESENCE

a. Presence and Recognition

I turn now to the third of the related questions with which the resurrection event is being addressed in this chapter: "How" does Jesus come to stand in the world as God's agent, engaged in the work of reconciliation? In what "mode" or "modes" is he now present? In posing this question, which is undoubtedly the most difficult of the three,[83] I shall

82. *AJN*, pp. 127-128, 171-172 (Eng. trans., pp. 124-126, 167-169).

83. I am not, however, willing simply to abandon the "how" question and limit the discussion to the question, "Who is Christ?", as Dietrich Bonhoeffer advocates in *Christ the Center*, pp. 30-31, 45. The reason is that the questions of identity ("who") and modes of presence ("how") are inseparable. We cannot pose the "who" question without also posing the "how" question, unless we assume that Christ's presence is utterly unique, shattering the structures of all human experience. In denying that assumption I do not propose to dissolve the mystery of Christ's presence, but rather to bring it into view *as* mystery—a mystery, however, that we ourselves experience and in which we share.

attempt to weave together in strictest fashion the claim that the resurrection involves both an action of Jesus and an action of men in community. For the modes in which Jesus makes himself present are constitutive structures of human existence-in-community: word, act, community, world.

The fundamental experience of Christian faith is that Jesus *himself* is present in the event called "resurrection." The "presence" in question, then, is a *personal presence,* the presence of a person to persons.[84] Nevertheless, the personal presence of the risen Jesus is a difficult matter to conceive since, on the one hand, the presence of a person always entails spatio-temporal or physical-historical locus whereas, on the other hand, the presence of Jesus is clearly not a matter of physical proximity to us. How can we think of Jesus' personal presence in a spatio-temporal sense without affirming his literal physical proximity?

At the outset, it is easier to specify what personal presence is *not,* rather than what it is. It is not a matter of physical immediacy as such. This is not to suggest that physical immediacy is not ordinarily an important condition of personal presence. But it is not the only condition or the crucial one. On the one hand, it is possible for someone to be physically proximate but not to be present as a person, e.g., someone fast asleep. The most extreme instance of this situation is the physical immediacy of a corpse. When the body ceases to be a medium of communication between persons, or between self and world, then it is no longer the body of a human being, a person. A body without word is not a human body but a corpse. On the other hand, it is possible to transmit personal presence spatially without physical immediacy. Such transmission can be accomplished not only by letters and other forms of writing, but also (in our time) by the various electronic communications media. The rejection of physical immediacy as essential to personal

84. Bonhoeffer, *Christ the Center,* pp. 43-49; and Hans W. Frei, "The Mystery of the Presence of Jesus Christ," *Crossroads,* Vol. 17:2 (Jan.-Mar. 1967), pp. 72-73.

presence means that we must dispense with all attempts to bring past historical figures into the present through some sort of realistic physical (or metaphysical) actualization, such as by relics, the veneration of saints, or the sacrifice of the Mass.[85] The traditional doctrine of the transubstantiation of the eucharistic elements represents an illegitimate attempt to prolong the physical presence of Christ, which, as we shall see, was already peripheral and unessential to the post-Easter faith of the first Christians.

Personal presence is not a matter of effective historical influence, for then a person is merely reduced to a power, a value, or an idea. Bonhoeffer sharply criticized this position, which he regarded as characteristic of liberal christology: "Christ is understood from his historical influence, he is essentially power, *dynamis,* and not personal. This *dynamis* can be envisaged in different ways; as the echo of historical activity or as the newly emerging picture of the ideal character of the man Jesus."[86]

A third misunderstanding is closely related to the second: personal presence is not a matter of psychological immediacy, an inner event in the minds of Jesus' followers. Here the emphasis is not so much on historical influence as it is on an immediate, ahistorical access to the idea of Christ, e.g., Wilhelm Herrmann's theory of an inner spiritual relation to the inner life of Jesus, or existentialist reductionism, which understands the resurrection *merely* as the rise of faith in Jesus on the part of the disciples.

The New Testament itself requires us to reject these misunderstandings. Most of the appearance traditions in the Gospels emphasize not the corporeality but the *verbal encounters* with the Risen One, encounters by means of which *recognition* is evoked. The thesis may be proposed that *personal presence occurs when recognition is evoked by means of word, including also verbal action or enacted word.*

---

85. See Ebeling's analysis of "realistic metaphysical actualization" in *WF*, pp. 33-35.
86. Bonhoeffer, *Christ the Center,* pp. 43-44.

For example, the appearances of Jesus in Matt. 28:9-10, 16-20, are verbal in character: Jesus encountered the disciples and was recognized by means of speaking, with no interest in his physical appearance. The same is true in part of the appearance traditions in the Fourth Gospel (especially Jn. 20:11-18, 29; 21:15-23).

But by far the most important evidence for this thesis is found in the Emmaus tradition in Lk. 24:13-35. In Paul Schubert's judgment, Luke probably took over and embellished an older Emmaus tradition, which came to a climax and conclusion in the "recognition scene" (vs. 31).[87] According to this story, two disciples were on the way to Emmaus when "Jesus himself drew near [ἐγγίσας] and went with them" (vs. 15). Despite his physical proximity, "their eyes were kept from recognizing him" (vs. 16). There ensued a lengthy conversation with him about the identity of the crucified Jesus (vss. 17-27; probably a Lukan addition, where the Evangelist weaves in his proof-from-prophecy motif). The story comes to a climax when Jesus finally was recognized in the action of the breaking of the bread: "When he was at table with them, he took the bread and blessed, and broke it, and gave it to them. And their eyes were opened and they recognized [ἐπέγνωσαν] him; and he vanished out of their sight" (vss. 30-31; cf. vs. 35). This is an action, furthermore, closely associated with words: both the word of blessing (vs. 30), and more especially all that had previously been said on the road to Emmaus ("Did not our hearts burn within us while he talked to us on the road, while he opened to us the scriptures?" [vs. 32]). In brief, the Emmaus story, both in its original and in its Lukan forms, associates the presence or "nearness" of Jesus not so much with a seeing as with a hearing and a doing. The seeing is further de-emphasized by the fact that Jesus "vanished out of their

87. Paul Schubert, "The Structure and Significance of Luke 24," *Neutestamentliche Studien für Rudolf Bultmann: Zu seinem siebzigsten Geburtstag am 20. August 1954* (Beiheft 21 of *Zeitschrift für die neutestamentliche Wissenschaft;* 2nd ed.; Berlin: Alfred Töpelmann, 1957), pp. 169-172, 174. Schubert suggests that the "original" story remains in vss. 13, 15b, 16, 28-31.

sight" as soon as they "recognized" him—as though to say that recognition has nothing to do with physical vision as such.[88] Finally, we may note the theological and ecclesiastical context of the Emmaus story, namely, the eucharistic celebration in the early church. The story represents a piece of theological reflection backwards from the Christian community's experience in the Eucharist, saying in effect: Jesus is present to us *there*, in the breaking of the bread; so also did he appear to his first disciples. The implication is that the community itself has become the "body" in which the risen Jesus is now present; in place of his own physical body it is the spatio-temporal form that "embodies" the words and acts by which recognition is evoked and by means of which, therefore, even now, he is personally present.

One of the central functions of the community is to preserve the *memory* of the Crucified One (cf. I Cor. 11:24, 25). For recognition implies some sort of prior encounter, which is recalled by memory. To "recognize" means to "know again."[89] A person is not fully present as person upon first or immediate encounter. Only as we are able to recognize him on the basis of previous encounters can we experience his unique, unsubstitutable presence. Memory is the matrix that cements these encounters together into a recognizable pattern of identity. There can be no recognition, and hence no presence, of the risen Jesus apart from memory of the historical Jesus. For the first disciples who experienced the risen Jesus, the relation to the historical Jesus was direct and personal. For us, however, this relation is of necessity mediated by the traditions concerning his historical word

88. Of course the Jerusalem appearance in Lk. 24:36-43 emphasizes the physical immediacy of Jesus with a vengeance. According to Schubert, its parallels to the story of Jesus' physical appearance in Jn. 20:19-20, 27; 21:5, 9-13, indicate that it is a fairly late and popular tradition, originally unassociated with the Emmaus story. It is not to be denied that Luke himself shared an interest in "this massive historicizing and naturalistic theology," an interest also expressed in Acts 10:39-41. But the physical seeing of Jesus was not a motif in the original Emmaus tradition and indeed runs counter to its entire thrust. (*Ibid.*, pp. 172-173.)

89. "Recognize" derives from the Latin *recognosco* (*re*, again + *cognosco*, to know).

and deed. Without these traditions there would be no means
of recognizing *who* is now present; in this sense, the risen
Jesus is "identified" by reference to the historical Jesus.
Because it possesses spatio-temporal extension, the community is the essential bearer and preserver of memory.

According to the Emmaus tradition, word, act, and community are the essential structures in the event of recognition by which Jesus' personal presence is constituted. To
these three may be added "world" as the context and goal
of the community's mission. I shall now examine these four
modes more closely, paired in two groups.

b. *Jesus' Presence in Word and Act*

Word is the most fundamental and decisive mode of Jesus'
personal presence. I have already noted the verbal aspects
of recognition in the Emmaus story and in the appearance
traditions in Matthew and John. To these may be added
Paul's own personal experience, as well as his theology of
resurrection. In Gal. 1:15-17 Paul describes his Damascus
experience with the concept of "revelation," which itself is a
fundamentally verbal concept and is here associated with
God's *calling* to a ministry of *proclamation.* The encounter
with the risen Lord takes the form for Paul of a revelatory
word-event. According to Bultmann at least, Paul general-
ized this experience to argue that the resurrection as such
is a word-event, an event taking place in the proclaiming
and hearing of the word, and that therefore it is transposed
out of the dimension of "cosmic-natural event" into that of
"genuinely historical event."

The reason for the centrality of word as a mode of Jesus'
personal presence is that word as such is the medium of
presence. In Sec. 3, Chapter 3 I argued that the essence
of word is its power to gather into presence temporally
and spatially, to make present what is not at hand, even
what is deeply hidden in space and time. Word gathers into
presence *spatially* by establishing "horizontal" communication between men, primarily in virtue of its quality as sound.

But such spatial presence ordinarily requires temporal simultaneity. Thus it is difficult to think of the spatial presence of a past historical figure except in the sense that he may be said to be present at the *place where* his word is brought to speech anew. This place, for reasons I shall specify shortly, is communal rather than individual; it is a place where horizontal communication is of the essence. Word gathers into presence *temporally* by integrating the modes of time, which is of more fundamental importance for understanding the presence of the risen Christ. Word is the event by which history happens; history is the unified event of the future coming through the past into the present, gathering time into presence by its forward call. In such an event, the past no longer remains a "dead past" but becomes a "living past," the past *presented.* When the call of the future comes to speech today, its coming to speech in the past is *re-presented* in a living, dynamic unity with the present. "History" as such, viewed as the total, unified structure of future-making-present-what-has-been, is the formal basis for understanding the possibility of Jesus' living presence in word. In Sec. 2, Chapter 2 I argued that the hermeneutical structure of history (the dialectic between critical and practical thinking) enables a past event to live and continue to function in the present, not just in the form of historical memory, but as a really present event. With the coming to stand of the risen Jesus in the world as the agent of responsible Christian word and practice, we have the fullest conceivable manifestation of this possibility. Thus the resurrection does not shatter the structures of history but fully actualizes them, far beyond the mode of our own historical experience. The resurrection itself is a "hermeneutical" process in the sense that it epitomizes the forward, practical-responsive movement from a definitive event of the historical past to the present and the future. The essence of the resurrection is historical *praxis,* by which the cause of Jesus is carried further and he himself lives as the agent of this *praxis.* It may be recalled that my basic systematic

distinction between Jesus as presence and as present followed from the hermeneutical structure of christology, i.e.,
from the dialectic between historical quest and present
responsibility. The present, risen Christ is related to the
past, historical Jesus (and vice versa) by the hermeneutical
power of the word.

But clearly it is no longer Jesus himself who speaks directly
and immediately in our midst. For speech requires an
embodied speaker, whereas the risen Jesus is not present in
his earthly physical body. Thus we can only conclude that
it is *we* who speak for him vicariously, we ourselves, we
together as a community. Just as Jesus is the "representative" of the word of God, so also are we "representatives"
of the words of Jesus. But if it is *we* who speak, then how
can we understand *him* to be *personally* present? Here
reference can be made to my earlier discussion of the
"homologous" relation between the word of God and the
word of man, which in turn was based on Heidegger's analysis of the "ontological difference"—the distinction-within-
unity of primordial language (the event of being) and human
speech.[90] I argued that the word of God is not a supernatural
word, which exists in another sphere of reality and is inserted into human speech "vertically from above." Rather,
it has its only being *there*, where man himself speaks in
faithful correspondence to the primordial word of grace.
The relation between the word of God and the word of man
is not one either of analogy or of sheer identity, but rather
one of correspondence or homology, a correspondence in
which the word of man functions as the "place" where the
word of God comes to speech. To speak *faithfully* means precisely to speak in homology with the word of God. When man
speaks faithfully (but *only* when he speaks faithfully), his
speech exists in a relation of "sameness" to the word of God, for
it is God's word of definitive grace that empowers faithful
human speech and utilizes it as the place of its historical exis-

90. See above, pp. 97-102.

tence *ad extra*. Faith means speaking a liberating, truthful, and salvific word by a power not at one's disposal. When applied to an understanding of the *person* of Jesus, this analysis permitted us to say that as *the* word of faith Jesus was also *the word of God*. But we may also apply this analysis to an understanding of the relation between Jesus and Christian believers. When *we* speak faithfully here and now, our speech exists in a relation of "sameness" or homology to the words of Jesus, for it is the faithful word of Jesus that founds, empowers, and defines our speech, utilizing it as the place of its contemporary occurrence. We exist *extra nos* in our faithful speech, in a peculiar relationship to Jesus, just as he existed *extra se* in his being as faith, in a peculiar relationship to God. Hence, just as God himself was present in Jesus' being-as-the-word-of-faith, so also Jesus himself is present—personally present—in our faithful speech and act. Likewise, just as the word of God is not a suprahistorical phenomenon but has its existence *ad extra* at the place where man himself is fully accomplished, so also the risen Jesus is not transported into an other-worldly heaven but lives in the words and deeds of the community of his faithful. In short, I am proposing an analogy between the being of God in Jesus, and the being of Jesus in the community. The essence of this analogy is the homologous function of word in both instances.

Word is the definitive mode of Jesus' personal presence. But for the New Testament (as indeed for Christian experience generally), the word by which Jesus is recognized and therefore present is always accompanied by act. For the Emmaus tradition in Luke as well as for Paul, this act is described as *sacramental action;* specifically, the celebration of the Eucharist. Sacramental action may be defined as action by which faithful word is embodied, given concrete form. In providing instructions for the Lord's Supper, Paul suggests that sacramental action is a form of *proclamation:* "As often as you eat this bread and drink the cup, you proclaim the Lord's death until he comes" (I Cor. 11:26).

Here Paul employs the same word, καταγγέλλειν, that he elsewhere uses for preaching (Rom. 1:8; I Cor. 2:1, 9:14; Phil.
1:17-18). This usage indicates, as Bultmann puts it, "that
the sacrament of the Lord's Supper like that of baptism is
also coordinate with the word-proclamation and ultimately
only a special mode of it. . . . Obviously, then, the efficacy
of the sacrament—in spite of the influence of mystery ideas
—does not really rest upon the elements, the bread and
wine partaken, but rests upon the doing of this act of
'proclamation.' "[91] The sacrament is a "doing" of the word
of proclamation; it is enacted or embodied word. The
enactment of word is important because a word that does
not issue in action or take the form of action is an abstraction. Action is the embodiment of word in the sense that
the man who speaks does so by means of his body and
bodily actions: verbal and bodily action are inextricably
intertwined in human experience. Hence we may say with
Bonhoeffer that "the word in the sacrament is an embodied
word." The sacramental form of Christ, in his view, counters
"the attempt to limit Christ to doctrine, to volatize him in
general truth." The word of God assumes the form of sacrament as well as of preaching because man exists in nature
and history as well as in spirit.[92] Thus, sacramental action
is not to be understood as an alternative or supplementary
form of presence to that of word-presence. The relation
between word and act may rather be thought of in terms of
concentric circles: word is the core of (specifically human)
action; action is the embodiment of word. That action is
"sacramental" which serves as the embodiment of *faithful*
word, word in which Jesus himself is personally present in
virtue of its homologous quality. It follows, then, that
sacramental action is not limited to the ecclesiastically defined sacraments (whether two or seven), but rather occurs
whenever and wherever an action serves as a sign, seal,

91. *ThNT*, Vol. I, p. 313.
92. Bonhoeffer, *Christ the Center,* pp. 54-55.

bond, or pledge, i.e., as a *sacramentum*,[93] of faithful word. Sacramental action is not ubiquitous, for Jesus is not present everywhere in nature and history,[94] but only in those words and acts which conform to the definitive word of faith, bringing it to expression anew. On the other hand, sacramental action is not to be limited to the formally defined sacraments. The latter may be taken as symbols or representations of a much broader scope of word-embodying action. They are the place where the sacramental function of such action is acknowledged and its relation to the action of Jesus made explicit.

Thus far I have considered word and action as the modes of Jesus' personal presence in a general way, with reference to both philosophical and biblical considerations. Now I shall attempt to define more specifically the *forms* of word and action by which Jesus comes to stand in the world and may be recognized as such. My orientation here is not to the traditional ecclesiastical forms of preaching, baptism, the Lord's Supper, and other sacramental or quasi-sacramental acts. These cultic forms, while by no means invalid or superfluous, are too confining, especially for an age in which the church is no longer the sole (or even a credible) mediator of the presence of Jesus. Moreover, it is inappropriate that ecclesiastical tradition should define the forms of word and action by which Jesus is present, for his presence shatters all traditional structures and requires ever-new formulation. This definition should be provided by Jesus himself, and that means by critical reference to the historical Jesus. The quest for the historical Jesus belongs to the essence of a resurrection theology, just as the latter provides the "practical" context for the pursuit of the former. The one who *was* presence is *now* present; hence the qualities of his past historical presence provide the criteria by which his con-

93. In Latin, *sacramentum* refers to that by which one binds oneself to another person or party, e.g., an oath, obligation, or dedication, or the pledge money deposited by the parties in a civil suit. It may still be used in English in the latter sense.
94. Bonhoeffer, *op. cit.*, p. 55.

temporary presence assumes form. My analysis of Jesus as the word of faith distinguished: (a) the *faithfulness* of his word as the word that is authoritative, truthful, and homologous with the word of God; (b) the content of his teaching *about* faith as the power that heals life and constitutes a new world (God's "kingdom"); and (c) his *enactment* of the life of faith in freedom, responsibility, and obedience, climaxed by the death on the cross. These qualities of presence, which designate Jesus as the one in whom God and man were definitively co-present, may also serve as the criteria for defining the forms of word and action by which he is present today. These criteria are not to be applied literally, for the presence of Christ does not occur by an *imitatio Christi* or by mere repetition. To bring Jesus' word and action to expression anew, we must speak and act quite differently. To speak the same word we must say it differently, not only because of the obvious difference in time and historical circumstance, but also because of the irrevocable difference between the one who was the witness and basis of faith and we who are disciples in faith. Jesus is present in terms not of a simple imitation of what he said and did, but of a responsible correspondence to his being as presence, a correspondence that comes to focus at three points: a new language, a new mode of existence, and a new *praxis*.

A new language. The presence of Jesus is above all a word-event, an event that constitutes a new world by a new language. This language is in the first instance the language of authority. True authority is not oppressive but rather liberates from tradition and inherited constraints; it manifests a power and a certainty that are peculiarly personal in character, based not on coercion and claim but on the incalculable power of the word. Such language is also truthful: it "unconceals" reality, disclosing the mundane world for what it is by cracking the shell of its everydayness and deceit, revealing the possibility of a new "logic," the logic of grace, justification, and reconciliation. By the "shock" of truthful word, a transformation of worlds comes about, anticipating the final transformation of the old into the new through God's universal kingdom. Authoritative and truthful word is fundamentally faithful word, word that is homologous with the word of God, serving as the place and the means by which God himself is present in word. Faithful word includes, of course, the word of proclamation and worship, but much more besides. Wherever and whenever an authoritative, true, and faithful word comes to speech— within the church or beyond its domain, in the form of preaching and the language of piety or in the parlance of the world—there the one who was *the* word of faith is present and active.

A new mode of existence. "Faith" rather than "anxiety" or "care" is the definitive mode of existence for those who share in the dominion of Christ, since their ultimate destiny is not death but life in the presence of God. Such faith is experienced as improbable power, the power of God himself, which is a gift *extra nos,* gathering life into wholeness, integrating man with himself (his past and his future), healing the social and political fractures of existence—in short, imparting "salvation" in an inclusive sense. By such faith we are open for and participate even now in the near kingdom of God, the new "world" constituted by God's presence. Because the kingdom of presence is an eschatological reality, faith remains the modality by which we presently exercise hope, love, and freedom. We hope faithfully; we love as those who anticipate in faith the final kingdom of reconciliation; and we are free by faith. Because of the eschatological structure of Christian existence, faith is the definitive mode by which the other Christian "virtues" must be practiced. The one who proclaimed faith is present in the occurrence of such faith.

A new praxis. The idea that the risen Jesus is present in the actions of his disciples was already found in primitive Chrstian tradition. The most striking instance is the account of the Last Judgment in Matt. 25:31-46. The righteous ones

ask: "Lord, when did we see you hungry and feed you, or
thirsty and give you drink? And when did we see you a
stranger and welcome you, or naked and clothe you? And
when did we see you sick or in prison and visit you?" Jesus
answers: "Truly, I say to you, as you did it to one of the
least of these my brethren, you did it to me."[95] A similar
idea is contained in such passages as Matt. 10:40-42; Lk.
10:16; and Mk. 9:37 par.: "Whoever receives one such child
in my name receives me; and whoever receives me, receives
not me but him who sent me."[96] These sayings represent an
effort on the part of the early church to define the modality
of Jesus' presence in action. Such action is seen to focus
primarily on deeds of mercy, compassion, brotherly love.
We may broaden this conception, however, to include the
several dimensions of Jesus' enactment of faith and thus to
propose that the new *praxis* takes three basic forms: freedom, responsibility, obedience. This *praxis* may be considered as "sacramental" in the broad sense designated
earlier; it is action that serves as a sign, seal, bond, or pledge
of faithful word, but is by no means restricted to the ecclesiastical sacraments.

The resurrection, according to Moltmann, belongs to the
history of the practice of Christian freedom. It is an event
that frees the present (liberating men from the personal,
social, political, and physical bonds by which they are
enslaved) and opens the future.[97] In view of the resurrection, Christianity may be defined as the "religion of freedom"
—a freedom qualitatively different from that found in either
Stoicism or Gnosticism. "This is not a freedom over the

95. Bultmann regards this saying to have originated in Jewish tradition, where
human action or inaction was referred to God. It was reworked by the
Christian community in the context of its Easter faith. (*SynT*, pp. 123-124.)
96. Of Mk. 9:37 par. and Matt. 10:40-42, Bultmann writes: ". . . here we
have an older [Jewish] saying so edited by the Christian tradition that it can
serve as a rule of the exalted Christ—for he speaks here—for the behaviour of
his people, and for his people in their mutual relationships." (*SynT*, pp.
142-143.)
97. Jürgen Moltmann, Lectures on Christology, University of Tübingen,
Winter Semester 1968-69. See also Ernst Käsemann, *Jesus Means Freedom*
(Philadelphia, Fortress Press, 1970), pp. 144-156.

world in eternity but a freedom from the slavery of this age for the future of a new, free world. The radical difference of Christian freedom from this world therefore ends neither in Stoic indifference nor in Gnostic libertinism vis-à-vis the world, but in solidarity with the whole groaning creation and is here lived as hope in the coming freedom of the whole."[98] With reference to the action of Jesus, I described such freedom as a revolutionary freedom *in* the world—a freedom that shatters the bonds of tradition and dehumanizing relations, yet does not succumb to the "law" of revolution. Although in the world it is not a freedom *of* the world, and therefore it transcends the various "freedom movements" in which it comes to expression. Moltmann describes this distinction in terms of the dialectic between emancipation and redemption. Emancipation is the immanence of redemption; redemption is the transcendence of emancipation. When these two creatively interpenetrate, then "the future of freedom can be neither the product of our Promethean strivings nor a chance gift from above."[99] The immanence of redemption in emancipation signifies, moreover, that Christian freedom is not only a private, inner possession, but a reality to be gained in the struggle for a liberated society. Jesus is present in the dialectic of alienation and reconciliation as it works itself out in the sociopolitical sphere.[100]

If freedom is a public as well as a personal reality, then the practice of freedom issues in the practice of responsibility for the world, which is the second of the modes of action in which the risen Jesus may be said to be present. From the model afforded by the earthly Jesus, responsibility is seen to involve compassion for the concrete plight of human beings and for the world in its worldly indifference, suffer-

98. Moltmann, "Die Revolution der Freiheit," *Perspektiven der Theologie*, p. 193 (this material is not in the English translation).

99. *Ibid.*, p. 209; see pp. 204-209.

100. Wolf-Dieter Marsch, *Gegenwart Christi in der Gesellschaft*, Chapters 1, 4.

ing in the place of others and on their behalf. We have already observed that the primitive Christian church experienced the presence of the risen Jesus most directly in acts of feeding the hungry, clothing the naked, welcoming strangers, visiting the sick and the imprisoned, and caring for children. The fact that love must assume the vicarious, self-divesting form of compassion ("suffering-with"), means that the reconciliation of mankind anticipated by the resurrection from the dead can be accomplished only by the willingness of the disciples of Jesus to take upon themselves the bondage of estrangement and indifference.

Thus responsibility, like freedom, has its basis in and is ultimately a manifestation of obedience to God, which is the highest form of Christian *praxis*. Such obedience takes the form of sonship, a sonship that must be maintained in maturity and responsibility for the world as inheritance, rather than being forfeited in the sinful abuse of the world as one's private property. Obedience also involves surrender and dedication to the will of God, even when such surrender leads to the God-forsakenness of the cross. Indeed, the cross remains the paradigm of all Christian *praxis:* it reminds us that freedom, responsibility, and obedience are exercised in a world where bondage, indifference, and pride remain the dominant modes of action. The kingdom of presence is coming in the midst of a kingdom of estrangement. Thus the Jesus who is risen and at work in the world as the agent of presence is risen precisely as the Crucified One.

The forms of word and action described here are for the most part non-religious in the conventional sense; they have to do with man's being in the world rather than with religious piety and ecclesiastical practices. This is quite in keeping, as we have noted, with Jesus' own concept of faith and of man's relationship with God. The word in which Jesus is present is not restricted to church proclamation but is found whenever and wherever an authoritative, liberating, and truthful word is spoken in the midst of uncertainty, bondage, and deceit. Faith as the definitive "existential" of human existence before God is not restricted to those who explicitly confess the name of Jesus Christ, but occurs whenever men experience the improbable power that gathers life into wholeness, "saving" it in the midst of anxiety and estrangement. The "sacramental" actions by which faithful word is embodied are not limited to the cultic sacraments but occur whenever freedom, responsibility, compassion, and obedience are practiced in the face of the manifest oppression, indifference, hatred, and pride that dominate the affairs of men. The presence of the risen Jesus occurs on *this* boundary—the boundary between freedom and bondage, truth and deceit, faith and anxiety, responsibility and indifference, obedience and pride—rather than on that between Christian piety and the world. The location of this boundary is fluid rather than static, for it is contingent on each new situation. It cannot be institutionalized or defined in advance by any theology but rather by the language and conduct of men, when as individuals or in the sphere of society and politics they show themselves prepared to assume responsibility for the world, to receive adoption as sons, and to enter (whether knowingly or not) into the body of Christ.

c. Embodiment of Jesus' Presence in Community and World

Action is the embodiment of word. But action in turn implies and requires the existence of a body. There is no such thing as disembodied action in the world, and for that reason no such thing as disembodied word. The body functions as the *vinculum* between self and world; it is this *vinculum* primarily in virtue of its capacity to speak. Word itself is a bodily gesture. But after Jesus' death his individual physical body obviously can no longer serve its word- and action-embodying function. An alternative form of embodiment is required if indeed he is to be recognized by word and deed. A basis for understanding what this might entail is provided by Karl Rahner in his monograph, *On the*

Theology of Death,[101] although in highly speculative fashion. Already during its lifetime, according to Rahner, the individual human spirit exists in an "open" relation to the world, so that the world as a whole functions as the body of man, in addition to or as an extension of his own body, and as the context for the latter. Through death and resurrection from the dead this world-relatedness is intensified and deepened: the spirit becomes *pancosmic*, not *acosmic*. The world as a whole becomes its "body," although the relations to this body are qualitatively different from those to the individual empirical body (cf. I Cor. 15:35 ff.). Self-identity is preserved, not by individuated physical continuity, but by participation in a community or a world-order in which the self is not lost but taken up into a higher unity or structure; here the self finds an identity that is founded *extra se*.[102] Rahner writes: "[The] relation of the soul to the world, if it is not exaggerated into a repetition of its earlier relationship to its own body, might imply that the soul, by surrendering its limited bodily structure in death, becomes open towards the universe and, in some way, a co-determining factor of the universe precisely in the latter's character as the ground of the personal life of other spiritual corporal beings."[103] If this notion were pursued in the categories I have been developing, it might be said that the risen Jesus becomes a co-determining factor in the present constitution of the world whenever and wherever an authoritative, truthful, and salvific word is spoken, and whenever and wherever action is informed by the qualities of freedom, responsibility, and obedience. The world as a whole, then, in its social and political fabric, functions as the "embodiment" of those words and actions by which recognition and hence the presence of Jesus is evoked. The community of faith may be

101. Rahner, *On the Theology of Death* (Quaestiones Disputatae, No. 2; 2nd ed.; New York, Herder and Herder, 1965), pp. 18-26. See also *ThI*, Vol. II, Chapter 6; and Vol. IV, Chapter 5.
102. I am indebted to Ernst Käsemann (Lectures on I Corinthians, University of Tübingen, Winter Semester 1968-69) for the formulation of this point.
103. Rahner, *op. cit.*, p. 22.

defined as the place in the world where this recognition is brought to explicit articulation by memory, cultic acts, proclamation, and mission. The community is the "body of Christ" in a more explicit, concrete sense, but only because it is the place in the world where the world itself embodies the risen Christ. The world itself embodies the risen Christ because it is re-constituted *as* world—the *nova creatio*—by his coming to stand in it.

On this theory, of course, such world-presence is possible for every human being after death. Indeed, Rahner's point in the monograph I have cited is that all men are in some sense co-responsible for the world and add something unique to it—in death as in life. Thus Jesus' resurrection from the dead is a specific instance of a universal human promise and possibility (which seems entirely consonant with I Cor. 15:12 ff.). Yet Jesus' is the more radical (and in that sense unique) presence by virtue of the absolutely fundamental way he co-determines the world,[104] which in turn is a consequence of the incomparable faithfulness of his historical word and the unqualified freedom, responsibility, and obedience of his historical deed.

The church is the community of those who participate explicitly in the dominion of Christ, but this is the case only because the world as a whole is the "embodiment" of the risen Christ. The church receives its definition, at least in part, from its relation to the world. It is the place in the world where the world's embodiment of Christ and his worldly dominion are acknowledged and made explicit. In Bonhoeffer's terms, the church is the "space" in the world where Jesus Christ takes form and is proclaimed. It is that section of humanity in which Christ has already taken form. Its purpose, then, is not separation from the world but the summoning of the world into the fellowship of the body of Christ, to which in truth it already belongs implicitly. The church's space in the world should be no larger than what

104. *Ibid.*, pp. 63-67.

is needed for the task of carrying forward its mission. It should not be in competition with the world for space, because its only justification in having space is to proclaim the agency of Christ. Its space is not an end in itself, something to protect or expand. The implication of this position is that there cannot be a static, spatial borderline between church and world. Eschatologically, church and world will become identical in the full realization of the kingdom of God. The movement of history is towards a progressive reciprocal infusion of the spheres of church and world.[105]

Edward Schillebeeckx has forcefully propounded the same theme in terms of a distinction between *implicit* and *explicit* Christianity. The dialogue between church and the world, he writes, is

> a dialogue between *two complementary, authentically Christian expressions* of one and the same God-related life concealed in the mystery of Christ, namely, the *ecclesial* expression . . . and the *worldly* expression of that identically same life, internalized within human life through man's free acceptance of grace. In other words, the *implicitly* and the *explicitly* Christian dimension of the same God-related life, that is, of human life hidden in God's absolute and gratuitous presence. In that context, this is what is meant by implicit Christianity; it is the human, earthly and profane reality assumed in its secularity into the God-related life which it proceeds to express objectively, even when that God-related life remains anonymous and implicit. . . . Within that God-centered life, albeit anonymous, the construction of the world and the promotion of peoples, those two great hopes of mankind on earth, become an activity which is not only intentionally but intrinsically relevant to the kingdom of God.[106]

In the process of secularization, Schillebeeckx sees an eschatological movement toward the identification of church and world. In the world there exists an inner thrust toward

105. Dietrich Bonhoeffer, *Ethics,* Eberhard Bethge, ed., trans. by Neville Horton Smith (New York, The Macmillan Co., 1955), pp. 20-21, 67-68, 72; and *Christ the Center,* pp. 59-67. See also Claude Welch, *The Reality of the Church,* Chapter 6.

106. Edward Schillebeeckx, "The Church and Mankind," *Concilium,* Vol. I: *The Church and Mankind* (New York, Paulist Press, 1965), p. 85. See also Karl Rahner's articles on "anonymous" or "implicit" Christianity in *STh,* Vol. VI, pp. 545-554; and Vol. VIII, pp. 187-212.

rendering explicit what has hitherto remained anonymous, individualized, and internalized, namely, a slowly emerging responsibility on the part of politics and secular culture for the liberation and humanization of life, the establishment of justice, the securing of economic well-being for all men, and the assurance of peace. Conversely, an "osmosis" of explicit Christianity has occurred from the church into the world. What was once regarded as the exclusive prerogative of the church (charity, education, healing, mission to underdeveloped lands) has now become an accepted feature of government and secular institutions.[107] To be sure, this process takes a jagged course, for liberty, justice, equality, peace, education, unity, and other goals of a humanized society are not directly attainable but can be achieved only in the context of the dialectic of estrangement and reconciliation as it works itself out in the social sphere. But this process need not be lamented as marking the end of the "Christianized era"; rather it should be welcomed as a sign of the coming of the kingdom of God. For the goal of the church is precisely to "lose" itself in the world, in the becoming explicit of the body of Christ in humanity as a whole.

Of course, as Schillebeeckx puts it, "the blurring of the boundaries between the Church and mankind can never abolish the dialectical tension between the two."[108] For during the course of history as we know it the old world and the new will continue to co-exist. Hence a place must remain within the old world where the new is acknowledged and becomes explicit, in recognizable continuity with the one

107. Schillebeeckx, "The Church and Mankind," *op. cit.*, p. 90. On the relation between eschatology and secularization, see also J. B. Metz, *Theology of the World* (New York, Herder and Herder, 1969), Chapters III, V. One may contrast the rather static conception of the relation between church and world found in the last chapter of Moltmann's *Theology of Hope*. There the coming of the eschaton seems to remain a purely transcendent possibility, rather than something to be accomplished at least in part through the dialectic of historical process. See esp. pp. 302, 308-310, 315-322, 324, 327-328. 331-333.

108. Schillebeeckx, "The Church and Mankind," *op. cit.*, p. 90.

and remains the witness, basis, and criterion of
. The danger always exists of confusing the world's
nous and demonic forms with an authentic embodi-
)f Christ. The church is not necessarily always the
place where this danger is avoided and where Christ's true
dominion is brought to speech and practice, as history has
so often sadly shown. But that, nevertheless, remains its
proper vocation and its continued *raison d'être* in the world.
The community may not be dissolved into culture and politics until the kingdom of God is fully present. Its full
presence, however, is an eschatological reality, not adequately conceptualizable in terms of our present experience of the structures of church and world. It means the
full and final presence of God, and hence the end of the
human pilgrimage.

In conclusion, then, four modes of the *one* presence of
Jesus as the risen Christ may be distinguished: word, act,
community, and world.[109] These are not discrete, supplementary spheres. Rather we may think of their relation in
terms of concentric circles. The word is the innermost circle,
the decisive mode of presence, as I have sought to establish
on both theological and philosophical grounds. Word is embodied by action, of which it remains the core. Word and
action together, as the first two modes of Jesus' presence
pro nobis, correspond to the two constitutive dimensions of
his past being-as-presence—his definitively faithful word and
his free, responsible, and obedient act. Action, however,
points not only "inwardly" to the word but also "outwardly"
to the community, the third of the circles, by which it together with word is embodied. After the death and resurrection of Jesus, the community becomes the "alternative"

109. My analysis has clearly been influenced by Bonhoeffer's discussion of
Christ's presence "in his *pro me* structure as word, as sacrament and as community," and by his conception of Christ as the "center" of human existence,
history, and nature (*Christ the Center,* pp. 49-67). Nevertheless, the details
of this analysis as well as my conception of the relation between these modes,
differ from Bonhoeffer.

form of embodiment by which his personal presence is constituted: in this sense it is the "body of Christ." Yet ultimately the community is nothing other than a "place" or
sphere within the world where Jesus' dominion is acknowledged and his presence recognized. Its eschatological destiny is to be merged into the world, which shall itself have
become the body of Christ, the kingdom of God. If word
is the innermost core of Jesus' presence, then world is its out-
ermost circumference. Word and world are the dialectical,
co-constitutive themes between which we must move in
seeking to understand the resurrection of Jesus of Nazareth.

4. PRESENCE AS AN ESCHATOLOGICAL REALITY

These reflections may be drawn to a close by noting an
etymological peculiarity of the word "presence." Our English noun derives from the Latin *praesentia*, which in turn is
based on the adjective *praesens*. *Praesens* is the present participle of *praeesse*, "to be before" (*prae*, before + *esse*, to be).
Hence *praesentia* and "presence" mean, in the root sense, the
act or condition of "being before." This meaning may be
construed not merely in the spatial sense (the state of "being
at hand," "being in view," etc.), but also in the temporal
sense. Rosenstock-Huessy has proposed that *prae-sentia*
means "being in anticipation," "fore-being" (*Voraussein*).[110]
According to Heidegger, the German word for presence, *Gegenwart*, in its root sense means "waiting towards," a sense he
sometimes brings out by hyphenating it (*Gegen-wart*). Thus
authentic "presence" means "waiting towards the future" in
resoluteness.[111] "Presence" is constituted by the *coming* of
being as future power through the past into the present,

110. Eugen Rosenstock-Huessy, *Die europäischen Revolutionen und der Charakter der Nationen*, 3rd ed. (Stuttgart, W. Kohlhammer Verlag, 1961), p. 558. I am indebted to Jürgen Moltmann for calling my attention to this reference.
111. *BT*, pp. 47-48, 374, 387-388.

gathering time into presence. Hence the act or condition of presence has an inherently *eschatological* dimension: it means "fore-being," being "before" the coming of being, being in anticipation, waiting toward the future. Man is gathered into presence in so far as he lives toward and out of the future. He is present to himself and to the world by standing "before" the coming of future power.

The dialectical relation between presence and future may be viewed from the point of view of the future as well. The future is related to the present as both *futurum* and *adventus*.[112] As *futurum* (from the future participle of the Latin verb *esse,* "to be"), the future is "that which shall be" —that which develops out of what has been in the past and now is. Here the image is that of development towards a *telos* that already is contained in potency by the original seed. Man has a measure of control over and responsibility for this process and thus his own destiny. The characteristic categories are evolution, continuity, prediction, planning, projection. This view of the future was given classic expression in Aristotelian teleology. As *adventus* (Latin, "arrival," "coming"), the future is "that which comes"—the *novum,* the not-yet, the *parousia,* which shatters present expectations. Now the image is that of a "coming" of the future into the present—a coming by which the future "calls" or "pulls" the present forward into new possibilities, exercising power and independence vis-à-vis the influence of the past. The characteristic categories are revolution, discontinuity, innovation, movement forward by leaps or breakthroughs. The future is not concealed in the hidden core of human development but is present in the mode of *parousia*— advent, arrival, coming. It is a peculiarity of the Greek language that the word *parousia* contains within itself the dialectic between presence and future. The word means

112. The English word "future" derives from *futurum,* whereas the German word for future, *Zukunft,* relates to *adventus* because it derives from the verb *zukommen,* "to arrive," "to approach."

literally "presence," "being-with" (παρά, with + οὐσία, being). But in ancient writers it became a *terminus technicus* for the visit or arrival of a king, and in the New Testament it was used to describe the second coming of the risen Christ, whose *parousia* would bring the end of history. Heidegger has played on this ambiguity by suggesting that the *parousia* of being—its advent or arrival as future power—is precisely the mode by which it is present with us and gathers into presence.[113] The future qua future is *parousia*, being-with, arrival, advent; and the present qua present is *praesentia*, being-before, waiting-towards.

In every historical event a dialectical interaction between *futurum* and *adventus* is taking place. The future comes *(adventus)* into the present, exerting its forward pull, its call forward, in the context of a projection out of past possibilities *(futurum)*.[114] Every occasion of human experience is constituted by the interaction between the causal influence of the past and novel possibilities for the future, which lure it beyond mere repetition of past experiences.[115] In some events, the element of tradition, of continuity with the past, prevails, but never to the exclusion of the occurrence of the new, the unpredictable, the uncontrollable, never to the exclusion of the power and the spontaneity of the future vis-à-vis the present. In other events the element of discontinuity, the shattering power of the *novum*, prevails, but never to the exclusion of the past, the regularities of a causal nexus, and man's projects for the future. All events in history exhibit the influence of both these forces, and the distinctive character of each event is determined by the way they interact in it. Technological planning on the one side and theology on the other side are inclined to forget

113. Heidegger, *Hegel's Concept of Experience* (New York, Harper & Row, 1970), pp. 30, 40, 45, 48-49, 75, 78-79, 84-85, 148-149.

114. For this Heideggerian formulation, see above, pp. 87-89.

115. See John B. Cobb, *God and the World* (Philadelphia, Westminster Press, 1969), pp. 49, 54-55, 81-82, for a Whiteheadian formulation of the same theme.

that *both futurum and adventus* are essential structural elements in the dialectic of historical process.[116]

The "presence" that constitutes human life, the presence of which Jesus of Nazareth was the definitive exemplification, is eschatological not only in the sense of meaning "living toward the future" and being constituted by the advent of the future. It is also eschatological because such presence is not yet fully realized: it is the human promise, not the prevailing human condition, except in anticipation. The presence accomplished in Jesus, too, is ultimately proleptic in character.[117] Jesus himself is not simply to be identified with the final consummation of humanity as a whole in God; he is the absolute anticipation of this consummation in a mode appropriate to a single individual. He represents the point at which God's self-communication in word is established as *irrevocably* present in the world and is clearly recognizable as such; in his person "the history of the world has reached—not indeed its full and absolute perfection—but its unsurpassable final phase of perfection."[118]

In the preceding pages I have specified the proleptic element in Jesus' being as presence in two ways. (1) I have defined Jesus as the word of faith and have argued that "faith" means the proper mode of openness for and participation in the kingdom of God here and now. The kingdom of God is "near," not immediately at hand, for its essence

116. The contemporary philosophers who have most adequately described this dialectic are Heidegger, Whitehead, and Jaspers. Ernst Bloch, despite his powerful arguments for the hiddenness and novelty of the future, ultimately reduces the future to *futurum*—the essential human core. See *Man on His Own* (New York, Herder and Herder, 1970), pp. 147 ff. Possibly in overreaction to Bloch, theology of the future has tended to eliminate the element of *futurum* and restrict Christian hope to *adventus*, the arrival of the qualitatively new. See Jürgen Moltmann, "Antwort auf die Kritik der Theologie der Hoffnung," in *Diskussion über die "Theologie der Hoffnung" von Jürgen Moltmann*, Wolf-Dieter Marsch, ed. (München, Chr. Kaiser Verlag, 1967), pp. 210-211; and "What is 'New' in Christianity: The Category *Novum* in Christian Theology," *RRF*, Chapter 1.

117. *JGaM*, pp. 53-66, 106-108; Jürgen Moltmann, *Theology of Hope*, pp. 82-83, 202-203, 225.

118. Karl Rahner, *ThI*, Vol. V, pp. 11-15, 174-175, 179-183, 188; cf. *STh*, Vol. VIII, pp. 223, 229.

is an eschatological reality, the "kingdom of presence." Jesus is the final word of faith, not the final act of love. Love is fully realized only in the being of God, whereas for man it remains always an eschatological virtue. We can say that "God *is* love" but not that "God is faith." "Love" may be defined as eschatological presence, presence-as-such; "faith" constitutes the modality by which we love here and now; and "hope" functions as the mediating link between faith and love: "So faith, hope, love abide, these three; but the greatest of these is love" (I Cor. 13:13).[119]

(2) I have contended that the resurrection is not only a present event but also a future promise. Although the experiential basis of the resurrection is in the present, and the term "resurrection" means Jesus' coming to stand in the world as agent, engaged in the practice of presence, nevertheless the direction and goal of Paul's argument in I Cor. 15 is from the present through the past to the future. That future which we are promised by being raised from the dead, in Christ and with Christ, is God himself—who *is* presence because he *has* word (the power of the future) absolutely. *We* have presence and life in so far as we participate in the presence and life of God. *God* is our future. That is the promise of the resurrection: that "in Christ all will be brought to life," that Christ shall reign until even death is brought under his dominion, that "when all things are thus subject to him, then the Son himself will also be made subordinate to God who made all things subject to him, and thus God will be all in all." Or, as Paul also expresses it: ". . . We too believe, and so we speak, knowing that he who raised the Lord Jesus will raise us also with Jesus and bring us, together with you, into his presence."

---

119. Karl Rahner, "Zur Theologie der Hoffnung," *STh*, Vol. VIII, pp. 561-579, on the Pauline ordering of faith, hope, and love.

INDEXES

INDEX OF BIBLICAL REFERENCES

GENERAL INDEX

Pannenberg, Wolfhart (*Continued*)
63, 67n., 69-72, 122n., 130n.,
154n., 159n., 182n., 184, 187n.,
188n., 200, 223, 233-237, 239n.,
245, 290n.
Parables, 151, 160-166, 185-186
Parmenides, 75, 90
Paul, the Apostle, 145, 195n., 198,
200-203, 207-209, 211-212, 222-
223, 226-230, 239, 251-256,
261-263, 270
Paul of Samosata, 62
Perrin, Norman, 138, 143-144, 154n.,
182n.
Personal presence, 266-268, 272-273
Personhood, 65-66, 106-109, 123-
128, 136
Peter, the Apostle, 227-228, 264
Philosophy, and theology, 113, 116n.
Pöggeler, Otto, 84n., 85, 112-114
Portmann, Adolf, 187
Power, 151-153, 168-174, 277
Practice
as an element in historical thinking, 31-40
as a function of christology, 41-44
as a mode of faith, 150-152, 188-
190; *see also* Resurrection, as
praxis
Prejudice (Forejudgment), 33-36, 41
Presence, 19-20, 24, 57n., 87-90, 94,
120-121, 153-155, 176, 256-258,
266-267, 287-289
as an eschatological reality, 287-
291
to God, 110, 151-153, 166-168, 256
horizons of, 104-110, 149-153
loss of, 108-109, 130-135, 175-176,
179-180, 197-198
to oneself (temporal presence),
104-106, 107-108, 125, 152-153,
156-160, 192
qualities of, 149-153
to the world (spatial presence),
93-95, 106-109, 125, 152-153
Procksch, Otto, 77

R
Rad, Gerhard von, 25, 213n.
Rahner, Karl, 10n., 63, 65, 68, 70,
105, 107-108, 117-118, 120, 123,
126, 200, 281-283, 284n., 290n.,
291n.

Rationalism, 35, 39, 51-52
Recognition, 267-269
Rengstorf, K. H., 233
Responsibility
as a function of christology, 40-48,
56
historical, 39-40
as a mode of faith, 153, 188-190,
195-199, 201-202, 208-209, 279-
281
Resurrection
as an action of community, 242,
258-269
as an action of God, 242, 254-258
as an action of Jesus, 224-225, 241-
254
as coming to stand, 243-250
of the Crucified, 214-217, 241
as the death of death, 214-215,
257-258
as future promise, 237-241, 291
interpretation of, 220-225, 228-
230, 248
as life, 248, 252-256
modality of, 265-287
as past occurrence, 231-237
as *praxis*, 49-50, 52-53, 220, 223-
225, 229-230, 241-243, 271,
277-281
as present event, 223-225, 229-
230, 240-241
time of, 221-223, 241
Revelation (Unconcealment), 84-85,
128-131, 228
Revolution, 190-191, 288
Richardson, William J., 90n., 97, 102,
115, 117n.
Ricoeur, Paul, 95, 98n.
Rosenstock-Huessy, Eugen, 84n., 287
Rubenstein, Richard, 3, 18

S
Sacrament, 230-231, 267, 268-269,
273-281, 283
Salvation, 151, 169, 174-175, 178-
180, 251-252, 260
Sartre, Jean-Paul, 96n., 187n.
Scheler, Max, 187
Schillebeeckx, Eduard, 10n., 284-
285
Schizophrenia, 104-105
Schlatter, Adolf, 81, 141n.